Language Teaching with Video-Based Technologies

This book explores the implications of technology-mediated project-based language learning for computer-assisted language learning (CALL) teacher development, focusing on the role of video-based instruction in elucidating challenges and opportunities to promote learner creativity in the language classroom.

The volume builds on existing literature on project-based language learning by extending the focus on the affordances of machinima, digital videos created by teachers and learners to capture the experience in three-dimensional immersive games or virtual worlds. Drawing on data from a large-scale research project featuring case studies that examine different facets of CALL teacher education, the book calls attention to language learning and teaching strategies that encourage both learners and teachers to develop innovative approaches in the language classroom and how such approaches promote the integration of lifelong learning skills alongside traditional linguistic competencies.

Offering a dynamic contribution to the growing literature on the interface of language learning and teaching and technology, this book will appeal to students and researchers in applied linguistics and language and education, as well as those interested in the latest developments in CALL.

Michael Thomas is Professor of Education in the School of Education and Chair of the Centre for Educational Research (CERES) at Liverpool John Moores University in the UK.

Christel Schneider is Managing Director and Founder of CSiTrain and Senior Research Assistant at the University of Central Lancashire, UK.

Routledge Studies in Applied Linguistics

For more information about this series, please visit: www.routledge.com/Routledge-Studies-in-Applied-Linguistics/book-series/RSAL

Language Teaching with Video-Based Technologies

Creativity and CALL Teacher Education

Michael Thomas and
Christel Schneider

Routledge
Taylor & Francis Group

NEW YORK AND LONDON

First published 2021
by Routledge
605 Third Avenue, New York, NY 10017

and by Routledge
2 Park Square, Milton Park, Abingdon, Oxon, OX14 4RN

First issued in paperback 2022

Routledge is an imprint of the Taylor & Francis Group, an informa business

© 2021 Taylor & Francis

The right of Michael Thomas and Christel Schneider to be identified as authors of this work has been asserted by them in accordance with sections 77 and 78 of the Copyright, Designs and Patents Act 1988.

Publisher's Note
The publisher has gone to great lengths to ensure the quality of this reprint but points out that some imperfections in the original copies may be apparent.

Library of Congress Cataloging-in-Publication Data
A catalog record for this book has been requested

ISBN: 978-0-367-43453-3 (hbk)
ISBN: 978-0-367-54254-2 (pbk)
ISBN: 978-1-003-00331-1 (ebk)

DOI: 10.4324/9781003003311

Typeset in Sabon
by Apex CoVantage, LLC

Contents

Acknowledgements

The book derives from a project that was externally funded by the European Commission Lifelong Learning Programme Key Activity 3 ICT (€487,895) (Project number: 543481-LLP-1–2013–1-UK-KA3-KA3MP). The information in this publication reflects the views only of the authors, and the Commission cannot be held responsible for any use which may be made of the information contained therein.

We would like to thank all the pupils, students, teachers, colleagues, partners and researchers in all the countries involved in the research leading to this book. The University of Central Lancashire and Liverpool John Moores University generously gave us the research time that enabled us to complete this work on time. We give a special thank you to the Education, Audiovisual and Culture Executive Agency of the European Commission for its support throughout all stages of the project. We are grateful to LinguaTV.com for its permission to reproduce Figures 4.1 to 4.6. All other images included in the book are done so with the kind permission of the authors.

Abbreviations and Glossary

ActiveWorlds	A platform for delivering real-time interactive three-dimensional (3D) content over the web (www.activeworlds.com)
Asynchronous	Events that do not happen at the same time such as time displaced discussions in a forum
Avatar	A graphical representation of a user in a 3D virtual environment
Camtasia Studio	Screen-recording software, which allows video editing in 3D worlds
CALL	Computer-assisted language learning
CALL-IS	Computer-Assisted Language Learning Interest Section
Callout	A short text in a box or speech bubble that provides information about a scene, picture or graphic
CEFR	Common European Framework of Reference for Languages: Learning, Teaching, Assessment. An international standard for describing learners' language skills across six levels: A1, A2 (beginner); B1, B2 (intermediate); C1, C2 (advanced)
CLIL	Content and Language Integrated Learning
CLT	Communicative Language Teaching
CoP	Community of Practice
CPD	Continuing Professional Development
Destination	In-world locations and resident creations of simulations of places
Dropbox	A cloud service to keep or share data (https://www.dropbox.com/)
EAP	English for Academic Purposes
Emote	Facial animations in Second Life
ESP	English for Specific Purposes
Green screen	A technique to remove the background in a film and replace it with another

Holodecks	Changeable environments where various scenes can be stored, opened by a click of a button and closed by typing the word clear into the textbox in a 3D context
HUD	Head-up display, used to present data within Second Life
ICT	Information and communication technologies
Island	A virtual region
IMVU	An avatar-based social network on the web, where users can choose avatars, build spaces and communicate (www.imvu.com)
In-world	A term used when referring to being in a virtual environment
Inventory	A collection of all the stored items that users in a virtual world own or have access to
Item	Asset types in an inventory, such as clothes, landmarks or objects
Lag	A colloquial expression for slow reaction time when using the internet
Landmark	A shortcut to a place stored in the Inventory parcel: the smallest division of land
Linden Lab	The creators of Second Life
Lip-syncing	An abbreviation for lip-synchronisation, which is a technical term for matching lip movements with pre-recorded sung or spoken vocals that listeners hear through speakers
Machinima	A technique for making films inside 3D virtual environments using real-time, interactive 3D engines to render a film instead of professional 3D animation software
Machinimatographer	A term used for somebody who makes machinima movies
Minecraft	A game that allows players to build using textured cubes in a 3D world
MMORG	Massive multiplayer online role-playing game
Moodle	A free and open-source software learning management system
MOOT	Machinima Open Online Training course
MOSP	Machinima Open Online Studio Project
MUVE	Multi-user virtual environment
Notecards	Inventory items used in Second Life to convey some information; they can contain text, or embedded textures, hyperlinks to locations, snapshots, objects, or other notecards

NPC	A non-player character which is controlled by the computer, not by a person
OpenSim	OpenSimulator, an open-source multi-user 3D application server (http://opensimulator.org/)
Open Wonderland	A Java open-source toolkit for creating collaborative 3D virtual worlds (www.openwonderland.org)
Overdubbing	A technique used to add supplementary recorded sound to machinima
PBLT	Project-based language teaching
PPP	Presentation–Practise–Production
Prim	Primitive: a 3D cube, sphere, or cone
Quake	A video game developed by ID Software and published in 1996
Rez	Or rezzing, a term used in Second Life and OpenSim for making something appear, such as a box, a bus stop, a hotel or any other object
Sandbox	Meeting space permitting practice, creativity and rezzing, depending on privacy settings
Sansar	A social virtual reality platform developed and owned by Linden Lab
Screencasting	A technique used to record a video of a computer screen
SLA	Second language acquisition
Sim	A simulator which can refer to a single region in Second Life or the hardware or software simulating one or more regions
SL	Second Life, a 3D multi-user platform created by Linden Lab and generated by its users (www.secondlife.com)
SLTE	Second language teacher education
SMEs	Small and medium-sized enterprises
STEM	Science, technology, engineering, mathematics
Synchronous	Something that is happening at the same time, such as instant messaging or live chats
TBLT	Task-based language teaching
Teleport	A way of changing location in-world
TESOL	Teaching English to Speakers of Other Languages
There	A social virtual world where users interact in a 3D environment (www.there.com)
Texture	Image to put on the faces of a prim or object to change its appearance
TMPBLT	Technology-mediated project-based language teaching
Twinity	A free 3D world where people can create an avatar and interact with other avatars (www.twinity.com/en/)

VAI	Virtual Ability Orientation Island
VIRDA-MS	Virtual Reality Dyslexia Assessment–Memory Screening
VirtualPREX	Virtual Professional Experience. An innovative assessment using a 3D virtual world with pre-service teachers
VLE	Virtual learning environment
VWBPE	Virtual Worlds Best Practices in Education Conference. A free annual virtual conference that is conducted using simulated environments
WASD	The W, A, S, and D keys or WASD keys on a computer keyboard are used in place of the up/down/left/right arrow keys
Wiki	Server software that allows users to contribute to and edit web page content
WoW	World of Warcraft, a massively multiplayer online role-playing game

Tables

Figures

1 Introduction

Like the wider domain of educational technology, computer-assisted language learning (CALL) has been promising to revolutionise teaching and learning for rather a long time. Indeed, while CALL has taken significant steps as an area of independent academic enquiry under the broader umbrella of second language acquisition (SLA) over the last three decades, insights from its growing body of research have affected practitioners in the field with much less speed as the majority of research has focused on English (rather than other languages) and higher education (rather than schools, adult or vocational education). In place of the marketing hyperbole promising 'revolution', 'disruptive innovation' and 'transformation', empirical research suggests that the reality is often one of uneven integration and, in fact, marginalisation, regardless of the more widespread availability of such technologies in our social lives through the use of smartphones, social networking applications and video- and photo-sharing websites. Indeed, the reality for most language teachers around the world, particularly in developing and under-resourced CALL contexts, remains that of a computer attached to a projector displaying PowerPoint slides or web pages with interactive grammar exercises and quizzes. At the opposite extreme, there are abundant examples of technology being thrown into pedagogical contexts as a 'quick fix' or symbol that 'something needs to be done', particularly in areas of significant social disadvantage or inequality. The lesson reiterated again and again from any attempt to narrate the history of CALL is that access to technology infrastructure alone does not automatically lead to well-trained teachers or meaningful learning environments (Davies, Otto, & Rüschoff, 2013).

As has been widely pointed out in the growing body of work on CALL, the effectiveness of technology integration in a wide variety of contexts has been dependent on several recurring findings. These are that the technology (whether hardware or software) is subject to constant change, that technology should be driven by pedagogy and not *vice versa* and that the use of digital technologies in learning is fraught with challenges that some teachers prefer to avoid rather than risk 'loss of face' in front of their learners and/or colleagues if something unpredictable goes wrong (Kenning, 2007). Like research in the broader area of educational technology, CALL research is in danger of focusing only on the newest gadget from the latest trade event, showing teachers how to use the technology in question rather than addressing the underlying and longer term professional development needs of teachers (Hubbard & Levy, 2006).

In response, this book explores the potential of digital technologies in foreign language teaching, specifically a video-based learning approach called *machinima*, through the lens of research and practice on teacher education, by asking, What makes effective CALL teacher education in this constantly shifting terrain? Specifically, what are the elements of an effective framework for online CALL teacher education, in terms of the type of support and mentoring required by trainees?

While we explore the context of video-based approaches to learning and specifically examine the implications of teaching and learning with machinima, our goal is to understand the bigger picture of second language teacher education (SLTE). Our focus on video-based learning, then, is a way to explore how teacher training courses can help to rediscover the potential of teacher and learner creativity in an age in which so much of formal education, particularly in the schools sector for modern foreign language learning, is concerned with testing and performance-based measures of successful learning. In harnessing the evident potential of digital technologies in the language classroom (Plonsky & Ziegler, 2016), educators and policymakers need to be savvier about the history of education technology, its failings and its limitations (Cuban, 1993, 2003), as well as the educational technology and digital start-up lobby who promote a product-driven and corporate approach to education that does not always fit with process- or values-based models of effective teaching and learning (Player-Koro, Rensfeldt, & Selwyn, 2017).

CALL Teacher Education

CALL teacher education, according to Torsani (2016),

> is not only (and not much) about transferring notions and/or learning how to use a piece of software; its main objective is to develop in teachers the knowledge of the technological options available and the ability to combine them with their knowledge of language teaching.
>
> (p. xvi)

Viewed in this light CALL is not merely about the use of technologies in language teaching and learning, but as Garrett (2009), also reminds us, it "designates a dynamic complex in which technology, theory, and pedagogy are inseparably interwoven" (pp. 719–720). The word *dynamic* here conveys the need for a much more critically informed approach to

CALL research and practice, one that is context-dependent, historically aware and focused on the transferable skills required by teachers in their particular teaching environments (Hubbard & Levy, 2006).

Viewed through the lens of these principles, this book investigates the specific use of digital video and immersive environments such as Second Life (SL) and OpenSimulator in the foreign language classroom as a potential means of encouraging creative and collaborative forms of project-based teaching and learning (Hafner & Miller, 2011; Thomas, 2015, 2017; Gras-Velazquez, 2019), but it does so by addressing important considerations for CALL teacher education as a result of the development of an online teacher training course. The course was originally based on the format of a MOOC, or Massive Open Online Course, like those offered by FutureLearn in the UK or EdX in the US, which run over a period of approximately five weeks, and involve the use of short, video lectures supported by tasks and online discussion board activities. While MOOCs have become a popular, if sometimes controversial, format for online courses, they have latterly become more commercialised and are often seen as a gateway to premium content for which payment is required. Pedagogically, MOOCs have often been criticised for not following the original, rather radical intentions of the first course developed by Siemens and Downes along connectivist lines, as they have tended to utilise behaviouristic learning principles (Downes, 2006).

Offered as a variation on MOOC principles, the video project explored in this book is based on what we have called a MOOT, or Massive Open Online Training course, as it focuses more on the pedagogical design of the course along dialogical (Wegerif, 2007, 2013) and community of practice (CoP) lines (Lave & Wenger, 1991). This meaning is implicit in the acronym, which draws on the meaning of the word *moot* as indicated in its *Oxford English Dictionary* entry: to 'subject to debate, dispute, or uncertainty' (*adjective*), to 'raise (a question or topic) for discussion; suggest (an idea or possibility)' (*verb*); or an 'assembly held for debate' (*noun*). The origin of the word *moot* is the Old English word *mōt*, meaning an 'assembly or meeting', as well as the word *mōtian*, of Germanic origin, which means to 'converse'. The connection with Wegerif's (2017) definition of *dialogical* is clear as it includes both epistemological and ontological aspects and means more than a mere space for dialogue. It includes, as Wegerif outlines, a "dialogic form", as it opens "a shared dialogic space", and in the educational context, has the "aim of teaching for more dialogue or teaching dialogue as an end in itself as well as using dialogue as a means to knowledge construction". Wegerif elaborates on this definition of dialogical as follows:

> In teaching through the opening of a shared dialogic space, dialogic education draws students into participation in the processes through which shared knowledge is constructed and validated. In other

words dialogic education promotes dialogue as an end in itself. As a result of participation in dialogic education students are expected to become better at dialogue which means better at learning things together with others.

(para 12)

The MOOT online teacher training course explored in the book aimed to embed the dialogical approach among the moderators and trainees to foster "a shared dialogical space" in which thinking is done together and in support of one another (Merleau-Ponty, 1968). To achieve this, the course followed Hubbard and Levy's (2006) techno-pedagogical model of CALL teacher education and sought to familiarise teachers with the technologies and approaches that they will also expect their learners to use by making them actual users of the technologies involved.

Our exploration of the online course, then, offers a case study of a model of CALL teacher education based on an approach that can also be called 'situated learning' in that it was both practical and theoretical, as Torsani (2016, p. 77) points out:

> Online courses are important because they take the notions which were learnt within institutional and formal contexts onto the field, with the result that learners manage to get a precise idea of all the mechanisms (technical problems, relationship management etc.) which rule working with technologies – in this case, digital media – once again proving the importance of the latter in CALL renaissance. Practice in the field, both in the shape of situated learning and in that of *critical incident*, plays a crucial role in solving the problem of credibility for technologies and the activities related to them (see Egbert, Paulus, & Nakamichi, 2002). Furthermore, the building of communities of practice, with its stress on cooperation and exchange among participants, opens the way for the vast and indistinct world of extra-institutional learning, whose realisations, such as, for instance, informal learning, form one of the privileged channels for professional training.

Following Lave and Wenger (1991), by situated learning we refer to the process of involving learners in authentic settings in which they can acquire and apply their knowledge through social interaction in a community of practice such as a project team. A CoP is a group of people who interact regularly and share a passion or interest as well as the ability to learn from each other. Developing firstly from 'low-risk' activities, learners gradually become more independent and engage in more complex activities as they become more experienced.

Designed along these lines, the CALL online training course at the centre of the book demonstrates the need to move from a procedural model of teacher training (Hubbard & Levy, 2006) to a more holistic model, which derives from earlier work by Ide (1987) and integrates procedural, creative, pedagogical and technological skills as part of a natural continuum. Following Chao (2015) and Slaouti and Motteram (2006), in such a holistic approach, teachers are encouraged to develop a mindset of lifelong learning rather than one based on discrete and unconnected training, and trainers need to consider how the skills and competencies learned can be transferred to the trainees' actual teaching contexts. Within this lifelong learning approach to CALL teacher education, the trainee is presented with opportunities for extra-institutional interaction, participation in active communities of practice, to understand the importance of critical pedagogy and reflection rather than merely accepting technology integration and the importance of integrating CALL teacher education into the wider context of SLTE (Slaouti & Motteram, 2006). The online teacher training course was designed to test this breadth and depth model of CALL teacher education that aimed to function as a type of cognitive apprenticeship (Chao, 2015) in which scaffolding took place to help teachers understand and integrate the technologies involved. In this approach, technology is not seen as an add-on but as integral to the course; thus, the design moves beyond the primacy of technology to show how to connect technology and linguistics with transferable skills. The design of the online course involved interactive and collaborative projects, rather than a tutorial led approach, based on a 'learning by doing' approach that was more likely to engage participants in more complex tasks. The course incorporated tutorials, the process of guided instruction and complex projects, thus presenting the training course as a replication of the teaching context of the participants (Debski, 2006). Following Herrington and Oliver (1999), the course aimed to adhere to the following core principles (as cited in Torsani, 2016, p. 115):

1. It envisaged real contexts, reflecting the modalities in which knowledge will be used in real life;
2. It envisaged authentic tasks;
3. It envisaged experts' performances on which to model processes;
4. It envisaged different roles and perspectives;
5. It supported cooperative knowledge building;
6. It promoted reflection so that abstractions may be made;
7. It promoted articulation in order to allow implicit knowledge to become explicit;
8. It envisaged opportunities for coaching scaffolding on teachers' part in critical moments;
9. It envisaged real learning evaluation within task accomplishment.

The model of CALL teacher education that underpinned the teacher training courses was therefore not based on mastering particular skills but, given the dynamic nature of the environment and field, was attuned to identifying and comprehending the complex factors that impact on the integration of technologies in unique language teaching contexts. It also explored the importance of other support networks for CALL teachers, such as social media communities, continuing professional development and mentoring (Bauer-Ramazani, 2006). While the book offers several specific case studies on CALL teacher training, CALL is recognised as a highly innovative and fast-moving field (Kessler, 2006), and the challenges and opportunities identified will also be relevant to teacher trainers, trainee teachers and more established teachers who work in the wider context of teacher development in education and/or educational technology in schools, colleges and higher education (Kessler & Plakans, 2008).

Digital Video and Machinima

While foreign language teacher development is a central focus of the book, other concerns include the role of foreign languages in terms of their place in the school and university curriculum (Brumfit, Myles, Mitchell, Johnston, & Ford, 2005; Mitchell, 2010). Although foreign language learning is often perceived as a valuable subject in that it provides learners with important skills for the global economy, its place is often still as a minor or marginal subject with respect to what are perceived to be more vital skills for employability in science, technology or mathematics. And while interactionism and communicative approaches have risen to the foreground in the last decade in foreign language pedagogy, traditional behavioural approaches still often dominate pedagogical approaches in formal educational contexts where modern languages are studied (Mitchell & Myles, 2019). Out of this context, one of the central concerns of this book, then, is the potential of cross-curricular instructional approaches to teaching and learning which combine a variety of disciplinary perspectives on a topic, theme or project in such a way that they enable learners to harness their communicative, collaborative, critical thinking and civic engagement skills to solve a problem or series of challenges (Barnes, 2005, 2015; Dooly & Sadler, 2016; Gras-Velazquez, 2019). As Burns (2015) argues, "in terms of curricular provision [project-based learning] demonstrates the importance of connecting children's understanding of processes of representation and their creative practice across the range of what school curricula constitute as distinct disciplines" (p. 17). Sefton-Green (2014) simply called this 'connected learning' in which teachers and learners create new approaches or 'mash-ups' by mixing pedagogies across the distinctive structures that often separate the arts, humanities, media literacies and sciences.

The use of digital video in education first came to prominence in the 1980s and 1990s, initially through CD-ROMs and latterly through the World Wide Web, although its initial use was restricted due to slower bandwidth (Shrosbree, 2008). From the late 1990s, this changed as speeds increased, and in recent years digital video has re-emerged in the CALL education context as developments in 3G and 4G have led to increased download speeds that have normalised video use via superfast streaming services on video-sharing sites such as YouTube. According to Shrosbree (2008), whereas formerly video capture and editing required a significant investment in expensive and difficult-to-manoeuvre equipment, filming and editing can now be achieved with far less effort and on a small scale with devices that almost everyone has in their pocket. In the age of Web 2.0 technologies and mobile devices like tablets and smartphones, digital video can be created, edited, disseminated and shared in ways that suggest there may be fewer infrastructural barriers to entry for novice teachers (Vandagriff & Nitsche, 2009). While most students use video in their social lives for obtaining information and informal learning outside of school via Wikipedia, YouTube and Google, it is evident as Brooke (2003) suggests, that more research is required on how it is being harnessed both inside *and* outside formal educational contexts (Hafner & Miller, 2011).

In order to explore how educators can bridge the gap between the inside and outside of the classroom and formal and informal learning in the context of foreign language education, this book critically investigates a language teaching approach that utilises *machinima*, which Morozov (2008) defines as user-generated digital videos created in an immersive environment such as a three-dimensional (3D) digital game or immersive virtual world. Machinima are recordings of on-screen activity and interaction made by users in such environments and permit, for example, medical students studying English to fly through a virtual model of the human heart by following the flow of blood in an artery, students of German to walk the streets of virtual Berlin in the 1920s and talk to the people they meet in the target language or airline pilots studying English for Specific Purposes (ESP) to control a flight simulator in the language of their choice. According to Muldoon and Kofoed (2009), the affordances of 3D immersive environments mean that it is possible to *experience* learning first-hand in an authentic and meaningful way and to *learn by doing* in the process (Henderson, Huang, & Grant, 2009; Hew & Cheung, 2010; Jauregi & Canto, 2012).

For CLIL (Content and Language Integrated Learning), ESP or EAP (English for Academic Purposes) students, doing these activities while using a second language provides opportunities to immerse themselves in a realistic 3D context in which the target language is being used naturally and the learners are confronted by real-word challenges, tasks and problems.

The filmmaking involved in machinima can be planned meticulously to incorporate locations involving actors and extras (in this case, played by other learners or teachers) and the development of scripts and complex narratives or can be made 'on the fly' to record synchronous language learner interaction in the form of role-plays or conversations as they happen naturally (Brown & Holtmeier, 2013; Shrestha & Harrison, 2019). Outside of education, machinima regularly attract millions of hits on video-sharing websites such as YouTube, where gamers of school and university age create complex productions filled with content knowledge for communities of practice that have grown up around immersive social games such as World of Warcraft (WoW) or The Sims. Indeed, supplemental fan-fiction communities in the shape of wikis, blogs and social networking sites, as Sauro (2017) has suggested, have been created by learners around the activities, thereby generating opportunities for further discussion, engagement and skills development in reading and writing (see also Sauro & Sundmark, 2016). Such environments are not devoid of educational content and knowledge then; rather, they present learners with potentially significant opportunities to discover, explore, collaborate and create products and solve real-world tasks in ways that may lead to knowledge acquisition across a range of disciplines (Catak, 2010). Gee (2004), for example, has called this approach 'distributed learning', by which he means an approach to learning that is driven by the creation and sharing of knowledge by individuals in such a way that it advances the collective knowledge of the participants of a knowledge community as a whole.

Arising from a range of themes that are highly relevant to educators in the modern teaching and learning landscape, this book is situated in a wider pedagogical context in which as Brooke (2003), Schneider (2014a) and Shrosbree (2008) have argued, video has become a medium for language educators who seek to harness the potential of visual forms of communication. While we are critical of generalised attempts to homogenise today's youth under such labels as the 'digital generation' or 'digital natives' (Prensky, 2001), primarily because such terms erase differences within and between individuals such as socio-economic class, race, nationality and gender (Thomas, 2011), it is evident that many young people utilise digital devices in the form of smartphones, tablets and computers as a gateway to communication, collaboration and interaction (Palfrey & Gasser, 2010); it is how and why this happens that is worthy of further investigation and critical analysis in this book.

In terms of a pedagogical approach, machinima can be explored in the context of project-based learning in that learners look at a problem through the lens of several disciplines (Charara, 2016). Starting from a focus on project-based language teaching (PBLT) and a multidisciplinary approach to cross-curricular learning (Barnes, 2015), the book explores a vision of foreign language education for the digital age in which learners and instructors have the opportunity to integrate several skills (e.g., skills in the technical area, digital literacy, intercultural communication and project management) in addition to those associated with traditional forms of language instruction such as learning vocabulary and grammar or fluency, accuracy and complexity (Dooly & Sadler, 2016). This approach has been defined more broadly as project-based learning in the general sense, as it incorporates multiple rather than single unconnected tasks, or following González-Lloret (2017) technology-mediated project-based language teaching (TMPBLT), as it identifies a key role for collaborative digital technologies in the process language development. Thus, the book examines a vision of foreign language learning that moves the discipline from the margins of the school or university curriculum, in which it may occupy one or two hours per week in the curriculum in a dedicated space or language lab, to one that is at the centre of an interdisciplinary or theme-based approach to learning (Barnes, 2015; Ward-Penny, 2010). Particularly in the school sector, but also in the further and higher education context, this repositioning or reconceptualisation of language learning means that pupils and students can use and learn about a variety of interconnected disciplines at the same time. This approach is positioned in such a way that does not simply oppose employability skills with those developed by a liberal arts education, which is focused on individual self-development and cultivating an organic relationship with the communities and society in which their educational institutions are positioned. In this sense, the book considers the argument advocated by Gray (2019) among others, that language learning should not be viewed as a 'luxury' subject or one that is not quite legitimate because its use value cannot be immediately determined within an increasingly neoliberal educational system. As such advocates of machinima argue that its potentially original and significant contribution to debates in this field emerge from its advocacy of an approach to language learning in which students acquire the key skillsets necessary for today's multicultural global context. Moreover, as education in immersive environments also deals with intercultural competence, it is not merely focused on the *products* that learners produce; it is also focused, as Wegerif (2013) argues, on the *process* of personal self-development and self-discovery that learners experience and acquire as part of open-ended critical enquiry. Set in this context, the vision of project-based language learning is explored with respect to the potential it has for promoting a values-based approach to learning, enabling students to learn about their own culture through learning about other cultures and other ways of life, as well as promoting values of respect, wisdom, compassion for others and multiculturalism.

Methodology

Teacher education in CALL is central to the book's investigation of the integration of digital technologies in foreign language learning. Language teachers may be increasingly aware of the technologies available and how students use them in their social lives outside school, but more opportunities are required, as Hegelheimer (2006) has argued, to understand the range of methodologies needed to use them effectively.

The case studies explored in the latter parts of the book critically examine the influence and impact of the outputs and research arising from a large, European Union–funded project on video-based teaching and learning. The two-year project involved consortium partners from universities in the UK, the Czech Republic, Poland and Turkey and small and medium-sized enterprises (SMEs) within the digital start-up sector from Germany, the Netherlands, Belgium and Poland. From the pedagogical perspective, the video project began with four macro-level objectives:

1. to explore language learning in authentic immersive virtual environments;
2. to investigate how teachers and learners develop the skills to produce real-time video productions in immersive environments (i.e. machinima);
3. to understand how to design machinima and lesson plans across a range of languages (English, German, Polish and Turkish); and
4. to evaluate two iterations of an open online CALL teacher education course aimed at helping teachers to learn the pedagogical and technical skills required to design, create and use machinima in their pedagogical contexts.

The video project was the first to analyse the available research in the field of machinima and foreign language learning in immersive education and several stages were integral in the project's life cycle. First, a needs analysis of teachers and learners involved in the use of video-based learning was undertaken, and this led, in turn, to the identification of guidelines for teachers about how to integrate video-based language learning materials and resources into their classroom teaching contexts. Next, example machinima were created for language teachers to use with their students prior to field testing by a variety of educational providers across different sectors in the project's partner countries. Results from the field-testing phase of the project were then used to design and develop an open online teacher training course or MOOT offered in the Moodle virtual learning environment (VLE) to train teachers about the pedagogical and technical processes involved in the design, production and integration of machinima in their curricula.

The findings arising from the video project's use of machinima suggest that teachers felt empowered to produce materials for language learning that emphasised learner creativity, underlined the importance of collaborative forms of teaching and learning and advanced machinima as a cost-effective means of producing digital video that enabled teachers and learners to develop a diverse skill set including technical, literacy, intercultural and language-related skills. These were primarily connected with advancing language learner creativity and exploring the potential of collaborative forms of learning using digital technologies to encourage lifelong learning. The potential of digital technologies and applications associated with virtual and immersive environments and the role of user-generated video production formed the core of these concerns. The key questions informing the project's use of digital video involved the following:

1. How can teachers create learning environments utilising digital video for their students?
2. How can teachers develop students' abilities to learn and practise at their own pace?
3. How can teachers encourage students to learn about the target culture?
4. How can teachers work with students to jointly create digital resources in an engaging way?
5. How can teachers stimulate learner engagement in the language learning process to develop key digital skill sets?

In exploring these aspects of the project's approach, the book critically investigates its use of a mixed-methods approach consisting of case studies and examines its findings on CALL teacher education with respect to current debates about the role of technology-mediated project-based language learning (González-Lloret, 2017) and cross-curricular forms of teaching and learning (Barnes, 2015).

One of the core areas of the research involved observing participants in the online teacher training courses, which aimed to provide teachers with the skills to create machinima and the pedagogy to apply them in their everyday teaching contexts. Observation was carried out during synchronous training sessions in the 3D virtual world of SL and the videoconferencing application Adobe Connect and included class recordings, analysis of lessons and focus group discussions. Further observations took place in the Moodle course management platform which was used to host the asynchronous training sessions and included documentation of all activities and discussions, analysis, feedback, focus group discussions, self-assessments and questionnaires. Skype and in-world interviews with expert machinimatographers and language teachers using machinima in their classroom were also conducted (see Appendix VI).

The field testing of machinima, which were specifically created for educational use, was evaluated through the analysis of interviews, reports, focus group discussions and questionnaires. The field-testing events were conducted with a variety of large and small learner groups conducted by the project's partner institutions in five countries (Turkey, Poland, the Czech Republic, the Netherlands and Germany). The testing groups recruited in these countries were university students, learners in vocational education, Erasmus students and military staff and focused on different language levels and skills, such as vocabulary and grammar, cultural differences and mathematics in the CLIL course. The lessons were provided in English, German, Polish and Turkish. Five of these teaching events were chosen for case study research to investigate the variety of learning contexts, and to identify examples of good practice within different scenarios (Hoffman, 2006). The following five case studies were selected to demonstrate a range of genres and potential uses of the machinima utilised during the pilot testing:

a.   Case 1 examined two web-based language courses which used machinima for adult learners of German, levels A1 and A2 according to the Common European Framework of Reference (CEFR). The study compared an independent set of machinima with a set of interrelated episodes.
b.   Case 2 evaluated machinima on health and safety used by a group of engineering students at B1-level English studying in higher education in the Czech Republic.
c.   Case 3 investigated how the Pythagoras theorem could be explained via machinima in a CLIL-informed mathematics lesson in the medium of English.
d.   Case 4 piloted machinima with learners of Turkish at a university in Istanbul.
e.   Case 5 explored machinima in a military university in Poland.

The book thus explores the aim of providing language teachers with the technical and pedagogical knowledge to create interactive and authentic machinima that could be adapted to their specific needs and learning contexts. Based on the aim to investigate learning in virtual worlds and immersive environments, the book evaluates the effectiveness of the project with respect to (a) the technology-mediated project-based learning approach and (b) the online CALL teacher education course, in order to identify implications that can be used by CALL teacher trainers and trainees in future.

An Overview of the Book

In order to understand the potential affordances of 3D immersive environments in terms of project-based learning, it is important to begin our discussion of the field by first examining the broader context of existing research.

Having established the context of the book in the introduction, Chapter 2, 'Immersive Education and Machinima', presents a critical review of existing research on immersive learning environments, video-based learning and machinima production in educational contexts. This chapter explores how foreign language educators have been using immersive environments over the last decade to investigate behavioural factors influencing second language development, such as learner anxiety and learner confidence, as well as the potential of collaborative learning, and how to design authentic and meaningful tasks in such environments. Various definitions of machinima are explored which explain how it emerged as a fusion of several creative platforms such as filmmaking, animation and 3D game technology; to this we might also add language learning skills.

The next sections of the chapter explore research on how to create machinima and how it has been integrated into education to date (Muldoon & Kofoed, 2011). Other sections deal with the potential of using immersive worlds for teaching special educational needs (Drigas & Ioannidou, 2013), CLIL as an approach that enables learners to study substantive content as well as learn or improve their knowledge and understanding of a foreign language, experiential learning which is used to underpin the design and creation process (Morozov, 2008), as well as the benefits and challenges presented by machinima (Johnson & Pettit, 2012).

Chapter 3, 'Technology-Mediated Project-Based Language Teaching', outlines the relevant research context on project-based learning and discusses its origins in task-based language teaching approaches. Task-based language teaching has steadily developed over the last three decades, and increasing amounts of research on the subject have emerged covering a range of subtopics from assessment to curriculum design. The chapter first defines project-based language learning in terms of its core group of characteristics which focus in particular on real-world activities. Following this, the chapter turns to consider the role of twenty-first-century skills and language education as the relationship between technology and task- and project-based learning has become increasingly prominent since the emergence of Web 2.0 technologies (Wang & Vasquez, 2012). The chapter concludes by examining research on CLIL in this context and discusses connections with CALL teacher education as the lens through which to explore video teacher training courses.

Chapter 4, 'Creating and Field Testing Machinima in the Language Classroom', explores the pedagogical potential of machinima in several contexts, each representing different educational sectors. A variety of machinima in formats were piloted by three universities in Turkey, Poland and the Czech Republic, as well as a secondary school in the Netherlands and a commercial language school in Germany. Key aims of the video project are investigated as a result of the field testing: how it sought to aid communication in the target language of the partners; its focus on learning foreign languages such as English, German, Polish and Turkish; the importance of CLIL and the role of foreign language instruction in teaching technical subjects in science and technology; how the project sought to develop a range of digital skills for teachers and learners and promote an awareness of metacognitive skills associated with learning to learn; the importance of interpersonal and intercultural communication skills alongside traditional language learning skills; its vision of the learner as a creator of content rather than a passive receiver; and the assumption that language learning promotes opportunities for cultural knowledge acquisition and the development of important values such as mutual understanding. Important in evidencing these outcomes was the research framework, and this is discussed in this chapter in terms of its mixed-methods model which used a case study approach (Boellstorff, 2008; Mawer, 2014; Tellis, 1997; Yin, 2014) to analyse and evaluate the engagement of language teachers in learning to create machinima. Furthermore, the methods explored the potential added value machinima provided for language learning and teaching. Observation was also part of this as the project focused on small groups and individuals, following a holistic approach as outlined by Cohen, Manion, and Morrison (2007) and Yin (2014) utilising observation during the training courses, interviews and focus group discussions as qualitative research methods.

The chapter discusses the findings from the field testing in relation to five case studies: case study 1 explores using machinima in independent stories in a commercial language learning context in Germany; case 2 examines teaching English for engineering focusing on health and safety in the Czech Republic; case 3 focuses on the teaching of mathematics with machinima via the work of a Dutch CLIL teacher who taught mathematics to 13- and 16-year-old students in English at a secondary school in the Netherlands; case 4 explores machinima at a university in Istanbul, Turkey; and case 5 investigates teaching machinima in a military university in Poland.

Chapter 5 discusses trainee feedback on the two CALL teacher education courses in which data were collected from questionnaires, interviews and focus group discussions in order to investigate teachers' experiences, their digital literacy skills and their familiarity with the concept of machinima. While the first part of the chapter focuses on the pilot iteration of the CALL teacher education course, the second part examines the changes made as a consequence and the data collected from the second iteration. For the interviews and focus group discussions, a semi-structured approach was adopted.

This preliminary research was carried out during a series of introductory seminars in the Czech Republic, the Netherlands, Poland and Turkey and aimed to address groups of teachers interested in and open to innovative developments in language teaching. The seminars aimed to familiarise teachers with machinima and raise their awareness of and interest in participating in the teacher training courses. The results were used to help design and organise the MOOT pilot course according to learners' identified needs. Furthermore, the aims of the teacher training course are examined in the context of a needs analysis that was used to identify teachers' own interest in learning to create machinima. All the teachers who responded to the needs-analysis questionnaire, interviews and discussions already had a pedagogical background and teaching experience, although the majority of respondents were not familiar with 3D learning environments or machinima. Thus, the course structure and participants of the course are described, and some key themes such as machinima and time management, lessons learnt from the first iteration and immersion in virtual environments are discussed, particularly in relation to the expected level of quality in machinima production, feedback and end-of-course discussion.

Finally, Chapter 6, 'Afterword: Implications for Project-Based Teaching and Creativity', explores the impact of the project in relation to a wide range of outcomes related to project-based and cross-curricular learning and the key findings of the research are summarised in terms of the machinima created in SL as well as ready-made machinima used in the physical classroom. In this respect, the study was based on the hypothesis that teachers who immerse themselves in virtual worlds understand the values and benefits of this learning environment better than those who merely use machinima without being involved in the production process. How machinima are used as a tool for assessment and feedback is also explored in relation to how machinima could be utilised for self-reflection. The visual form of feedback made available by machinima emerged as a potentially valuable tool for reflection, as this allowed learners the opportunity to review their interactions as well as their linguistic and extra-linguistic performance. The quality of the machinima, with regard to the expected outcomes of the machinima productions and the way machinima were perceived by users, was also important, as was the time and effort required in relation to the machinima productions. Consequently, a central question examined to what extent the creation of machinima was worth the time and effort in relation to its value-added dimension. As discussed in the case studies, the creation of machinima was an extremely time-consuming process, especially because of the technical challenges involved.

In the closing sections of the chapter, the limitations and recommendations arising from the research are explored in order to investigate the unique challenges and opportunities presented by the project-based approach and the implications for designing CALL teacher education courses. Recommendations about further studies that include a more significant qualitative dimension and deploy ethnographic approaches to understand learner and teacher perceptions and behaviour in immersive VLEs and online CALL teacher training environments are also outlined.

2 Immersive Education and Machinima

Introduction

Over the last decade, a growing body of research has identified how 3D immersive environments have the potential to enable collaborative and personalised forms of language learning (Jauregi & Canto, 2012; Panichi & Deutschmann, 2012; Zheng, Newgarden, & Young, 2012). Immersive environments provide much more depth than traditional VLEs do by offering students 3D models of real-life simulations in an environment that is graphically rich with interactive content and based on models of social interaction (Blyth, 2017; Yamazaki, 2018). While many studies have explored the use of immersive worlds for learning, few have examined their potential for teacher training. Further research needs to be undertaken on how they can be used to embed them as a mainstream teaching environment (Torsani, 2016). A series of challenges in this respect are evident in terms of the technological expertise, support structures, research ethics and project management skills required, as these are central to pedagogical tasks and projects involving machinima.

Most machinima production has taken place in 3D virtual immersive environments such as SL and OpenSim or gaming environments like WoW and later Minecraft, and research on these platforms has been essential to the early stages of machinima integration in educational contexts (Shrestha & Harrison, 2019). Founded in 2003, following the emergence of Web 2.0, SL became the most prominent immersive virtual environment in the first decade of the new millennium. During this period, it was often buffeted by grand claims about the number of registered users it had, a trend that hit a peak in media hype between 2005 and 2008 when Linden Lab claimed the site had more than 12 million participants. Regardless of the hyperbole and marketing hype that has often surrounded it, SL has been one of the most successful multi-user virtual environments (MUVE; Warburton, 2009). Others include sites such as ActiveWorlds, IMVU, There, Twinity, Open Wonderland and OpenSimulator. Unlike SL, which is not considered a digital gaming environment, WoW is currently one of the world's most subscribed to massively multiplayer online role-playing game (MMORPG) with more than 5 million subscribers (Statista, 2019), whereas the number of users in SL has declined from its peak of 1.1 million monthly users to an estimated 800,000 to 900,000 users as of 2018, and it is clearly in decline. Nevertheless, it is not clear to what extent this is an accurate figure as it is difficult to determine how 'active users' are defined or how 'active' is understood in relation to the frequency of user activity. In order to understand the role played by machinima in 3D virtual worlds such as SL to date, it is important to begin our discussion of this field by first examining the broader context of research on immersive digital environments and clarifying the key debates that have emerged. While SL has failed to disrupt education in the ways originally envisaged, valuable lessons can still be learned from critically examining findings arising from research studies in which it has been a central concern (Kim, Lee, & Thomas, 2012; Sadler, 2012; Sadler & Dooly, 2013).

Prior to exploring the research on immersive education and defining machinima more closely, the first section of this chapter examines CALL teacher education, as this is a central concern of the book and the teacher training course discussed in Chapter 5.

CALL Teacher Education

The research on teacher training with information and communication technology (ICT) over the last three decades has generally provided positive if limited evidence to support the integration of technology in education (Hubbard & Levy, 2006; Kessler, 2006). According to Hubbard (2008), the main reasons limiting the development of CALL teacher education include the lack of qualified and experienced trainers, insufficient understanding of methodology and the absence of the relevant infrastructure and time. Even today, teacher training courses do not always equip trainees with the required skills to utilise learning technologies in the language classroom. To address this gap, more research has focused on technology implementation, the characteristics of the learners or the potential of the technologies (Chapelle, 2005). The challenges associated with integration have generally centred on five main factors, as Mumtaz (2000, p. 319) has identified:

- factors that discourage teachers from using technology;
- the nature of pedagogical organisations;
- the factors that encourage teachers to utilise technology;
- how the roles of teachers and ICT impact on pedagogy;
- how teachers learn to integrate technology into their pedagogical activities.

The factors influencing teacher use of ICTs have remained consistent over the last few decades and more research is required on how the increasing correlation between technology and 'innovation', which is often perceived through the lens of economic discourse associated with marketisation, has shaped them (Player-Koro et al., 2017). Teachers consistently highlight their lack of ICT experience, deficiencies in on-site technical support, lack of appropriate hardware, limited time in their workload to adequately integrate technology and lack of financial resources as key factors in the process (Rosen & Weil, 1995). Likewise, early research that identified teacher profiles remains relevant today. Evans-Andris (1995), identified three predominant types, including avoidance, technology integration and teachers who develop technical specialisation. Cuban's (1993, 2003) research on the use of technology remains prescient in this respect, as he identified the power of cultural beliefs about what teaching is and their importance in shaping more conservative approaches to technology integration. Second, the continuing reliance on late nineteenth-century models of 'age-graded' education may restrict opportunities for adaptation. Three dominant profiles of teachers emerge, namely, the technophile, the preservationist and the cautious optimist. In the first situation, increasing availability of hardware has transformed teachers into mentors and coaches that enable students to learn more effectively to overcome difficulty. In the second, the structures of the institution are maintained, and technology has become a tool for teachers and learners to use. The cautious optimists are identified with a steady change in an institution's organisational structures resulting in more profound changes in approaches to teaching and learning. Cuban's approach to teacher profiles critiques the notion of teacher resistance which is a commonplace stereotypical assumption which often conceals the fact that teachers are willing to change if provided with the necessary support rather than reinforcing identities that suggest teachers are inept or incapable of harnessing technologies effectively. The research suggests that there are three key factors that are often recurrent in findings relating to the educational institutions, the resources they provide to teachers and the beliefs, expertise and expectations of the teachers themselves.

Over the last decade CALL teacher education has attracted a steady increase in research interest (Egbert et al., 2018). The increasing availability of low-cost and easy-to-use technologies is one reason for this, as well as a growing recognition of the accompanying need for language teaching practitioners to stay abreast of these opportunities and to adopt more research-informed and less *ad hoc* approaches to the use of technologies (Chun, 2017). The unsatisfactory trial-and-error approaches that often accompanied earlier stages in CALL integration were typically left up to teachers themselves, and few had opportunities for structured in-house training in educational institutions or in pre-service contexts. With the rise of the web and online training, there are more courses available for language teachers interested in CALL, but it is important for structured training to be developed in both pre- and in-service language teaching contexts (Leahy, 2006; Hong, 2010).

Like the wider field of educational technology, CALL has often been perceived to be a technology rather than a pedagogy-based domain in which intuition and tacit knowledge often take precedence over theory-led approaches (Hubbard & Levy, 2006; Stockwell, 2007). Guided by a heavily deterministic logic that owes a great deal to the prevalence of technology industry marketing, technology is often mistakenly perceived as being capable of influencing any teaching context into which it is introduced (Bax, 2011b). Indeed, while the rhetoric of technology education is often underpinned by the language of innovation, the mere presence and use of digital technologies does not mean that the use will lead to effective integration. While technology has become more widely available in students' out-of-class social contexts, digital technologies have become increasingly normalised in terms of tools for communicating and students may be less willing to perceive their uninformed use as motivating in themselves (Bax, 2003). The so-called wow factor, as Bax (2011b) pointed out, may also lead to learners who expect more from their mere appearance, and teachers are expected to have relevant skills and a clear rationale for digital technology usage than may have been required a decade ago.

CALL teacher education has developed significantly over the last decade, and there are now a variety of options available within institutions or offered by certified providers or by special interest groups and national and international language educator and CALL associations (Iskold, 2003; Son, 2002). These courses have developed an emphasis on several key areas, including teachers' technological and digital literacy skills (Robb, 2006), to develop their confidence and technical infrastructure. It is evident from research on the topic that technology use does not always lead to innovation (Kessler & Plakans, 2008) or the required balanced perspective that derives from a fuller understanding of the context of the learning environment (e.g., a profile of the needs and expectations of the learners, learning objectives and, crucially, understanding that different learners will use different technologies in different ways rather than uniformly; Levy & Stockwell, 2006). Building on these two approaches, namely, to technology skills and the needs analysis, it is evident that CALL teacher education can encourage different research approaches as well, such as the use of diary studies, as well as research on the mentor–mentee relationship. Most studies conducted tend to be qualitative in dimension given the focus on ascertaining teachers' perspectives on their teacher development (Chun, 2017).

Some teachers faced with CALL technologies choose to use those they are already familiar with such as email rather than risk adopting those that may leave them feeling uncomfortable or that require more specialised technical skills. As Stockwell (2013), suggests, however, convenience may be a leading factor but may limit the pedagogical underpinnings of the technology usage, which has typically been led more by such factors as ease of use, cost and availability. To mitigate this risk, teachers need to develop a critical perspective on technology usage as indicated by their use of diary-based approaches to integration, as well as their ability to draw on a research-informed approach through the use of relevant CALL journals and data-driven studies and reports (Egbert et al., 2018).

Teachers attempting to integrate technology may be supported by a more capable other or mentor or undertake peer observation (Mann, 2005). Nevertheless, both approaches can present challenges in the workplace and may lead to loss of face in front of students or colleagues if not handled sensitively (Wajnryb, 1992). The support in evidence in mentoring and peer observation may also contribute to teacher support groups or communities of practice, which may be face-to-face or virtual or a combination of both modes of delivery (Boon, 2007). Where there is limited support from educational management within institutions, particularly when CALL teachers are working abroad, bottom-up teacher development and support infrastructure may need to be established by teachers themselves. Stockwell (2013) identifies three main implications for CALL teacher education. These include recognising that results will not be instant and that teachers need to cultivate resilience and perseverance in order to develop the required appreciation of and skills necessary for dealing with digital technology integration. In this respect, a trial-and-error approach may be useful but one that is informed by relevant knowledge of CALL research. Second, communities of practice can help in providing the confidence to experiment and the discussion fora to exchange opinions. Finally, teachers need to develop a critical pedagogical perspective in which they critique normalised assumptions and do not merely accept the easiest possible route. Teacher resilience is based on an acceptance of failure as well as taking responsibility for being an active agent of change and self-development.

Moving from the wider context to the specific CALL teacher development context, there are several consistencies across much of the research. While CALL has developed significantly in terms of support structures over the last two decades, particularly as a result of web-based discussion groups and national and international teacher associations as well as more dedicated CALL modules on training courses up to master's level, the overwhelming majority of teachers still accrue the majority of their skills through informal sources (Kessler, 2007). This continues to cause challenges to teachers' confidence and the more advanced skills required to be proficient. While digital literacy skills and how to use a technology are important, they often do not provide a framework for successful integration from the pedagogical point of view (Kern, 2006). Indeed, Egbert et al. (2002) suggest that teacher preparation courses need to be ongoing rather than one-off events. Kessler (2007) also indicates that trainee teachers are likely to learn using older technologies and programs and therefore are not always best prepared to integrate newer technologies. The research on dedicated teacher training courses identifies the need for a positive attitude from trainees and a willingness to challenge existing conventions in terms of what is accepted technology usage (Kadel, 2005), and an openness to constructivist approaches has helped teachers to be adaptive to new technologies (Becker & Riel, 2000). Nevertheless, Vodanovich and Piotrowski (2004) point out that institutional barriers to entry may impact on teachers' positive behaviour, namely, the time required to plan and integrate the technologies. A central theme of many of the research studies on CALL teacher education has focused, as a result, on developing teachers' confidence and specific technology skills. This, however, remains a difficult task given the frequency with which technologies change and develop, and it is important that teachers have a deeper understanding of the technology available and the contexts into which they seek to integrate them (Kessler & Plakans, 2008). Confidence with technology comes with repetition and an environment in which teachers are given the freedom to experiment and take risks without fear of being unable to deliver on quantitative measures of student achievement. Kessler and Plakans (2008) found that highly confident CALL teachers did not necessarily use technology more than teachers with lower levels of self-perceived confidence. In fact, highly confident teachers tended to use CALL technologies less in terms of frequency and less in terms of appropriateness; when they used CALL, it was often in an *ad hoc*, unconnected or unplanned way. Less confident teachers, on the other hand, tended to use CALL technologies in a more deliberative fashion that strongly correlated with institutional expectations and norms and the curriculum. Kessler and Plakans's findings indicate that teachers who are highly confident may not always transfer this into teaching innovation, which corroborates earlier research by Galloway (1997), thus deconstructing more generally accepted views that confidence levels are connected with expertise. Confidence with CALL technologies are based on several recurring factors in the research, including familiarity with technology, the existence of effective written instructions, effective preparation (Hegelheimer, 2006) and the ability to deal with single or multitasked environments (Kessler & Plakans, 2008).

As indicated in the preceding discussion, opportunities for training have multiplied, particularly as a consequence of online professional development and principally as a result of perceived cost and time-efficiency savings (Compton, 2007). Such courses are required to enable high degrees of communication and interaction (Hampel & Stickler, 2005).

Immersive Digital Environments

In relation to immersive digital environments, it is important to begin by first defining our key terms, as the field has led to a growing body of work across several disciplines, and this has not encouraged a standardisation of terminology. Schroeder (2008), for example, defined virtual and immersive environments as "a computer-generated display that allows or compels the user (or users) to have a sense of being present in an environment other than the one they are actually in, and to interact with that environment" (p. 25, cited in Warburton, 2009, p. 415). According to Meyers (2014),

> [c]ommunication in a virtual world is . . . dependent on two levels of meaning making: in-world comprehension of digital action and a translation of that meaning to out-world significance. The two levels of meaning combined become a "literacy" of digital play. To be fluent in this kind of literacy requires immersion in the culture of the space.
>
> (p. 670)

Central to most definitions is the idea that immersive worlds enable teachers and learners to create or use 3D objects so that they can model and explain complex and dynamic phenomena (Panichi & Deutschmann, 2012). Such activities include conducting real-world experiments in non-high-risk environments or in those impossible to re-create in the real world. The types of collaboration and interaction enabled by immersive environments may aid learner development, a key principle of SLA. Central to interaction in immersive environments is social presence, which is typically defined as the notion of 'being there' or the 'salience' of other people participating in a mediated form of communication (Kim et al., 2012). The principles underpinning education in immersive environments owe a great deal to the constructivist approach in this respect (Huang & Liang, 2018), which stresses the importance of personal engagement, reflection and interaction as part of the learning process. Being part of the virtual environment means fully immersing in it so that learners and teachers feel part of it. Building on ideas related to social presence, other researchers have identified the importance of immediacy and intimacy. Whereas the immediacy is evident in the use of synchronous technologies, for example, to enable communication at a distance. Intimacy, on the other hand, is often related to physical proximity, such as eye contact and facial proximity and other factors evident in presence-based or face-to-face interaction (Panichi, 2015). Immersive environments can help to sustain presence through creating authentic tasks and this is a further connection with constructivism, which is not concerned with learning for the sake of it but with fostering a type of learning that has a direct practical application. Knowledge is constructed based on personal experience, personal reflection and metacognitive skills, and students work with peers to share the knowledge construction process (Sadler, 2012).

It is clear that virtual reality and immersive environments have evolved rapidly during the last decade and been used to address a diverse range of complex problems and challenges in education. Different definitions of immersive environments have also evolved, from virtual reality to immersive reality to those using head-mounted displays (HMD) and a plethora of terms have developed in response. In HMD, participants are stimulated to feel that they exist within the environment even though it is artificial. This presents the potential for participants to experience and explore training in safe environments in contrast to the real world which may present hazards or risk to health and safety.

While SL has become very well known as one of the leading immersive environments used by educators, there are a number of other prominent worlds. These include OpenSim (www.opensimulator.org) or OpenSimulator, which is an open-source multiplatform, multi-user 3D application server; There (www.there.com/), a social virtual world which attempts to enable participants to integrate emotion, body language and voice into real-time communication; Twinity (www.twinity.com/en), an online virtual environment that complements and amplifies the interests of young people by focusing on music, pop culture, fashion, celebrities, self-expression, communication, community and social networking; Entropia Universe (www.entropiauniverse.com/), an advanced 3D online virtual environment with a developed planetary system and a universal real cash economy; and Active Worlds (www.activeworlds.com/), which offers a comprehensive platform for delivering real-time interactive 3D content over the web. Within these worlds, participants can communicate with high-fidelity, immersive audio; share live desktop applications; and collaborate in an education, business or government context.

One of the attractions of the virtual environment is the feeling of presence they generate, as Edirisingha, Nie, Pluciennik and Young (2009, p. 459) argue, as "a 3D MUVE such as SL, has the potential to generate a sense of presence among peer learners via their avatars in a 3D environment through real-time interactions that may facilitate relationship-building, learners' engagement and motivation". At the centre of the virtual experience is the digital representation of the self through the use of an avatar. Via this 3D representation, users may imagine or create a new identity or identities for themselves (Ushioda, 2011) and, in turn, enable them to experience reality in a new way. As Falconer (2011, para 1) suggests, the

> advent of virtual worlds has provided another interface we can now inhabit; that between the virtual and the real. And, particularly, that the notion of in-betweenness becomes significant when virtual worlds are used for education through simulations of real life experiences and activities.

The avatar represents an opportunity for users to refashion him- or herself, and they often spend a significant time shaping and reshaping their avatars, which, as Savin-Baden's (2010) research has suggested, leads them to experiment on avatar identity and to adopt different genders or roles.

Indeed, as the preceding research indicates, users in virtual worlds often choose their avatars for a variety of complex reasons. According to Sant (2009), some users choose idealised versions of themselves in order to engage in anonymous forms of role-play, whereas others design their avatar's looks to reflect their real-life selves to enable them to conduct 'real-play' activities. As a result, Ushioda (2011) argues that users may feel that their avatars enable them to portray other aspects of their character and thus feel less inhibited than they would in real-world classroom environments. This approach may lead to fewer inhibitions, and students may be more outspoken or willing to take more risks in these environments (Peterson, 2010, 2011). One reason for this could be that they are potentially more individualised or student-centred (Coffman & Klinger, 2008), and the virtual world may enable learners to multitask in a way that is not possible in the traditional classroom, particularly as students can speak to others orally and via text chat separately or simultaneously (De Jong Derrington, 2013). Language learners may be able therefore to use the affordances of virtual worlds to socialise with native and non-native speakers and collaborate using a variety of learning strategies such as problem-based learning, collaboration and cooperation, as well as game-based learning. Utilising more authentic approaches to learning presents opportunities for them to communicate in real time (Edirisingha et al., 2009). Drawing on constructivist approaches to learning (Kluge & Riley, 2008) enables a more personalised approach to individual and group-based learning in which the participants themselves can contribute creatively to the environment in which they learn in order to create new and authentic learning content (Molka-Danielsen, 2009; Keskitalo, Pyykkö, & Roukamo, 2011; Salmon, 2009), thus aiding their ability to become independent and active learners and to engage in experiential learning approaches.

Teaching Foreign Language Learning in Immersive Environments

According to SLA theorists such as Krashen (1987), successful language learning is based on rich input that is compelling for learners and at the same time authentic. Language learning is not merely concerned with attention to grammatical competence but also engaged with a range of other important skills such as intercultural and pragmatic awareness (Ellis, 2005a). Moreover, according to Warburton (2009), immersive environments such as virtual worlds present learners with opportunities to experience these important aspects of language learning, including exposure to linguistic content as well as cultural artefacts. Immersive environments provide opportunities to stimulate interaction in rich visual contexts and through the use of avatars, this can lead to an emotional engagement with the experience. More significantly, immersion can enable learners to create objects and through this experience ownership and responsibility for particular spaces and places (Zheng et al., 2012).

While there are many potential advantages, engaging with virtual and immersive environments inevitably presents numerous challenges to learners and instructors alike. Kluge and Riley (2008) and Warburton and Pérez-Garcia (2009), for example, identified a range of problems including technical challenges, how a virtual identity might impact on an individuals' actions and sense of self, misunderstandings related to cultural codes and rules and how they are used to promote collaboration and build trust between participants and digital literacy skills, in particular those related to checking permissions for intellectual property and copyrighted objects.

With these opportunities and challenges in mind, let us now turn to consider how machinima have developed in 3D virtual worlds as a form of video production and how techniques have been developed to utilise them in the educational context. First, it is important to define the term *machinima* which is central to the video-based learning activities in immersive environments analysed in later chapters of the book.

Defining Machinima

The term *machinima* is a neologism derived from merging the words *machine* and *cinema* and was first used in the late 1990s (Carroll & Cameron, 2005; Hancock & Ingram, 2007; Marino, 2004; Kirschner, 2005; Snelson, 2010; Thomas, 2014), after one of the earliest Quake movies titled *Diary of a Camper* had been recorded; this is often described as the first machinima movie (Snelson, 2010). Arising from this context, machinima refers to

> The use of real-time computer graphics engines to create a cinematic production. . . . In a broad sense, any piece of linear audiovisual content such as a short film or series made with settings, characters, or video game engines can also be seen as machinima.
> (Machinima, n.d., para. 1–26)

Such in-world recording techniques were made possible through the inclusion of recording functionality in 3D games from around 1994, which enabled players to record and share sequences of gameplay in order to provide tips and tricks about how to succeed or progress to the next level in the game (Carroll & Cameron, 2005). As Marino (2004, p. 1) explains machinima is therefore "a mixture of several creative platforms – filmmaking, animation, and 3D game technology", in that visual narratives are created by recording events and performances (filmmaking) with artistically created characters moved over time (animation) within an adjustable virtual environment (3D game technology platform or engine). Machinima are able to "represent any conceivable object or sequence or event, while incorporating rich narrative structures, as well as graphical and text-based content, using visual and aural modalities through images, music subtitles and voice-overs" (Morozov, 2008, p. 9). They can be viewed as a creative visual form that requires users to develop their digital literacy skills as "anybody can record and edit unique visual experiences incorporating 3D character models and objects, set designs, graphical textures, camera angles, special effects, weather filters, custom lighting . . . with unlimited variations on plot, settings, and characters" (Morozov, 2008, p. 5899).

Whereas Picard (2006) defines machinima simply as making films from video games, which were originally associated with the game industry and created exclusively by gamers, Marino (2004) and Hancock and Ingram (2007) describe machinima as animated filmmaking within virtual environments using 3D videogame engine technology. For them, it is simply a technique to capture events in a virtual environment and to edit and publish the product with the same technology used for capturing 3D computer games. Morozov (2008), however, sees machinima as establishing a new era in technologies for designing audio-visual narratives, while Ng and Barrett (2013) differentiate between machinima and 3D animation. The latter associate machinima filmmaking with puppetry, which allows users to manipulate the characters and act out their role in a real-time sequence, thus requiring a certain amount of flexibility in shooting; this approach is in contrast to 3D animation in which users have total control over everything they see.

Brown and Holtmeier (2013) argue that even though machinima originated from both films and games they do not fit comfortably into either category. They claim that machinima differ from computer games as they generally follow different planning strategies, such as scripting and storyboarding, which provide detailed instructions about the story line and characters, and the dialogue between the characters is considered a more complex process (Snelson, 2010; Thomas, 2014). Moreover, Kirschner (2011) differentiates between people who create machinima to produce something with a particular game they like and those who use the technology without connection to a specific game who try to design and produce their own unique ideas. This is why the 3D virtual world of SL potentially differs from other machinima platforms as its content is user-generated and not 'rule-based' or 'goal-oriented', and therefore, it cannot be considered a game (Pinchbeck & Gras, 2011). This definition is also evident in the work of Dellario, who defines machinima as "the convergence of filmmaking, animation and game development. By combining the techniques of filmmaking, the flexibility of animation production and the technology of real-time 3D game engines, machinima makes for a very cost- and time-efficient way to produce films" (Dellario cited in Spiller, 2004, p. 3).

As these differing perspectives show, it is important in the context of educational technologies to be aware of their history in order to give a balanced – rather than over-exaggerated or understated – view of their potential and limitations (Bax, 2011b). New video-based technologies such as machinima are no exception in this respect. Machinima production techniques started around the turn of the new millennium due to advances in digital technologies and video production. Through technological advances in miniaturisation and developments related to the portability of equipment, the cost of design, production and hosting of video work of this type, the genre became increasingly accessible by a larger number of interested users (Shrestha & Harrison, 2019).

Machinima production derives from techniques in cinematography and according to Morozov (2008, p. 5906), a thorough knowledge of this approach is valuable in understanding

> the visual attention of the viewer, the appearance, facial expression and gestures of the characters when they are talking, the duration and placement of each scene in the overall composition, the camera angle and focus, lighting, the mood of the surroundings, the soundtrack and considerations relating to ambient noise.

In this context, it is important to understand the variety of production techniques available to machinimatographers, including straight recording, puppetry, recamming and scripting (Kelland, Morris, & Lloyd, 2005). Whereas straight recording is a simple process of recording online activity in the immersive environment, puppetry concerns the use of a structuring narrative to aid the performance of avatars. Recamming is a more sophisticated version of puppetry in which additional avatars, scenery and camera operations are integrated. Scripting, on the other hand, is a more advanced combination of all these aspects leading to the design of how avatars perform. As these techniques became easier due to increasing speeds of technology and cheaper production costs, machinima developed from around the late 1990s (Marino, 2004), with many new and original machinima productions emerging from the early 2000s (Middleton & Mather, 2008), leading to the greater recognition of the term in 2002 through the establishment of the Academy of Machinima Arts and Sciences (Marino, 2004). In particular, growth was evident as a result of interest in video games which has grown exponentially over this time. Machinima developed from recording techniques used by players of video games who used the on-screen recording technique to demonstrate particular tips and tricks or how to advance in the game. As a consequence, the narratives or game sequences became gradually more advanced through the use of different player perspectives and as the graphics' capabilities of the games improved alongside video editing software and storage capabilities (Morozov, 2008).

In terms of the teaching and learning skill sets required, machinima-tographers need a complex understanding of what Gee (2003) has called semiotic domains, namely, gestures, symbols, written languages and images to develop twenty-first-century literacy skills promoted by the New Media Consortium (Morozov, 2008). In the general education context, machinima are valuable because the production techniques enable educators to create current materials that are based on constructionist philosophies. The immersive environments associated with them enable the development of authentic and realistic simulated learning contexts and situations (Lombardi, 2007). These skills are associated with an understanding of "procedural language, problem solving, discussion, social pragmatics, storytelling, and code-switching between different genres of writing" (Lansiquot & Rosalia, 2008, p. 2661). The immersive environment of virtual worlds like SL promote such skills through their in-built functionality which enables users to personalise the use of cameras, scenes and locations and to design activities such as collaborative role-plays (Lansiquot & Rosalia, 2008). It is therefore possible to promote experiential learning, the ability to collaborate in group environments that can be based on task- and problem-based approaches to learning, and to design and create objects and spaces that can be used by other teachers and students to engage in active forms of learning (Morozov, 2008).

Significantly in this respect, as Muldoon and Kofoed (2009) indicate, this style of creative learning is best identified as encouraging an apprenticeship-style learning process in the classroom as it involves the engagement by instructors and learners in domain-related practices and the ownership of inquiry by those involved. It places a strong emphasis on coaching and modelling good practice and, related to this, the development of digital literacy skills around collaboration and social learning, as well as the development of a motivating learning context for the apprenticeship skills to develop (Barab & Duffy, 2000). The different stages in the development of the apprenticeship model are developed by the machinima production process through "the embedding of critical stages of apprenticeship in a classroom environment and at the same time minimiz[ing] the risk of extraneous cognitive load, the stages of apprenticeship are creatively entwined in the story, i.e., modelling, scaffolding and fading" (Muldoon & Kofoed, 2009, p. 2246). This definition in particular highlights the relationships between teachers and learners as well as within groups of learners themselves, which develop as a natural part of the machinima production process, where the focus is on promoting creativity between the various experts and novices involved.

Creating Machinima

Having explored the origins of machinima and its various definitions, it is important to examine how different areas of research on the subject have emerged. Research has examined the applicability of several methods to collect data in immersive environments in order to move beyond the traditional reliance on qualitative data from interviews and observation (Meyers, 2014). This has included research on how to design scenarios for machinima to encourage new digital literacies (Lacasa, Martinez, & Mendez, 2011), research on the role of avatars to communicate with students to develop emotional intelligence (Conkey, 2010), the motivational aspects of machinima production (Jones & Munro, 2009), the use of machinima in oral history projects (Fujimoto, 2010) and the role of machinima in the digital arts movement and its future implications (Harwood, 2011). Turning to students, other research has explored how students could benefit from synergies between digital gaming, cinema and animation (Catak, 2010), how the use of computer games and machinima in new media linked to their socio-educational experiences (Wendt, 2013), the different role-playing strategies that can be developed by students (Carroll & Cameron, 2005), what constitutes effective digital storytelling in machinima (Johnson & Runo, 2011) and how machinima emerges as a practice-based approach to learning which challenges students and instructors to develop their digital skill sets and competencies (Harwood, 2013). Other research has explored how visual scenes, actions and narratives from digital games can be used to produce sophisticated machinima narratives (Hsiao, 2013) and how machinima can be used by students to visualise their learning experience (Gregory, Gregory, & Gregory, 2013).

According to Constantinides (2012), Ng and Barret (2013) and Middleton and Mather (2008), the basic procedure of making machinima follows the same method and uses similar techniques as the production of real-world films. The process of creating machinima includes assigning different roles and responsibilities within the production team, such as film director, actors, camera operator and film editor. In addition, information about venues, props, ambience, lighting and sound effects need to be considered prior to filming (Rainbow & Schneider, 2014; Snelson, 2010; Thomas, 2014). Constantinides (2012) discovered that some of the steps involved in traditional filmmaking could also be adapted to the process of machinima production, whereas others needed to be refined, as there are different challenges involved in filming in a 3D immersive environment. One difference is that a screencasting application is needed instead of a video camera, but the post-production stage is similar to any video-editing process. Drax (2015) also considers the creation of machinima as very closely related to processes supporting independent filmmaking. He differentiates between something that is recorded and streamed in 3D, like the first demo recordings of games (e.g., Quake movies), and machinima that go through the entire life cycle of design, production and editing. Hancock and Ingram (2007) argue that real-life film shoots may be of better quality generally and therefore are more likely to be accepted by end users as a result. However, they also found that shooting machinima may be much faster and that the production process much more cost-effective overall. Snelson (2010), Spiller (2004) and Rainbow and Schneider (2014) agree with this assessment, because one person alone can produce machinima videos by assuming the roles and responsibilities indicated earlier in place of a full production team. While this approach may lead to low production costs (Hancock & Ingram, 2007; Rainbow & Schneider, 2014), this is not always the case, however, as conventional 3D production that includes detailed animation techniques can be just as expensive as real-life productions in that they require the use of specific animation software applications and may, in fact, require more time for editing overall (Ng & Barret, 2013).

Even though Ng and Barrett (2013) argue that anyone can make machinima, as it merely involves learning techniques to control avatars and film them, this might be a difficult challenge for novices as opposed to professional machinimatographers (Snelson, 2010). According to Morozov (2008), filmmaking is a complex process that requires a number of skills, such as scriptwriting, creating dialogues for the characters, set design, finding and preparing appropriate locations in immersive environments, acquiring permission for filming, recruiting characters and editing and producing the final film. Indeed, producing a relatively short two- or three-minute machinima can take a significant amount of time, effort and computer storage space, as a lot of footage is required (Drax, 2015).

Several other limitations relating to quality are also worthy of further consideration. Hancock and Ingram (2007) point out that computer-generated characters are rarely as convincing as a real-life person, even though animated speech gestures are increasingly available to use with avatars to make them more realistic. They argue that the movement of characters does not always look natural or smooth and therefore cannot be compared to real-life actors. Nevertheless, Johnson and Pettit (2012, p. 34) suggest that it is important to continue pushing the boundaries of this technology and to "experiment with techniques such as pose animations, lip-syncing, and some basic scripting techniques" in order to express human emotions through avatars. At the same time, however, they admit that this requires sophisticated knowledge and advanced skills of what is possible in immersive worlds. To mitigate some of these challenges, Conkey (2010) further identified how active listening can be critical in virtually mediated environments where body language and facial expression are key to understanding the communication expressed in machinima-based narratives (Farley, 2016).

Galani (2016a), on the other hand, argues that such deficits can be compensated for by other cues, such as the timbre, tone or volume of voice; the pace of speech; breathing; laughter; or even facial expressions such as a smile; this is all functionality that is increasingly being added to avatars to make them more authentic and realistic. Similar to Conkey (2010), Yogeswar (2015) discovered that animated avatars or characters are becoming popular in VLEs, because they add a "human touch" to online courses in which no human facilitator is available to the students. Conkey (2010) further observed that animated non-human characters are frequently used by companies and in businesses and expected that it was only a question of time until they would be fully integrated into everyday life. On the other hand, as Jauregi, Canto, De Graaff, Koenraad, and Moonen (2011) point out, learners in 3D environments who are used to their own and other peoples' alter egos in the form of their avatars, experience lifelike social interaction while at the same time engaging in meaningful learning. This means that encouraging learners' immersion in 3D environments by facilitating their interaction is key for a positive and meaningful learning experience (Farley, 2016).

Machinima in Education

Based on the discussion so far, it is evident then that machinima can potentially develop skills that are not always evident in traditional face-to-face education. As we have seen in the previous examples, machinima may offer opportunities for authentic learning, or what Muldoon and Kofoed (2011) term situated learning, in which learners are able to develop higher order critical thinking skills through the use of technology-enhanced learning environments. Indeed, their research suggests that student engagement and motivation may increase as a consequence. Thomassen and Rive's (2010) research on mixed-reality environments using machinima further confirmed the idea that virtual worlds may stimulate the feeling of close proximity which results in increased tacit knowledge exchange. Moreover, Barwell, Moore, and Walker's (2011) study of machinima production involving the MMORPG WoW, demonstrated the importance of designing technology-enhanced spaces in which the emphasis is on the *process* rather than the quality of the *product* produced. Their case study–based research involving students from two arts disciplines collaborating via WoW, demonstrated how it was possible to produce a complex animated interpretation of a work of literature, in this case Chaucer's *Canterbury Tales*, that motivated learners to engage creatively with the subject matter in place of an approach based on standardised testing. Such approaches have been further developed by Sauro (2017) in her research on online fan-fiction communities using literature in the language classroom.

This emphasis was also evident in Middleton and Mather's (2008) discussion of the educational value of immersive virtual worlds, as they highlighted how digital media works most appropriately alongside a blended curriculum where the media are designed specifically to address challenges, seed ideas or illustrate problems. In this context, involving learners in machinima production may enable learners to find value in the production process as a result of the stress on learner creativity, the reusability of open educational resources and materials and by utilising the 3D environment to aid the visualisation and simulation of important ideas and concepts (Shrestha & Harrison, 2019).

Special Educational Needs

One of the areas of educational research that has potential for significant further development in the field of immersive environments is its use with learners who have special educational needs, learning disabilities or challenges in learning (Drigas & Ioannidou, 2013). Preliminary research in this field suggests that immersive virtual environments can help overcome some of the challenges associated with communication, interaction, sensory and physical development, as well as emotional and social development. A range of developmental disorders are typically connected with communication skills and social integration skills. Disorders such as those on the autism spectrum have led to the development of specially adopted technology-enhanced learning environments in immersive worlds in which the affordances of the 3D immersive experience can ameliorate some aspects of their condition. Research by Smith (2010), for example, identifies how the Autism Society of America Island in the virtual world of SL contains several facilities that can be used to facilitate collaborative spaces for autistic people, their carers and their parents. Other sites such as Island Brigadoon in SL have also been especially designed to provide safe environments where autistic learners can develop their communication and social skills as well as self-confidence. Learners who experience challenges in traditional environments, for example, may benefit from the use of more visual 3D spaces where they can experience the illusion of authentic objects and learn at their own pace in a more personal and individual fashion (McKinney cited in Smith, 2010).

Across a range of learning disabilities, the affordances of machinima may enable learners to engage in role-playing situations in authentic environments, a factor that stands out as one of the central advantages of the technology (Parson & Mitchell, 2002). The virtual world thus presents learners with a non-threatening environment in which to simulate and engage in taught activities that they may encounter as more stressful in the real world (Mitchell, Parson, & Leonard, 2006). Moreover, role-play activities in the virtual world may help students with learning disorders such as Asperger's syndrome providing opportunities to practice social skills in a safe environment, either with others or with therapists, based on the principles of learner-centredness as described earlier (Parsons et al., 2000; Smith, 2010).

For other learning disorders such as dyslexia, which involves challenges associated with reading, writing and concentration, virtual environments may be used to aid the development of alternative pedagogical approaches utilising video, storytelling, mind-mapping, physical representations of learning materials and developing non-threatening collaborative group environments that are multisensory (Hall & Velez-Colby, 2011; Smith, 2010) or Virtual Reality Dyslexia Assessment–Memory Screening (VIRDA-MS) that help to detect specific memory characteristics in adults with dyslexia during their interaction in immersive environments (Kalyvioti & Mikropoulos, 2012). Overall, this is an area with significant potential for further research and may be seen as one part of a wider field of digital health. Numerous other examples exist, such as City University of London's use of a virtual environment called EVA Park to encourage interaction between patients who have suffered strokes and developed aphasia (Amaya et al., 2018).

Experiential Learning

As we have seen, then, machinima productions allow the creators to design videos on any topic and genre. Morozov (2008, p. 5905) discovered that making a machinima production across the whole cycle, from "casting to cutting", increased his understanding of the filmmaking process. The experience of being involved in the entire filming process, being in charge of choosing the characters, their movements and dialogues, the camera angles, light, ambient sounds and surroundings, made Morozov aware of the quality of other machinima.

Such an understanding foregrounds the important question of whether it is really necessary to experience the affordances of an immersive environment and whether learners who are exposed to the process benefit more from such an experience, particularly where machinima is involved. In this respect, Kolb's theory of Experiential Learning (Healey & Jenkins, 2000), which provides a holistic model of how students learn, may help to answer these questions. Kolb identified four stages of learning which can easily be applied to machinima-based experiences (Conkey, 2010; Rainbow & Schneider, 2014). The first phase, *concrete experience*, relates directly to learners' experience with machinima. During the second phase, the *reflective observation*, learners reflect on their experience, analyse it, ask questions and engage in discussion with others. During the third phase, *abstract conceptualisation*, learners try to understand the process and compare their newly gained knowledge with other familiar concepts. In the final phase, *active experimentation*, learners try out what they have learnt and experiment with it (Rainbow & Schneider, 2014).

Indeed, providing learners with machinima in order to reflect on their achievements and provide them with the opportunity to analyse and revise their performance is one of the most effective and rewarding ways of using machinima for student feedback (Corrigan, 2014; Galani, 2016a; Schneider, 2014a). In this vein, Dreher and Dreher (2009) also value machinima as an "effective form of visual presentation and feedback" which has the added advantage for students to "repeatedly review in order to permit a deeper level of reflection upon what has been done, how to improve and what has been learned" (p. 449). Furthermore, according to VirutalPREX (2012), the use of machinima as an assessment tool allows students to develop their critical thinking abilities and related skills such as self-critique and reflective judgement. These reflective processes may be better developed in pedagogical contexts through communities of practice in which learners and teachers can develop meaningful learning spaces designed to support and scaffold experimental forms of learning.

Machinima Events

Like many areas of educational technology, Lowood and Nitsche (2011, p. vii) consider machinima to be a "moving target" in that it is constantly being "pushed and explored" and in the process reinvented. According to Morozov (2008, p. 5905), this ongoing developmental process is enhanced by various informal 'maker' communities and groups that have developed as a result of machinima production. These informal communities of practice have enabled the development of an extraordinarily inventive community of educators, technicians and amateur machinimatographers to exchange ideas, support each other and acquire peer feedback on their productions. In Morozov's (2008, p. 5903) view, machinima "would not exist in its current form without a community of producers and consumers" to support its growth. While these groups have been instrumental in leading the development of machinima, recent changes also include the disappearance of popular communities such as Machinima.org, Machinimag.com and 3DFilmmaker.com, as well as the very popular Machinima Open Online Studio (MOSP; Aeon, 2015a). Some significant challenges faced by machinimatographers with regard to generating interest in their work may be responsible for this and include the fact that distributors are more focused on gaming and gameplay than artwork channels (Harwood, 2011, 2014). While the annual machinima contests of the University of Western Australia ended in 2015, there are other websites and blogs which continue to provide access to expertise in filmmaking, animation and video games. There are also other new developments, such as the Linden Lab Sansar project (Altberg, 2016; Charara, 2016) and the rapid progress in technology that aims to improve facial animation and develop more natural movements for avatars, which will also create more interest in the genre (Aeon, 2015b).

Apart from the machinima communities mentioned, there are also annual festivals and conferences that reward the best machinima productions, such as the Machinima Expo (2015), the annual ISTE Machinima Fest (ISTE, 2015), the Virtual Worlds – Best Practices in Education (VWBP, 2015) and SLanguages (2015). Many examples of machinima can be found on websites such as Machinima.com, Machinima Archive and YouTube (Snelson, 2010, p. 16). Based on the development of these 'maker' and sharing communities of practice, Fosk (2011, p. 26) states, that machinima have matured over the last decade, expanding to new genres of film-making with a particular focus on "story-telling and art-based work", and this is underlined by Harwood (2011, p. 6), who describes machinima as "an art form in evolution".

At the same time, machinima have begun to gain attention from language educators, who have discovered the value of creating virtual films for educational purposes. Spiller (2004, p. 2), for example, sees great potential in the use of machinima in language teaching as more and more teachers seek "new ways of engaging their students", suggesting that machinima would be particularly useful in classes with less commonly taught foreign languages as there is often a lack of material available to support them. Over the past few years, a significant number of machinima have been developed in different genres that are now available for teachers and learners, including lesson plans and teaching guides. The popularity of these materials is a result of their reusability and the materials can often be adopted and adapted to the individual context of the teachers (Middleton & Mather, 2008). To support the development of reusable content a series of regular events and training programmes have emerged over the last decade, and this is evidenced by *MachinEVO* (2012–2015), a free five-week workshop for language educators developed as part of TESOL's Computer-Assisted Language Learning Interest Section (CALL-IS).

Benefits and Challenges

Across all the previously mentioned areas, as we have seen, there are several benefits and limitations to the use of 3D immersive environments in educational contexts and the role machinima can potentially play within it. Some of the unique features of machinima identified by Morozov (2008, p. 5905) relate to the creative possibilities they offer in comparison to real-life videos. As Amsterdam suggests, machinima have "the potential to transform your story, characters, plot device and dreams into reality" (Johnson & Pettit, 2012, p. 44). In a machinima production, for example, weather conditions, such as wind, snow and storms, as well as light settings from daylight to night, can be controlled and manipulated according to the specific purpose of the machinima. Dangerous situations, like accidents, earthquakes and explosions, can be simulated and captured in machinima without causing harm to participants. Another advantage of machinima identified by Morozov (2008, p. 5905) is that they can

> be utilised as a stand-alone medium of original creative expression and communication, by gamers and non-gamers alike. The virtual reality environments, serving as development platforms for machinima movies, offer tremendous flexibility for representing (virtually) any conceivable object or sequence of events, while incorporating rich narrative structures, as well as graphical and text-based content, using visual and aural modalities (through images, music, subtitles, and voice-overs).

Creating interesting machinima for pedagogical purposes implies that facilitators new to 3D worlds need to change their views and establish different perspectives when acting in a virtual environment. Indeed, it is often reported that novices to virtual learning replicate their physical environment in virtual worlds rather than pursue aspects of the technology that may be truly disruptive of existing practice (Collins, 2008; Rainbow & Schneider, 2014; Thomas, 2010). In order to take full advantage of the potential offered by immersive environments teachers and learners new to them need to be encouraged to use 3D worlds in a way that applies their teaching or learning to the affordances of virtual worlds and to adjust to new virtual skills, methods and approaches accordingly.

To aid this process, for example, Lim (2009, p. 7) suggests six types of appropriate learning strategies in his framework of SL teaching. These types of learning could be applied to machinima-based content for language learning, as suggested by Rainbow and Schneider (2014). For example, *learning by exploring* could be utilised for exploring places like museums or art galleries and studying artefacts found there. *Learning by collaborating* could be facilitated by working as a part of a film team to plan a guided tour or reconstructing a house together that has fallen apart. *Learning by being* could be explored through role-plays in specific role-plays or individually *rezzed* scenes that establish different identities for the characters involved. *Learning by building* could be facilitated by setting up an exhibition or building props to use in a role-play. *Learning by championing* could involve making machinima to share information about a new tool. Finally, *learning by expressing* could be utilised as a significant resource to present an in-world event, for example.

While these different approaches provide many opportunities for further development and engaging in creative activities, it is evident that novice users of virtual environments generally feel overwhelmed by the opportunities for creativity afforded by machinima, as Morozov (2008, p. 5905) suggests:

> [Filmmaking is] . . . an immensely complex art form, encompassing a variety of areas of knowledge, from scriptwriting, to set design, to

post-production. Writing a good dialogue for the characters, even for a 2-minute film, can take a significant amount of research, time, and effort.

In this respect, Snelson (2010, p. 28) also considers machinima-making as a challenging process, especially with respect to interactive educational productions, as they require a "complex interplay of skills", knowledge and creativity from all involved. Snelson experienced similar problems to those described by Morozov in her project *Save Princess Dot*, which was created by a person experienced and skilled in SL, YouTube and video production. She assumes that more time would be required for such a production by someone not familiar with such processes whereas Warburton (2009, p. 423) argues that "even simple things can take a long time", referring to the intellectual property permissions often needed for filming, designing the content, and including teaching activities, all of which require multiple skills. It is evident then, that both learners and teachers will need to develop the necessary digital literacy skills to work effectively and safely in these environments.

Apart from the time constraints that users are likely to face during filmmaking, there are several technical challenges that need to be addressed by educators when designing, creating, integrating and using machinima. These include insufficient bandwidth, hardware or firewall and security issues (Conkey, 2010). The quality of equipment in educational institutions, such as the resolution of graphics on computers is also often seen as a problem for using machinima in the classroom (Spiller, 2004). Similar challenges have been reported from schools' field testing of machinima for the video project and are discussed further in Chapter 4. Moreover, to the "machine-related client-side issues", Warburton (2009) identified other problems users might have with managing the client interface, including a lack of competence with regard to navigation, creating objects and moving and changing avatars in the virtual environment. Such issues could have a negative impact on users' learning experience. Machinima requires an intensive engagement particularly near the beginning of the process and throughout the project if developing high-quality products is an expectation. A heavy cognitive load may be placed on learners and instructors, and this may, in turn, divert the focus of attention away from the primary object of learning, for example, the foreign language. While envisaged as a collaborative form of CALL, machinima production relies on a principle of collaborative teamwork, and this may not always work smoothly, depending on the age group of the learners and/or their technical expertise, character and commitment (Koenraad, 2005). Effective training and preparation are required in order to mitigate these technical and pedagogical challenges and to enable users to familiarise themselves with the immersive digital environments in effective ways (Lu, 2011). Further barriers discovered by Warburton (2009) with regards to identity, culture and collaboration may also play a role in influencing the context of immersive education in complex ways in the language classroom. Nevertheless, Warburton (2009, p. 424) concluded his assessment of the affordances of SL and its barriers by saying that "virtual worlds are attractive spaces for education". Despite the challenges addressed, 3D virtual worlds also present potentially new opportunities to discover different methods and fresh pedagogical designs that encourage language learning and teaching in virtual environments and trigger positive experiences utilising machinima (Warburton, 2009). Furthermore, facilitating teaching and learning through digital technology by creating machinima in 3D environments provides teachers and learners with powerful experiential learning opportunities (Thomas, 2015).

Summary

This chapter has explored how machinima has developed from its origins in filmmaking and game-based recordings to a stand-alone medium that can be utilised to stimulate communication in education more widely and the language classroom in particular. A great variety of visual narratives, resources and performances that have been produced over the past decade have been identified. Furthermore, different views with regard to the process of making machinima have been discussed, indicating not only the advantages with regard to cost-effectiveness and saving time but also the disadvantages concerning technical challenges, quality and lack of non-verbal cues compared to real-life filmmaking. The generally positive experiences and benefits of immersive learning in virtual environments through autonomous, collaborative and project-based learning, following Kolb's (Healey & Jenkins, 2000) holistic model of experiential learning, including the use of machinima as a tool for feedback, appear to potentially outweigh the challenges addressed. However, some considerations such as time management, the lack of non-verbal cues, missing emotional expressions or culture-specific gestures in machinima will need further attention by immersive-world researchers. Nevertheless, it is highly likely that with the rapid change and improvement in technology and learners' motivation and engagement, there will be fewer issues of this kind in the near future.

Through this review of pedagogy, it is evident that teachers and learners immersing themselves in virtual worlds understand the values and benefits of this type of learning environment better than those who merely use machinima without being involved in the production process. Therefore, we have argued that being immersed in the virtual environment and being part of the collaborative creation process of machinima production have had a significant impact on learners' autonomy and motivation while improving their language skills and digital literacy (Schneider, 2014b). In order to further consider this, a number of research questions can be identified arising from this stage of the literature review. First, what added value do machinima offer for language learning? This question has a number of related questions such as in what ways does immersion in the virtual environment influence teachers' acceptance of and engagement with machinima? How does the creation and use of machinima affect students' motivation, active participation and learning outcomes in language learning? And in what ways could machinima be utilised for self-reflection, feedback and assessment? Moreover, it is important to consider the qualitative element in relation to the materials produced as they tend naturally to focus on the process of second language development and communicative competence far more than on learning outcomes. What level of quality is expected by learners and instructors from machinima? Sub-questions in this respect are what are the reasons for either accepting or rejecting machinima? What impact does the level of quality have on whether machinima are ready-made or self-created? And in what ways does the quality of machinima affect language learning? Finally, we need to consider the specific factors that impact on the machinima-making process. What impact do time and effort have on machinima productions and their acceptance? And is the creation of machinima worth the time and effort in relation to the added value to teaching and learner performance?

It is evident that machinima are viewed by some researchers as an independent experience akin to a video game (Morozov, 2008), and this may help to engage with students who may not be motivated by formal learning environments. Deploying machinima in educational contexts presents opportunities for language learners in particular to experience a range of valuable contexts in which they can learn in stimulating ways, so that language learning is not merely concerned with traditional grammar-focused activities. Machinima can be used to stimulate authentic learning environments and interaction so that, as Herrington and Oliver suggest, "the abstract knowledge taught in schools and University is not retrievable in real-life situations because traditional approaches (lectures and tutorials) ignore interdependence of situation and cognition" (Herrington & Oliver, 1999, p. 23, cited from Muldoon & Kofoed, 2009, p. 2243). In this way, machinima can be allied with a form of project-based learning in which learner creativity can be encouraged alongside a range of other complementary skills, in place of the compartmentalised school system that divides subjects to avoid overlap between them. Evidence suggests that machinima can augment levels of learner engagement (Muldoon & Kofoed, 2009) and enthusiasm, producing less inhibition in the language learning process. Through the use of video and voice-enabled communication in immersive environments, it is possible to engage learners in powerful learning experiences that involve their emotional, as well as cognitive, intelligence as they engage in intercultural communication and stimulating forms of project-based enquiry and learning. As we have seen, the rich interactive environments that can be created in immersive worlds and environments mean that foreign language learning may be taught alongside CLIL approaches and therefore used to extend language learning to a range of other disciplines from the humanities to the sciences in order to stimulate learner engagement, critical enquiry and collaborative forms of digital literacy.

3 Technology-Mediated Project-Based Language Teaching

Introduction

Project-based approaches to teaching and learning are not a recent development. Indeed, they have a long history in the wider field of education and draw on the experiential learning philosophy of Dewey (1959, 2011) and social constructivist theories associated with Vygotsky (1978). In the context of language education, project-based language teaching (PBLT) owes a great deal to prior research on task-based language teaching (TBLT) which has grown steadily in significance over the last three decades. Whereas tasks are micro in nature, projects tend to integrate several or more individual tasks into a larger and more sustained piece of work that may also involve the collaboration of several other students and/or teachers over extended periods both inside traditional and more formal learning contexts as well as spanning external, informal learning practices (Bülent & Stoller, 2005; Gras-Velazquez, 2019). It is essential therefore that the series of tasks within the project are clarified at the outset for all learners (Grant, 2017). Moreover, in projects the collaboration may take place within or between learners located in different classrooms, either within a particular institution, country or across different countries, in the manner of telecollaborative activity (O'Dowd, 2018; Luo & Yang, 2018). According to Beckett and Slater (2019), "participating in projects can build decision-making skills and foster independence while enhancing cooperative work skills, challenge students' creativity, and improve problem-solving skills" (p. 2). In the context of learning technologies, this may include extra-curricular activities as well as different digital and media literacy practices as learners engage in activities involving different forms of play that have become prominent in their social lives beyond the classroom (Beckett & Slater, 2019). The project may lead to the creation of a product that can be audio-visual, physical and/or digital, and it is usual for this to be shared with an audience of peers either in the classroom or virtually. Depending on the objectives of the project, the product may require the use of several skills in addition to linguistic knowledge, such as intercultural competence, digital literacy and civic engagement. In this context, students may adopt a variety of changing roles over the course of the project (investigator, peer evaluator, provider of feedback, content creator, quality control and project management), and teachers may work more, as Bax (2011b) indicated, as 'difficultators' rather than 'facilitators', problematising and de-familiarising normalised assumptions in order to stimulate learners to engage in higher order skills such as discussion, analysis and critique.

TBLT found prominence as a language teaching approach in the late 1970s and early 1980s, originally in the context of a project in India as a result of research by Prabhu (1987). Developing largely from a reaction to grammar-based exercises and activities typically found in language learning textbooks that were not related to real-world problems or challenges and continuing the interactional emphasis of communicative language teaching (CLT), in Prabhu's hands, the task-based approach aimed to further develop opportunities for learner interaction and meaning-focused activities that were authentic and communicative in orientation. Both TBLT and PBLT approaches derive from constructivist and experiential learning theories that seek to engage learners in learning from experience or 'learning by doing', engaging with others through meaningful interaction and reflecting on the processes and products they are involved with and individually and collectively create (Alan & Stoller, 2005; Beckett & Slater, 2018).

On the challenges side, both TBLT and PBLT have attracted the criticism that while they may have a positive impact on students' motivation to learn, it is not always clear to learners how their language skills are being developed adequately (Mosier, Bradley-Levine, & Perkins, 2016; Tang, 2012).

Developing from an understanding of this context and early history, this chapter builds on the research literature explored in Chapter 2 by examining the opportunities and challenges presented by TBLT and latterly PBLT, before turning to consider how the use of digital technologies may be used to address some of the limitations of both approaches and extend project-based learning through the innovative use of video and machinima production. In Chapter 2 we identified several prominent definitions of machinima and developed our understanding of how these video-based visual narratives are produced in 3D immersive environments such as games or virtual worlds. Continuing this theme, this chapter explores how the machinima production process may be used by language educators, students, and course and materials designers in the field of SLA to develop authentic, communicative resources that enable opportunities for interaction in the target language and thus lead to language development and exchange across a variety of languages and cultures. In the context of the larger scale tasks often involved in PBLT, machinima may be used in creative ways to enable learners to focus on a series of different cognitive tasks at different phases that result in clear communicative outcomes (Matthew & Butler, 2017), which, as Meskill, Anthony, Hilliker-VanStrander, Tseng and You (2006) have argued, can be seen as a powerful venue for second language development to occur. Such configurations, in combination with well-designed and orchestrated language learning tasks, represent opportunities for learners to manipulate interdependent chunks of the target language in complex ways over extended periods. Prior to exploring this potential in more detail, let us first turn to consider the provenance of the task-based approach as this provided the infrastructure for PBLT to emerge.

Origins of TBLT Approaches

TBLT has steadily developed since the early 1980s and increasing amounts of research on the subject have emerged covering a range of sub-topics from assessment to learner autonomy and curriculum design. TBLT now has its own dedicated biannual conference, several book series and a network of leading international academic researchers and practitioners in many countries. Research has been conducted in Asia (with particular focus on Hong Kong, Singapore and the Chinese mainland; Thomas & Reinders, 2015), and there is a growing interest in the Middle East, Europe and North America, bolstered by educational reforms that seek to challenge more traditional forms of education and the central role of the teacher which normally supports them. While many definitions of the word *task* have emerged over the last three decades, none, understandably, have achieved universal acceptance as more and more nuances have emerged in the research and as a result of varying approaches to implementation. Among these definitions, Skehan (1998), for example, outlined an influential definition which incorporated the importance of meaning, stipulating that there was a clear connection between the identified tasks and the real world and stating that the outcome of the task is what is important in terms of assessment. Nunan agreed with this emphasis, arguing that learners involved in TBLT are much more likely to be engaged in active forms of learning as a result of this by "comprehending, manipulating, producing, or interacting in the target language", and as a result, their activities are more meaning-focused rather than form-focused (Nunan, 1989 cited in Ellis, 2003, p. 4). This emphasis was taken further by Ellis (2003), a leading advocate of the approach across several key studies and monographs, who identified six defining characteristics of tasks which have since proved to be influential and retain relevance and popularity. For Ellis, tasks begin with work plans or lesson plans made by the teacher and which embody his or her expectations about what students should do when processing individual tasks. Ellis places a primary focus on meaning, and this is underpinned by the integration of real-world tasks that reflect the types of processes that people in authentic (e.g., non-classroom-based language use) contexts are likely to address when communicating in a particular target language (Ellis, 2005b). Such tasks may include addressing a gap in knowledge or exchanging information or opinions in order to solve a problem. According to Ellis, learners are required to use their own linguistic (e.g., knowledge of the language) and non-linguistic (gesture, pictures, posture) resources to complete the task. This is different from more traditional language teaching approaches in which the central aim of the teacher is to provide the learners with the language they think is required. In task-based approaches, on the other hand, learners are expected to create the language required to complete the task from their own linguistic resources. Finally, the completion of the task needs to lead toward a communicative rather than purely linguistic outcomes. That is to say, the task is not merely focused on the learning of linguistic structures or the use of the target language for its own sake. The task-based approach develops implicit knowledge and is focused on trying to stimulate the use of the type of language that will be used outside formal instructed contexts in more authentic situations. Long (1985, p. 89) captured the 'authentic' nature of tasks well in the following extract, where he argued that a task is

> a piece of work undertaken for oneself or for others, freely or for some reward. Thus examples of tasks include painting a fence, dressing a child, filling out a form, buying a pair of shoes, making an airline reservation, borrowing a library book, taking a driving test, typing a letter, weighing a patient, sorting letters, making a hotel reservation, writing a cheque, finding a street destination and helping someone across a road. In other words, by 'task' is meant the hundred and one things people do in their everyday life, at work, at play and in between.

For Long, the tasks are non-linguistic and non-technical. They may not involve any form of language use and may be part of a longer series of tasks or sub-tasks, all of which are geared to solving a problem or accomplishing an objective.

A further important aspect of SLA in the TBLT approach is that language acquisition is 'incidental'; that is to say, it is not deliberatively targeted by the teacher or the learner prior to the start of the tasks. Reflection on the grammatical structures which present problems during the interaction are typically addressed in a post-task reflective activity to raise awareness in the minds of the learners. This approach contrasts with alternatives in which grammatical structures are taught at the beginning of the activity and prior to any interaction. The disadvantage of this approach, and one which led to the development of TBLT, is that teaching the grammatical structures first may inhibit the learners by making them unduly conscious of accuracy at the expense of fluency.

While detractors of TBLT have argued that the approach might only be relevant to certain types of language user (e.g., advanced proficiency learners) in a particular location (e.g., Europe rather than Asia) or language skill (e.g., speaking rather than writing or reading), Ellis indicates that TBLT can be used by teachers around the world in relation to all four language skills, as it engages cognitive processes and, crucially, has a clearly defined communicative outcome or product. Not only does it involve tasks in which small groups of learners or pairs are expected to participate in the communicative activity, but it may also involve teachers interacting with an entire class. For Ellis, learners can also learn a new language while they are engaged in a meaning-based task; the focus on meaning is not exclusive, so it is also important that students learn new linguistic forms, regardless of the types of task, whether input or output-based in orientation (Gass, 1997, 2005; Shintani, 2012). It is important therefore to critique some of the misconceptions that have emerged about task-based approaches, which suggest that it is meaning-focused only and that there are never any opportunities for teachers to intervene and provide correction with respect to linguistic form when necessary and the occasion presents itself, even during the processing of the tasks in question, without disturbing the fluency of the task process. TBLT may then also be done with large groups or with learners of different proficiency levels, but this may depend on the type of task, whether input or output, for example, and the extent to which the teacher can manage the size of the classroom and learners effectively and monitor what they are doing. For Ellis, then, several misconceptions about TBLT need to be addressed, not least the idea that it is mutually exclusive with respect to all other approaches. On the contrary, Ellis maintains that it may be combined with other approaches when required but that the task focus needs to be a significant part of the approach if a communicative outcome is uppermost in the teacher's list of objectives. This communicative outcome cannot be as effective if only one intentional approach such as PPP (Present–Practise–Produce) is used in an exclusive way and fails to recognise that much of language learning can be considered to be incidental, as TBLT suggests. The context of the instruction is an important consideration for Ellis and like-minded advocates of TBLT, and it may be the case that a balance has to be found between TBLT and other approaches which may be used in a complementary rather than exclusive fashion rather than seeing it as *the* only approach which needs to be adhered to and as a complete replacement of all other approaches.

These characteristics are echoed and further developed by Thomas and Reinders (2010), who add the importance of other skillsets to Ellis's emphasis on the traditional four language skills. These include digital literacy, media literacy and multimodal communicative skills, a development which acknowledges the role that digital technologies now play in the lives of many language users around the world, both inside and outside the classroom, in formal and informal contexts (Lacasa, Cortes, Martinez-Borda, & Mendez, 2012). In turn, this emphasis underlines earlier research done by Chapelle (2001) in CALL, who recognised that second language learning has changed dramatically as a result of digitally mediated communication which is now a staple of our everyday communication practices and that language teaching approaches need to respond to these changes in innovative ways if they are to remain relevant to modern society. The use of 'computer-based tasks' should therefore be a priority in order to improve learners' understanding of new communication practices and to familiarise them with the ways that digital technologies are changing both the frequency, mode and complexity of global communication in the target languages they are learning.

As we have seen, then, TBLT derives from a response or reaction to some of the dominant theories of SLA that were prominent in the 1970s and, according to Doughty and Long (2003), combines elements from both cognitivist and interactionist approaches. Researchers have built up a considerable body of work as a consequence about this approach, and this includes research on the sequence of tasks and their complexity, the theoretical implications of TBLT approaches and efforts to improve the methodological aspects of the research; research examining the effectiveness of teacher training in order to overcome the challenges involved in their implementation in a variety of cultural and pedagogical contexts and traditions; and, as Chapelle and Thomas and Reinders, have indicated previously, more recently, research has considered the relationship between digital technologies and computer-mediated communication and task-based approaches, which has given fresh impetus to the field as a whole (González-Lloret & Ortega, 2014; Shintani, 2016; Shintani & Aubrey, 2016) as it has sought to address some of the misconceptions and limitations inherent in non-technologically mediated interpretations of TBLT.

Historically, TBLT draws on forms of authentic and experiential learning, then, in which while learning may take place in a classroom environment or outside in fieldwork settings, it is strongly positioned in relation to engaging students to solve real-world problems rather than complete abstract exercises to score higher on an end-of-term test or examination or learn the target language for its own sake. Moreover, solving problems through a communal approach or collaborative community of practice is central to the task-based approach with respect to authenticity. Due to the influence of constructivist ideas, task-based approaches encourage learners to develop higher order critical thinking skills and use their cognitive abilities to solve complex problems by interacting with other learners in the target language. Building on the interactionist paradigm, tasks also encourage learners by giving them comprehensible input and use feedback strategically to promote enhanced performance over time.

Interactionist approaches rely on input to lead to dialogue and negotiation of meaning and focus on form, noticing of key structures and repair (Hanaoka, 2007; Hanaoka & Izumi, 2012). Research on TBLT, in this respect, has focused on investigating the role of tasks in enhancing fluency, accuracy and complexity (Foster & Skehan, 1996; Ortega, 1999), particularly in relation to task-planning activities (Bygate, 1996; Hsu, 2015) and language proficiency (Lochana & Deb, 2006), as well as considerable research on learner motivation (Willis, 1996).

Informed by these common concerns, it is evident that task-based approaches have several intellectual precursors. Most notably approaches focus on attention to grammar (the so-called grammar translation method) or the 'audiolingual' method. Both owe a great deal to behaviourist theoretical approaches that were concerned largely with reading and writing rather than with integrating the four skills, receptive and productive, in a holistic fashion. Likewise, audiolingualism was based on rote learning approaches stressing memorisation of input rather than cognitive processing (Leaver & Willis, 2004). Due to the limitations of drill-based approaches that often provided limited opportunities for interaction and target language practice, CLT developed, and a clear break can be discerned between it and the assumptions of behaviourist learning approaches (Van den Branden, Bygate, & Norris, 2009). The following extract from Savignon (1993, p. 263) captures the essence of the communicative approach well:

> In Europe, during the 1970s, the language needs of a rapidly increasing group of immigrants and guest workers, and a rich British linguistics tradition that included social as well as linguistic context in description of language behaviour, led to the Council of Europe development of a syllabus for learners based on functional-notional concepts of language use. Derived from neo-Firthian systemic or functional linguistics [language was viewed] as meaning potential [in order to maintain] the centrality of context of situation in understanding language systems and how they work . . .

This approach led to fundamental changes to the way language educators and syllabus designers viewed the development of language acquisition, initiating a movement away from prioritising structural or lexically organised syllabi in favour of reaching a new relationship among content and process, form and function (Breen, 1984). As Savignon (1993, p. 163) continues, as a result of CLT:

> a threshold level of language ability was described for each of the languages of Europe in terms of what learners should be able to *do* with the language. . . . Functions were based on assessment of learner needs and specified the end result, the *product*, of an instructional

program. The term *communicative* was used to describe programs
that used a functional-notional syllabus . . .

From the late 1970s and early 1980s, communicative approaches positioned interaction at the heart of language learning and teaching activities, promoting and adopting new roles for teachers and learners and, in
particular, giving learners much more of a role in developing their own
independent learning experience through syllabus design. The work of
Candlin (1978) was foundational in promoting learner choice and autonomy, enabling learners to

> define their own learning path through principled selection of rel-
> evant exercises . . . to ask for information, to seek clarification, to
> use circumlocution and whatever other linguistic and nonlinguistic
> resources they could muster to negotiate meaning . . . to speak in
> other than memorized patterns.
>
> (Savignon, 1993, pp. 264–265)

The behaviourist grammar-focused methods and psycholinguistic approaches
of a previous generation clearly played a key role in producing the communicative reaction and to a new role for social context and learner
autonomy (Holec, 1979).

From this communicative context, TBLT developed. Samuda and
Bygate (2008, p. 57) have argued persuasively that in this respect, TBLT
can be described as an opportunity to "return to the conceptual foundations of CLT . . . rather than [as] a radical departure or innovation"
(Samuda & Bygate, 2008, p. 57). Communicative approaches such as
PPP still tended to focus too much on grammar input and gave little
time for authentic language practice and production activities (Van den
Branden et al., 2009). Task-based approaches continued to gather pace
and momentum throughout the 1980s, thus enabling a critical perspective on current approaches to develop (Candlin, 1987). While more
advocates and research on TBLT emerged, this diversity led to a plethora
of definitions, and this has tended to obstruct its advancement in some
parts of the world due to a range of rather fundamental misconceptions
(Candlin, 1987; Ellis, 2003; Long, 1985; Prabhu, 1987; Skehan, 1998;
Samuda & Bygate, 2008). At the heart of the task-based approach is the
emphasis on learners being able to learn language skills in such a way
that they can acquire practical communication skills in the target language (Allwright, 1984). Such an emphasis is evident in the work of TBLT
theorists such as Willis (1996), in which a task is a goal-oriented activity
which uses the target language to solve authentic problems by adopting
a purely functional approach (Long, 1990) or emphasising learning by
doing (Skehan, 2002). TBLT is thus critical of a "tradition of abstraction
in linguistic inquiry" which "contributed to the neglect of social context

in both language teaching and language acquisition research, hindering understanding and acceptance of communicative competence as a goal for learners" (Savignon, 1993, p. 273).

In order to achieve this focus on meaning-based tasks, it is also important to consider research on the sequence of tasks that are taught to students. According to Willis (1996), an effective sequence incorporates pre-tasks, tasks and post-task language-focused reflections. The pre-task phase engages learners in activities related to vocabulary and the intended task plan. This phase raises students' awareness in preparation for the main task in which learners adopt a more autonomous disposition and often work individually or collaboratively as part of a team such as a dyad or triad. The instructor may play more of an independent role and offer guidance or operate more distantly, observing the students with no strategy for intervention. Following these two preliminary stages, the final stage, frequently called the reporting stage, provides opportunities for learners and instructors to re-engage with one another and to reflect on the performance or product produced. In this latter stage, reflection on grammar and form may re-emerge as an important element. Nevertheless, it needs to be acknowledged, as we will later see with project-based learning approaches, that these constructivist learning approaches are advancing the importance of skills that cannot be neatly researched or evaluated by traditional pre- and post-test methodologies or within existing classroom contexts.

Based on the above understanding of different tasks, it is clear that they are not seen as mere 'activities' or 'exercises'. Indeed, as Samuda and Bygate (2008) suggest, tasks are designed to play a more significant role by driving classroom activity and, in turn, shaping and defining the curriculum and the mode of assessment used to evaluate them. Tasks are therefore an organising principle of syllabi and not merely peripheral to it. They are seen as integral to SLA by promoting authentic modes of learning and assessment. Tasks are much more specific than mere exercises or activities in the language classroom, though this has often led to a good deal of confusion among novice teachers who are learning the task-based approach for the first time.

To aid the process of clarifying what tasks are, Ellis (2003) has helpfully sought to differentiate between task-supported language teaching (TSLT) and task-referenced language teaching (TRLT), which offer are two related but different interpretations of the task-based approach, particularly with respect to the role of assessment. For task-supported learning, as the name suggests, tasks are important elements, but they are not the most important; indeed, this interpretation has sometimes been seen as akin to a form of PPP as it retains an important role for teaching linguistic structures (Tomlinson, 2015). As indicated earlier and unlike these two variants, the more mainstream task-based approach does not seek to consciously target specific linguistic or grammatical structures. Rather, in order to try to maintain the authentic language learning environment, the focus on relevant grammatical structures is allowed to emerge from the interactions 'incidentally' in a way that is not predetermined by the learner or the instructor prior to the actual interaction (Samuda & Bygate, 2008). This shift in focus underlines the importance of the task which derives from the real world rather than from the artificial world of the language classroom environment, such that tasks should be those that are not typically done by applied linguists (Long, 1985) and are closely connected with problem-solving activities (Candlin, 1987) which can be undertaken by learners themselves following a process of cognitive engagement (Prabhu, 1987). All these elements together are incorporated into Skehan's (1998) influential definition of task as "[a]n activity in which meaning is primary; there is some communication problem to solve; there is some sort of relationship to comparable real-world activities; task completion has some priority; [and] the assessment of the task is in terms of outcome" (p. 95). While this definition is comprehensive, a term missing from this list of characteristics is *collaboration*, a term which reflects the influence of constructivism on language learning pedagogy over the last two decades in particular. Collaboration is important as it may lead to surprising outcomes with respect to task completion which may not have been envisaged by the instructor in his or her original work plan. Indeed, the distinction between the work plan or original lesson plan formulated by the instructor and the outcome of the task produced as a result of the interaction between the students has been an area of much discussion and debate in the TBLT research literature (Ellis, 2003; Samuda & Bygate, 2008). Significant re-interpretation is often the product of task processing by students and it is evident that tasks place a strong focus on creative problem-solving.

As is evident from this description, task-based approaches therefore have a significant emphasis on cognitive problem-solving as evidence of real-world engagement. As such tasks emerge clearly as more holistic than those which are focused merely on individual activities. The process may involve both linguistic and non-linguistic challenges, but it is concerned with a clear objective in which the use of language and learner agency are integral (Van den Branden, 2006). Above all, the focus on the tasks means that as a result of the approach, the instructor aims to consciously promote language as a product and/or process (Samuda & Bygate, 2008). While other language teaching approaches have tended to be top-down or to favour the role of the instructor as an expert, TBLT aims to empower teachers *and* learners. In order to achieve this successfully, classroom research needs to be undertaken to understand the sequence of tasks and the importance of timing in relation to instructor decision-making. There is a gap in the research in this respect, and more studies need to be conducted to understand the perspectives of learners as they grapple with task completion processes in real classroom learning environments rather than experimental contexts. Research has explored various ways in which how learners acquire a second language and the different aspects of how tasks are influential in this process (Samuda & Bygate, 2008; Van Lier, 1996). These strategies include how more and/or less capable peers may interact with language learners so that the interaction takes places in an equitable way, harnessing all necessary resources in order to succeed. It may also affect the role of the instructor prior to, during and following completion of the tasks. Given such variation in the types of task-based teaching used to date, TBLT cannot be considered a methodology but an approach that combines common elements such as a clear objective, a focus on productive meaning and a role for collaborative learning and interaction. While this definition relies on a holistic view of tasks, it is necessary to consider how the different types of task may contribute to this goal. As an illustration of this point, tasks may be further described as convergent or divergent, focused or unfocused, input- or output-based (Izumi, 2002). Moreover, tasks may involve the exchange of information or the attempt to fill a gap as a result of sharing missing information (Pica, Kanagy, & Falodun, 1993). While in some tasks students are required to find one common solution based on consensus, in others, they may apply their creative skills to multiply the number of potential solutions, or they may produce hybridised solutions that combine several different approaches (Ellis, 2003; Newton, 1991). Given this diversity of task type, it is equally important that researchers are aware of the complex factors that influence how tasks are completed by different types of students (Samuda & Bygate, 2008). This includes factors such as task familiarity, the ability to plan, the way tasks are repeated and how the learners' roles are decided and adapted. For example, a lack of familiarity with a particular task type or types may produce outcomes and opportunities for task processing that were not expected by instructors or designers but might still have led to meaningful output, interaction or products (Pica, Young, & Doughty, 1987; Plough & Gass, 1993). Indeed, exploratory tasks may present communicative opportunities not foreseen in the task-as-work-plan (Samuda & Bygate, 2008). Such communicative opportunities draw on research relating to the negotiation of meaning, which is defined in terms of repair sequences that learners engage in to check, clarify and understand turns in a conversation (Samuda & Bygate, 2008; Long, 1985; Gass & Varonis, 1985; Pica & Doughty, 1985). The negotiation of meaning, namely, confirmation checks, clarification requests and comprehension checks, addressed by research on the negotiation of meaning underlines the importance of learner interaction and collaboration, and this is evident in the research on how social constructivism has aided research on tasks. According to this framework, the emphasis is placed firmly on the types of processes that aid understanding of collaboration, but social constructivist–inspired research is often more ambitious in exploring interaction as it adopts a much more detailed and fine-grained approach to collecting data arising from the communicative interaction (Samuda & Bygate, 2008). Findings suggest that peer-to-peer scaffolding and other forms of analysis on collaborative interaction can provide significant insights into the potential opportunities presented by students' collaborative talk, which, in turn, can improve outcomes and produce language use, although more research is needed on the specific role of tasks in this process (Blake & Zyzik, 2003; Duff, 1993; Samuda & Bygate, 2008). As implied earlier when we identified the distinction between the task-as-work-plan and the task-as-process, research suggests that learners may complete tasks in ways not originally envisaged by their instructors, due to their own creativity and heuristic approaches (Ellis, 2003). TBLT is therefore highly unlike behaviourist approaches in which learners are not allowed to explore their creativity and because it enables learners to engage in unplanned activities in both formal and informal learning contexts. Regardless of these seemingly positive aspects of the approach, challenges remain, however, particularly in relation to assessing learning outcomes, as TBLT switches focus to the process of learner collaboration, interaction and engagement rather than the production of easily quantifiable outputs. This leads us to consider some of the weaknesses associated with the TBLT approach as envisaged by Swan (2005) among several other researchers.

Critical perspectives on task-based approaches have addressed a range of potential weak points, from classroom management, pedagogy and administration to assessment perspectives. Where tasks are the main organising principle of lessons, this may lead to an over-concentration on functional language at the expense of the range of language interaction and linguistic structures available. Where learner creativity is emphasised, it is equally possible that this may restrict the type of learners who could engage with it, favouring Western cultural stereotypes, rather than Asian learners, for example, who may be more reticent to engage with open-ended forms of enquiry-based learning (Guo, 2006; Pennycook, 1994; Takeda, 2015). The argument that Confucian Heritage approaches are incompatible with TBLT is frequently based on essentialist ideas of identity that are not corroborated by the research on such skills as critical thinking, and indeed, more recent research suggests more communicative approaches are being increasingly used in Asia (Thomas, 2017).

Several responses to the first argument can be made as tasks are inherently creative forms of language learning, and this is not restricted to lower proficiency levels or to different types of skills, as tasks may be used in an integrative way and are not specific to any one type of learner (Ellis, 2003). They may, of course, be used in hybridised ways alongside other approaches in a mixed approach, and this presents teachers with greater flexibility depending on the personal needs of the learners (Ellis, 2015). Likewise, the idea that TBLT is restricted to artificial types of language instruction because it is instrumental in orientation effectively fails to recognise how a classroom environment may restrict authenticity for all types of formal instruction. Tasks have the advantage of promoting opportunities for authentic in-class and out-of-class learning, as well as hybridised approaches involving different methodologies that are based on a more personalised approach to individual learners rather than a one-size-fits-all approach.

Defining Project-Based Language Learning

Based on the definitions of task-based language learning outlined in the preceding discussion, it is clear that a core group of characteristics can be identified, including, in particular, the focus on real-world activities (Beckett, 2002). According to Grant (2017), "previous studies suggest PBLT is well suited for providing meaningful language interactions to facilitate second language acquisition. PBLT also appears supportive for developing a range of life long skills and student autonomy" (para 14). Unlike task-based learning which has typically focused almost exclusively on the language education field, project-based learning has been adopted across a range of different disciplines from the arts to the sciences (Hutchinson, 1991). From a plethora of different definitions similar in range to those we saw earlier relating to task, Desiatova (2008) defines a project as a series of 'extended' tasks and distinguishes a project according to its ability to 'integrate' several different language skills and types of activities within its scope. Grant (2017) defines PBLT as an "extended series of activities utilizing a combination of different language skills in pursuit of a goal or outcome" in which the "series of activities should be meaningful and bring about opportunities for comprehensible language input and output between interlocutors" (para 2). In a project, the overall effect is one of moving towards a commonly agreed-on goal in a structured process that includes a recognisable cycle of activities (Beckett, 2006). These activities are common to project management, in general, and include planning and scoping, the collection of relevant evidence and information, followed by a processing phase in which a particular problem or problems are solved, with the cycle culminating in a reporting phase in which the product or results are communicated (Rooij, 2009). This cycle is particularly appealing to language educators as each stage of the process when undertaken largely or exclusively in the target language could lead to significant opportunities for language development, negotiation of meaning and discussion and analysis in an authentic context (Baş & Beyhan, 2010). At the heart of this approach, then, is the ability of the language learner to engage creatively with the target language while performing the interconnected tasks, often in collaborative ways (Beckett & Miller, 2006). Table 3.1 shows how the skills associated with project-based language learning can be linked to Bloom's taxonomy of cognitive domains. According to Farouck (2016), learners learning within a PBLT

Table 3.1 Bloom's Cognitive Domains and PBLT

Level	Linguistic Acquisition Activity
Creating	Students were able to give presentations to their audience and produce independent reports to their instructor by using the English words and phrases with appropriate grammar that they have learned.
Evaluating	Students were able to negotiate or argue on a chosen word or phrase or grammar in order to choose the best ones for their presentations. Students were able to evaluate their peers' presentations and give feedback.
Analysing	Students were able to compare words and phrases or grammar in order to select the best ones for their presentations.
Applying	Students were able to apply words and phrases to the contexts of their projects. They did this with project partners and feedback from their peers and adult guide.
Understanding	The students were able to classify words by parts of speech and to recognise sentence patterns with the support of their peers and adult guide (e.g., instructor, parent, etc.).
Remembering	The students were able to learn and memorise new words and phrases through different sources.

Note: Adapted from Farouck (2016, p. 15).

framework will be working at the higher levels of these domains, analysing, evaluating and creating as part of their language development.

Understood in this context, PBLT is akin to 'phenomenon-based learning' which has been introduced into the Finnish school system to engage learners with a theme-based approach in which several disciplines have been intertwined rather than relying on a single discipline to drive the curriculum. In this multidisciplinary approach, learners may learn about a variety of approaches combining history, geography, mathematics and English, while they solve a real-world problem in the medium of a foreign language. The collaborative and individual nature of the projects means that they demand engagement from learners at a higher level of cognitive processing and planning. According to the British Council (2013), project-based learning is an ambitious approach which is more learner-centred and places a significant emphasis on learners engaging in tasks for extended periods. They define projects in terms of a central topic to which all the tasks are connected, thus presenting learners who typically use the internet as a means of communication and research with opportunities to collaborate in order to produce a final product such as a report or visual narrative. Based on this definition, we can trace the origins of project-based learning to authentic forms of learning associated with creativity rather than a transmission mode of delivery (Beckett & Slater, 2005). This form of social learning theory is underpinned by learning by doing rather than prescribed forms of instruction and can be interpreted as a reaction against transmission-based, behaviourist and rote learning approaches (Bülent & Stoller, 2005). Based on research, experiential approaches, on the other hand, have been shown to stimulate learner engagement (Kotti, 2008). Experiential learning is associated with developing social inclusivity, and this is related to greater opportunities for developing second-language learner identity and collaborative literacy skills (Stoller, 2006). Project-based approaches demonstrate the same concern with promoting meaning-based activities and authentic problem-solving and combining diverse skill sets that engage learners in individual and collaborative tasks in order to lower learner anxiety and develop learner confidence. Projects therefore combine academic skills as well as opportunities for developing learners' social skills; with the longer periods involved in project-based learning, learners can experience less intense pressure to adhere to grammatical correctness and expected outputs in second-language learning contexts. Given the greater lengths of time involved, learners have more time to plan, produce and disseminate work, as well as incorporate appropriate time for reflection, peer review and evaluation. Instructors likewise are expected to not only reconsider their role, making it more learner-centred, but also adopt different subject positions depending on the phase of the project (Papandreou, 1994). While the learner and instructor roles are called into question, project-based learning also assumes that there are different stages involved in the development of projects. One example of this is from the work of Kriwas (1999), who suggested the appropriate use of four distinct stages, beginning with a 'speculation' phase in which themes and topics are identified for further exploration. The second stage involves assigning roles and responsibilities to project team members and agreeing on a work plan. The penultimate phase involves learners in completing their tasks in order to realise the finished project. In the final stage of the project cycle, learners evaluate, analyse and then present their project results. As is evident from the preceding description, project-based language learning presents many opportunities to learners and instructors for creative forms of learning in which they engage in making concrete products or projects that lead to clear outcomes.

Central to these developments is the role of social constructivist theory as it places engagement, collaboration and authenticity at the centre of the learning process. In the context of the foreign language classroom, it introduces the need for a broader understanding of literacy practices, including those related to the use of information, media and multimedia skills (Warschauer, 2006). These new electronic forms of literacy include computer literacy, information literacy, multimedia literacy and computer-mediated communication literacy. It is closely connected to problem-based and enquiry-driven models of education (Savery, 2015). Nevertheless, there are also rather idealised tendencies underpinning the use of social constructivist ideas in the narrower context of computer-assisted language learning. In particular, the freedom given to teachers as facilitators may not always lead to the most effective forms of instruction, depending on the level and ability of the learners to concentrate. Moreover, TBLT research has often attracted criticism regarding its ability to be used in different cultures which may not have the necessary flexibility regarding teacher and student roles. For example, there may be cultural and/or institutional factors that prevent learners and instructors from promoting this model of learning in their specific context. Moreover, a focus on meaning and communication at the expense of focusing on form and lexis may promote fewer opportunities for deeper engagement with the language, and collaboration may not suit everyone, particularly learners who prefer more autonomous or individual approaches as opposed to group work (Peterson & Nassaji, 2016).

Cultural considerations may also influence students' abilities and willingness to collaborate in teams. Indeed, collaborative environments may force learners to work against the grain of their natural proclivities and lead to challenges integrating dominant and less dominant personality types. Completing authentic tasks may lead to more significant cognitive demands and make learners who prefer to use their first language to scaffold their foreign language learning feel uncomfortable. While learners may feel thus more challenged and need relevant training and metacognitive skills to deal with the new demands of task- and project-based approaches, instructors equally may also face challenges, as in some interpretations of TBLT they may be on the margins of the classroom, while in others, they may be more drawn into the learning process as constant sources of encouragement and learner development. Research suggests that projects may increase the level of risk and uncertainty in classroom environments and make learners more difficult to manage at the same time as they tend to increase the level of overall noise in classrooms. Some consideration of the physical size and layout of the classroom is therefore imperative in order to provide an optimal environment. Consequently, there are several significant challenges involved in the process of creating effective project-based language learning environments, some of which may not suit all learners or instructors, and this is more obvious in environments that focus on outcomes-based data such as examination scores and proficiency testing.

Twenty-First-Century Skills and Language Education

The relationship between technology and project- and task-based learning has become increasingly prominent since the emergence of Web 2.0 technologies and applications and its related pedagogy of twenty-first-century skills from around 2005 (Wang & Vasquez, 2012). There appears to be a natural fit between these two areas given the focus on enhancing learners' creative skills, and this has attracted researchers in computer-assisted language learning as a consequence (Thomas & Reinders, 2010). Like the principles of TBLT and project-based learning described earlier, Web 2.0 embraces key principles related to collaborative learning, user-generated content and providing more agency to learners to create democratic learning spaces. Often referred to as encouraging an 'architecture of participation' based on bottom-up procedures, end users (in this case, students or teachers) adopt active roles as makers of content rather than mere passive consumers of information. This is evident in the range of so-called disruptive technologies that have become associated with the term, including wikis, blogs and social networking sites, all of which include millions of users in collaborative acts of real-time content creation and curation which can be tagged and searched for or geographically located (Richardson, 2010). Building on Web 1.0, which focused merely on one-way information flow, Web 2.0 provided opportunities for content generation and mass publishing and dissemination (Warschauer & Grimes, 2008). Translating this into education and specifically language education, whereas Web 1.0 may promote more behaviourist ideas related to reading, cloze exercises and memorisation in which instructors play a key role, Web 2.0 promotes collaborative task completion in which instructors may function more as a combination of a guide, coach, mentor or facilitator in real-world problem-solving situations to assist learners in a form of peer-based learning. In the case of the latter, there is clearly a certain degree of end-user or learner empowerment in terms of agency, and this may be related to an attempt to fashion what Lave and Wenger (1991) have called a community of practice in which learners, for example, support each other to achieve common goals. As was pointed out earlier, where we considered the criticisms often levelled against task-based approaches, the constructivist principles which underpin these frameworks may be perceived as Western in orientation and unsuitable for Asian learners. This distinction is rarely supported in the research, however, and it is clear that where trained and guided, Asian learners are equally capable of harnessing higher order critical thinking and cognitive skills (Thomas, 2017). In addressing some of the myths associated with Web 2.0, what is most important, then, is to recognise as Warschauer and Grimes (2008) have suggested, that it marks a significant contribution to agency and authorship-based education in which learners are situated at the centre of the process (Schrage, 2001). These characteristics are evident in various social applications that have become popular for educational purposes, chief among them being immersive or virtual worlds.

Virtual immersive environments are central to the video project discussed in the second part of this book and a review of relevant research in this context is integral to understanding their opportunities in the wider context of project-based learning. While in the UK terms such as VLEs have been used, there are several variations; in the US context, for example, the term *course management systems* (CMS) refer to the same type of applications. Such systems often refer to content information systems like Blackboard and Moodle, and although they have functionality for teaching, they often are used only for storage rather than as learning environments in the true sense. In contrast, the term may also encapsulate fully immersive online environments and digital games that involve large numbers of users. As 3D technologies have improved and their technical specifications and browser-based technologies have developed, immersive environments have become more feasible when used in conjunction with relatively inexpensive equipment (Peterson, 2010, 2011). These environments are based on informal forms of learning which stimulate collaboration and creativity in relation to building objects in the form of clothing, tools or even whole cities and solving problems and challenges. In the case of language education, these tasks and projects can be completed in the target language as is evident in approaches such as CLIL which involve digital technologies and computer-mediated communication (Sadler, 2012). The projects are in real time and provide opportunities for synchronous and asynchronous telecollaboration with learners and teachers from around the world. Drawing on self-designed virtual representations of their identity through the use of named avatars, immersive environments may enable individuals and groups to create or re-create physical environments that are of benefit to a wide range of disciplines and subjects. Communication can be undertaken in voice and text chat and avatars can be moved to display body language. This has led to new literacy practices as learners demonstrate their ability to communicate in diverse ways using authentic contexts and in diverse settings (Inman, Wright, & Hartman, 2010). A variety of platforms have become prominent, with SL and, later, OpenSimulator being perhaps the most successful, although a new wave of browser-based worlds have more recently emerged making it easier from a technical perspective. SL developed an extensive infrastructure of buildings and property renting making it easier for educators to develop their own resources and materials and activities based on an architecture of participation (Castronova, 2007). Research has suggested that this authentic environment promotes the development of real-world tasks and projects and learners' creativity may lead to ownership and increased agency in the target language, as avatars interact in role-play scenarios and different types of simulations are made possible (Davies et al., 2013). These include higher order critical skills according to Bloom's taxonomy as learners can engage in activities in and outside of formal contexts. Moreover, while the technical functionality of synchronous communication is important for language development, research also suggests that asynchronous communication promotes opportunities for reflection, which is equally important for the language acquisition process and other cognitive development. Students with learning disabilities or behavioural challenges such as anxiety or depression may also benefit from the reduced pressure evident in classroom environments through the use of digital avatars.

While the anonymity experienced in a virtual environment may be productive, then, they may also experience hurdles to communication through the lack of nonverbal cues, and online communication may result in abbreviated forms of speech (Davies et al., 2013; Molka-Danielsen & Deutschmann, 2009). The pervasive use of digital technologies may suit some learners but not all, as some perceive it as a type of gaming environment, or indeed, gamification may be used to motivate learners who prefer other styles of interaction. Gee (2003) has consistently argued that it is not the technology that is important in this respect, but the principles of learning that may be promoted by immersive environments that are potentially beneficial in relation to higher order literacy skills, real-world decision-making skills and the solution to problem-based learning through simulations. Learners may therefore accomplish real-world tasks in real-world environments (Whitton, 2014) while also supporting some students to develop their motivation and enjoyment of the learning process (Blumenfeld et al., 1991). It is, above all, the social dimension, and people dimension provided by these virtual worlds rather than the technology that makes them potentially attractive to second language learners and CALL teacher educators. Underpinning many of these arguments is the notion that the contemporary generation of learners can be distinguished by their intuitive grasp of key digital skills, and this is especially worthy of further investigation in the specific context of language acquisition, as much of the research has focused on non-discipline specific groups of learners (Tapscott, 2009).

Having established this context, let us now turn to consider the research linking tasks, projects and technologies in language learning contexts. Doughty and Long (2003) identified ten main principles in this respect that are still an important point of reference today. Central to these ten factors is that of authenticity which as we have seen is central to much of the research on situated learning as well as specific technologies that enable interaction and collaboration to take place between learners and instructors, such as video, animation and a range of multimedia content (Coleman, 1992; Heo, Lim, & Kim, 2010). Such a focus on creative learning and authentic learning environments and tasks aims to motivate a 'learning by doing' approach. Building on early work (Thomas & Reinders, 2010), tasks and technology have become an increasing focus of attention in recent years (González-Lloret & Ortega, 2014), and much of the research identifies how technology could be used productively to overcome some of the inherent weaknesses of a non-technology-based approach. Moreover, it could also aid learners' acquisition of language alongside other aspects of the learning process, such as developing motivation, aiding intercultural exchange and developing digital literacy skills. In this way, as Lamy (2006) has suggested, it may be necessary to consider the move to a broader conception of tasks in technology-mediated environments, which are "less structured" and "more inquiry-based" such that they aid "learners to exercise agency and enact identities" (p. 263). Lai and Li's (2011) influential meta-analysis of tasks and technology identified a range of research supporting how technology enhances language production (Sotillo, 2000; Sykes, 2005), improves language development (Ducate & Lomicka, 2008), equalises production by focusing on interruptions caused by error or correction (Ortega, 1997), provides opportunities for learners to interact during text chatting (Kelm, 1992), leads to less dominant roles for teachers (Fitze & McGarrell, 2008) and notices grammatical features and adds to lexical diversity and complexity (Sauro & Smith, 2010). More significantly, the reliance on asynchronous modes of communication such as text chatting may produce less teacher-centric environments and enable learners to experiment with their second language identities, particularly if they are failing learners or those whose second language identity is less well developed (Black, 2008), due to the inherent playfulness of the environment (Warner, 2004). While earlier research in the field focused on experimental studies, more recent research has attempted to investigate teacher and learner perceptions alongside a more robust and relevant approach to measuring any improvements in learning outcomes. The attempt to reconceptualise how to research projects and tasks using technology is a result of the recognition of the role of other skills in the mix, such as digital literacy, intercultural skills and learners' interpretive skills. The new affordances of digital technologies have therefore presented researchers with opportunities to investigate formerly marginalised areas, such as learner identity and how they interact in formal and informal environments during expected and unexpected forms of play.

In the context of language learning, however, it is apparent that by addressing these areas of learner identity, it may be challenging to measure actual learning gains or the effect of the intervention on the acquisition of linguistic structures. Tasks and projects may be unfocused and it is essential that course and materials designers explore other options, such as how the different task phases function in order to compensate for it (Abrams, 2006). In adapting to project-based learning utilising technology, learners and instructors need to adapt also. This may require a learner-centred approach in which they are willing to be creative and take risks or reflect in meaningful ways on what type of learners they are by engaging with their history (Lai & Li, 2011).

In addition to learners, instructors in technology-mediated project-based environments may need to grapple with several challenges, including a change of positionality as they take on a more flexible role as a facilitator. This may cause greater anxiety and challenges in terms of classroom management, particularly with larger groups that may constrain many learners from pursuing their own interests, as well as lead to loss of face for instructors as they confront challenging situations in which learners may be more knowledgeable than themselves (Kern, Ware, & Warschauer, 2004). The research has clear implications for teachers who are less willing to consider how their role may change as a result of project-based learning techniques and expectations at learner, pedagogical and administrative levels (Hampel, 2006). Faced with these more dynamic environments, it is equally necessary to consider how researchers engage with them to acquire reliable data in sufficient quantities and quality (Lai & Li, 2011). Projects engage learners in verbal and non-verbal interaction using technologies, and it is important for a range of data collection methods to be used that recognise the multimodal aspects of interaction (Seedhouse & Almutairi, 2009). Indeed, these new methodologies confirm the interest of SLA researchers who have turned their attention to learner identity rather than narrow research on learner gains. More innovative methodologies which combine several data collection approaches, such as video, screen capture and classroom observation, are needed in order to triangulate different data sets of a multimodal nature.

CLIL

CLIL is increasingly being advocated as an approach that enables learners to study substantive pedagogical content as well as learn or improve their knowledge and understanding of a foreign language. Content-based instruction or English medium instruction describes a teaching approach in which disciplines in the sciences or humanities are taught using a foreign language in an immersion programme (Dalton-Puffer, Nikula, & Smit, 2010). There are both soft and hard forms of CLIL, and it is best seen as a continuum in which content and language take precedence depending on the context of the instruction, and thus, the approach can be interpreted as neither exclusively one nor the other but more of a hybridised form or dual-focused approach. It is most important that both language and content are integrated as the title suggests and the relationship between them may change at different points depending on the aims of the course. In so-called hard CLIL, the emphasis is placed more on the content so that learners can immerse themselves in the specifics of the subject and almost forget that they are also listening, speaking and reading a foreign language as the medium of communication. In the 'soft CLIL', context learners' attention may be drawn more to the language or communicative elements at strategic points when dealing with particular aspects of the subject. In addition to these core principles, Navés (2002) identifies ten other attributes. These range from respect and support for learners' native language and culture so that they have time to practise both their first and second language to the use of multilingual and bilingual instructors to enable more effective integration of the two languages and the content of instruction, the use of CLIL-inspired forms of instruction as optional rather than mandatory in order to leverage investment from learners, instructors and parents. In this respect, CLIL instruction may benefit from a longitudinal approach rather than a short-term one in that the continuous and consistent focus on content and target language has been found to produce the most effective results (Navés & Muñoz, 1999). The close engagement of parents and other stakeholders, such as the educational institution and parents, is advocated as they can play a key role in supporting learners with a variety of motivational and other resources (Navés & Muñoz, 1999). It is clear that instructors need to have received effective training in language pedagogy, working in a multicultural language setting, as well as subject-specific knowledge and skills (Montague, 1997; Van de Craen & Pérez-Vidal, 2003). CLIL also tends to require high expectations and standards if it is to be successful so that institutions are aware of learners' goals (Marsh, 2002). Effective materials design processes are considered as important aspects of a successful CLIL environment as both language and content materials need to be integrated appropriately. All the stakeholders involved need to be clear about the different strategies required for CLIL, including effective predictive and anticipation, comprehension, classifying and analytical skills (Numrich, 1989).

In the context of the European Commission, CLIL has been advocated as an effective approach for furthering language instruction and developing content-based instruction. According to the Commission, language education plays a significant role in developing cultural integration processes, understanding and tolerance between and within different cultures, as well as promoting multilingualism and cultural exchange. The CLIL approach therefore has a strategic role to play in advancing the values and principles of multiculturalism. When explored from this perspective, the use of CLIL alongside visual digital approaches, such as machinima, to language learning and teaching requires further investigation as they are ideal spaces for the integration of authentic content-based instruction and language learning. Machinima is particularly important given its affordances for raising intercultural awareness and its ability to integrate a range of different cultural dimensions through immersive environments. Machinima may be of value potentially to instruction focusing on many content-based areas and disciplines, from history and geography to STEM (science, technology, engineering and mathematics) subjects and medicine, thus enabling instructors and learners to engage in the production or use of powerful visual narratives and artefacts in their teaching.

Given the wide range of requirements listed earlier, effectively integrating CLIL according to a balanced approach may also create several challenges for instructions, learners and institutions. Teaching two or more subject areas at the same time is naturally one of the most significant challenges CLIL presents to the novice teacher in this respect. This may create anxiety for the language instructor teaching a substantive subject area, depending on the level, as well as for the content-based instructor who needs to demonstrate subject knowledge in language instruction. Arising from this concern with the subject matter and the medium in which it is presented, effective assessment stands out as a significant challenge given the subject expertise of the instructors involved. It is advisable in the case of the latter, to have a team-based teaching approach to CLIL implementation in which team members derive from several areas of expertise and regularly engage with one another in planning phases. Furthermore, if CLIL is to be used in immersive environments or contexts requiring the use of significant forms of technology, then the team will also need to have sufficient technical literacy skills to deal with any challenges that may emerge. The use of technology to underpin or facilitate the development of the CLIL classroom has been called techno-CLIL, and further research is necessary on how CALL research can be used to develop the synergies between digital technologies and content and language integrated learning in a variety of languages utilising projects.

Summary

This chapter has discussed the rise of TBLT in the wider context of the turn to theories such as social constructivism and communicative language teaching; this might be characterised as the social turn in SLA (Block, 2003). Technology-mediated approaches that utilise tasks have led to more research in the last five years and have been shown to develop promising opportunities for overcoming some of the perceived weaknesses and misconceptions about task-based approaches (Ellis, 2009), as well as contributing to the creative potential of larger project-based learning (González-Lloret & Ortega, 2014; Thomas & Reinders, 2010). Ellis (2010) identified this potential, and it has proved to be influential in driving forward research into the use of technologically mediated forms of TBLT alongside higher order skills that encourage learners at all levels to engage with critical and analytical skills in the language classroom. By extension, project-based learning approaches when merged with the principles of CLIL appear to provide a framework for harnessing the potential of immersive environments in foreign language learning contexts, as they provide a variety of opportunities for scaffolded learning that is collaborative and communicative and deals with real-world problems and challenges in highly motivating, learner-centred ways.

4 Creating and Field Testing Machinima in the Language Classroom

Introduction

This chapter investigates the potential of machinima in five field-testing contexts, each representing different educational sectors. A series of machinima of different styles and formats were piloted by three universities in Turkey, the Czech Republic and Poland, respectively, as well as a secondary school using CLIL in the Netherlands and a commercial language school specialising in video-based language learning in Germany. The first part of this chapter examines the way immersion in virtual worlds influenced instructors' engagement with machinima in their language teaching. Special attention will be paid to the extent to which the use of machinima affected students' motivation, active participation and learning outcomes, as well as how the machinima were utilised for self-reflection, feedback and assessment purposes (Barwell et al., 2011; Catak, 2010).

Whereas some of the video project's field-test partners created their own machinima, others used machinima which had been created for them or adopted 'ready-made' machinima that were available on the web. The first set of machinima for the German commercial language school's online platform had been developed by language teacher trainers from a Polish university partner. They were based on three independent stories and included a set of language-related activities in several formats. As a result of feedback from these machinima, a second set was developed by the German commercial language school and involved a story line based on a crime scene, which also included a set of language-related exercises in several formats, such as listening comprehension, vocabulary and grammar exercises. The piloted machinima were originally planned for language teaching. However, some also involved CLIL courses, and machinima were specifically designed for and piloted within a CLIL course at a secondary school in the Netherlands. The Polish and Turkish universities produced their own machinima for their classes, which were either used in an ESP context, or they were produced and used as additional material following the language course curriculum like the ones used in Turkey. The research was based on the following questions:

- To what extent can machinima videos enhance language or CLIL teaching?
- Do students learn better with machinima than without?
- What is the difference between learning with real-life videos compared to learning with machinima?

Case study research was used for the field testing and was based on different methods of data collection as the research included different sized participant groups and unique teaching events to investigate several learning contexts. The observation of the different scenarios was used retrospectively to create five case studies:

Case 1: Using machinima in a commercial learning context in Germany
Case 2: Teaching English for ESP and general English in the Czech Republic
Case 3: Understanding mathematics with machinima and CLIL in the Netherlands
Case 4: Piloting machinima with learners of Turkish
Case 5: Using machinima in a military university in Poland

The data were collected from teachers and students who used machinima in their classrooms, based on quantitative and qualitative methods including questionnaires, interviews and focus group discussions (Boellstorff, 2008; Cohen et al., 2007; Mawer, 2014). The data were gathered before, during and after the lessons which used machinima in the classroom. The following sections explore each of the case studies in more detail. A full list of the machinima involved in the pilot testing is listed in Appendix V.

Case Study 1: Using Machinima in a Commercial Learning Context in Germany

Language Productions (LP) was a private commercial provider of online language courses based in Germany. The company's language courses targeted educational institutions, commercial providers and individual private customers, and it was a pioneer in the use of video-based instruction. It used video-based learning extensively throughout its course materials with the aim of creating realistic scenarios for language learning through the use of role-plays involving professional actors speaking in the target language. During the first field-testing phase, LP used ready-made machinima created by a partner university in the project team. Each of the machinima was self-contained (e.g., they were not connected in terms of actors, scenarios or content) and included several interactive exercises for learners to complete once they had watched the videos.

For the second phase of field testing, the LP film crew designed and shot their own machinima, which were based on a storyline involving a burglary in an art gallery, where a valuable picture had been stolen. Each episode led to a dramatic final-section or 'cliffhanger' scene which aimed to stimulate the viewer's curiosity to watch the next part of the story in a new episode. Each machinima episode also included interactive exercises such as 'gap-filling'- or 'mix and match'–style vocabulary exercises. No teachers were involved in either of the two pilot phases as the materials were designed primarily for independent online study. The first pilot course was designed for German learners at the A1 level according to the CEFR (a basic ability to communicate and exchange information in a simple way) and the second pilot course at the A2 level (the ability to express oneself in a limited way in familiar situations and to deal in a general way with non-routine information). To evaluate the field-testing events, participants' responses were collected through LP's dedicated e-platform, and no teachers were involved.

Field Testing With Ready-Made Machinima Online: Stage 1

The first set of field testing involved three machinima each related to a different topic such as sport, music and family provided by the Polish field-testing university. In the case of LP, the machinima were translated into German and contained a transcript of the spoken dialogue, subtitles, a dictionary and interactive exercises.

Figure 4.1 shows the machinima in the top-left part of the screen alongside a German transcript of the dialogue (right column) and subtitles under the video. The subtitles show the German phrase "Ich liebe es, am Strand zu sitzen, die Sonne zu beobachten und dem Meer zu lauschen", which translates into English as "I love to sit on the beach, to watch the sun and listen to the sea". Figure 4.2 shows a further example of the type of exercise used alongside a machinima, in this case a multiple-choice quiz. Students were shown excerpts of the machinima and were required to identify the correct response from a menu containing several options. In this case, the question was, "What did the girl in the video not like?"

Other interactive exercises were provided in a variety of formats, including falling words (*Wortfall*), in which words descending in the

Figure 4.1 Machinima "Reisen mit Musik" ("Travelling with Music")

Figure 4.2 Video Quiz With Comprehension Activities

middle of the screen were dragged by the students into the correct category according to the verb form. An example is shown in Figure 4.3, in which the student has to decide if a word was in its infinitive or conjugated form.

The infinitive form of the verbs, as has been correctly done with the verb *reisen* (to travel), has been dragged to the left of the screen, while the conjugated verb form was positioned in the right column. As indicated in Figure 4.3, the form *warten* (to wait) is in the incorrect column and is marked in red in the game. There was no limit for attempting the exercise.

Another supplementary exercise involved video dictation in which learners were requested to look at an excerpt of a machinima and complete an unfinished sentence in a text box as shown in Figure 4.4.

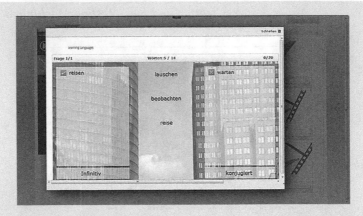

Figure 4.3 *Wortfall* (falling words quiz)

Figure 4.4 Video Dictation

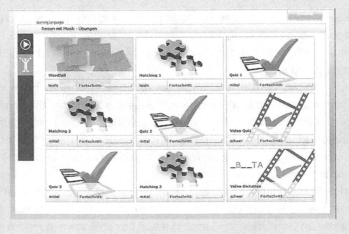

Figure 4.5 Exercises Offered Along With The Machinima

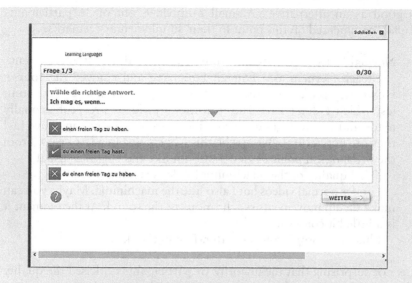

Figure 4.6 The System Shows Whether a Response Was Correct or Incorrect

Figure 4.5 provides an overview of the nine different types of quiz activity that accompanied the machinima, including *Wortfall*, three types of matching exercise, two video quizzes and video dictation.

For each question, feedback was provided by the activity once answers had been graded correct or incorrect (see Figure 4.6).

Post-Course Survey Findings

Following the end of field testing, 36 participants responded to a questionnaire (16 = m; 20 = f). The majority of the participants were between 32 and 36 years of age (28%), 22% were between 22 and 26 years old, 19% were between 27 to 31 years old and 17% were between 37 and 50 years old. Forty-four per cent had a background in higher education; the remainder did not respond to this question. The majority (91%) had learned about machinima 'through the internet', although none of the participants had previously created their own. The majority of learners (42%) felt 'sceptical' about learning with machinima, whereas 33% indicated satisfaction. Twenty-two per cent indicated that machinima had 'motivated their language learning'. Nineteen per cent felt 'curious and excited', whereas 14% felt 'confident', 'confused' and 'disappointed', respectively. The overwhelming majority of learners (89%) considered that machinima was not as effective as traditional video-based instruction, whereas 11% reported that they considered machinima to be 'just as good as an alternative'. A small number, 6 out of 36 participants (16%), commented on this point in their supplementary remarks:

> Normal Videos are better, the movements are different, more fluent.
>
> I teach German as a Foreign Language and enjoyed the course. However, I prefer the [traditional] videos. Machinima are like comics, which I don't like. The [traditional] videos are professionally made and . . . very good. These videos are not fluent somehow, [as] they are not natural. But maybe this can change in a few years. From the pedagogical point of view I did not like the videos as usual.
>
> [The] quality of the [machinima] videos is not good.
>
> I prefer normal videos but I also like the machinima. Maybe you can make the lip movements synchronous to the sound. At the moment it is a little bit confusing.
>
> I like the normal courses better. Doesn't look real.

It is not surprising that the majority of participants criticised the quality of the machinima as this was a commercial language learning context involving corporate customers. The example machinima that were filmed during training sessions were of low production quality in terms of the movement of the avatars and the use of audio; nevertheless, the participants also remarked that they found them to be highly engaging because their teachers had produced them and they recognised that the exercise enabled them to understand the challenges integral to the machinima creation process.

Participants' Statements on the Experience of Using Machinima

Respondents were asked to agree or disagree with a set of ten statements anchored on the following Likert scale: *strongly agree, agree, neither agree nor disagree, disagree* and *strongly disagree*.

Forty per cent 'agreed' (6% 'strongly agreed') with the statement '*I enjoy watching machinima in my lessons*'. Thirty-seven per cent were 'undecided', and the remainder 'disagreed' with this statement.

Forty-nine per cent 'agreed' and 20% 'strongly agreed' that "*short machinima are better to help me learn*". Thirty per cent were 'undecided', and only two respondents 'disagreed' with this statement. Forty-nine per cent were 'undecided' about the statement '*I learn a lot with machinima*'. Twenty-six per cent 'agreed' and one respondent 'strongly agreed' with this statement, whereas 14% 'disagreed' and 9% 'strongly disagreed'. Thirty-eight per cent 'agreed' and 9% 'strongly agreed' with the statement '*Machinima help me to learn new words*'. Thirty-eight per cent were 'undecided' about this statement; 12% 'disagreed' and 'strongly disagreed'.

The majority of respondents were 'undecided' about the statement *'Machinima help me to understand new grammar'*. Twenty per cent 'agreed' and 20% 'disagreed' with this statement. The majority of respondents were 'undecided' or 'disagreed' with the following statements: *'Machinima help me to improve my speaking'* and *'Machinima help me to improve my writing'*. Twenty-nine per cent 'agreed' and 6% 'strongly agreed' that *'machinima help me to improve my listening'*. Fifty-one per cent were 'undecided' about the statement, a few (9%) 'disagreed' and 6% 'strongly disagreed' with this statement.

Forty-six per cent 'strongly disagreed' with the statement *'Watching machinima is fun, but I am not learning anything'*, and only 11% 'agreed' and 6% 'strongly agreed' with this statement. Thirty-four per cent were 'undecided'. A majority 'agreed' (53% and 38% 'strongly agreed') that *'the avatars don't look natural'*. Forty-six per cent 'agreed' and 9% 'strongly agreed' with the statement *'I find it difficult to learn a language if the avatars do not show what they feel'*. Thirty-one per cent were 'undecided' about the statement, and 14% 'disagreed'. Forty per cent of the learners were 'undecided' about the statement *'I learn and understand the subject better with machinima'*. Thirty-seven per cent 'agreed' and 6% 'strongly agreed' with the statement, whereas 14% 'disagreed' and only one learner 'strongly disagreed' with this statement.

The statement *'I will continue learning with machinima in the future'* met with agreement by 26% of respondents, while 6% 'strongly agreed'. Forty-nine per cent were 'undecided', whereas 14% of the learners 'disagreed', and 6% 'strongly disagreed' with the statement. Thirty-seven per cent of the learners 'agreed' and 6% 'strongly agreed' with the statement *'Machinima help me to learn on my own'*. Thirty-four per cent were 'undecided', 17% 'disagreed' and 6% 'strongly disagreed' with this statement. In addition, several individual comments were also added as indicated in the following excerpts:

> I am not convinced about machinima. They are not professionally produced. If they could be improved, I can imagine that it is more fun.
> It is really difficult to say whether you learn anything with machinima.
> I like videos, but I am very sceptical about those new videos.
> I am not sure if I learnt something.
> Videos are not very good.
> I don't like this format. I think I stay with the 'old' courses.

The respondents were used to video-based instruction involving real-life actors in authentic contexts, and as a result, it is perhaps no surprise that they reacted critically to their first encounter with teacher-created machinima. Future research needs to take this context into consideration when evaluating machinima to enable a more balanced account of its potential based on a more longitudinal approach.

Field Testing With Ready-Made Machinima Online: Stage 2

In the second iteration of the course designed for German language learners at the A2 level (CEFR), a set of episodes was created about a storyline involving a burglary. Exercises were established involving a similar pattern to the first iteration with machinima which was designed for the lower language level of A1.

Post-Piloting Questionnaire

In total, 62 learners took part in the second iteration of the LP field-testing phase (39 = m; 23 = f), with all but one learner involved coming from a higher education background. The age group ranged from 22 to 26 years (23%), 32 to 36 years (26%) and 37 to 50 years (23%). As can be seen from Table 4.1, fewer than 37% were already familiar with 3D immersive environments, while a corresponding 37% were not. Eighty-four per cent had not created their own machinima, whereas 16% had. In relation to respondents' previous experience of technical problems associated with working in the virtual world of SL, 25% identified internet connection problems, 33% thought their involvement was time-consuming, 25% mentioned video-related technical problems and 17% highlighted audio as a source of problems.

In response to the statements in the questionnaire, the majority of respondents were very positive about learning with machinima as they enjoyed watching the videos in their lessons and agreed that short machinima (approximately 3–5 minutes in duration) were optimal for helping them to learn. The majority stated that they 'learned a lot with machinima', although there was also a fairly high rate of responses that indicated 'undecided' to the statements provided. The number of participants that disagreed with the statements was significantly lower.

The high level of positive agreement with the statements is noteworthy, and this may be a consequence of the fact that the participants had access to technically superior machinima in this iteration of field testing as well as a more integrated and stimulating narrative story line. The positive responses shown in Table 4.1 demonstrate that the majority of learners were satisfied with the machinima that they engaged with and felt confident and motivated to use them. Nevertheless, a few participants felt 'sceptical' (13%) or 'confused' (11%). Thirty-five per cent of the participants believed that using machinima was 'as good as traditional video-based learning', whereas 65% 'disagreed'; this division of opinion is a recurring pattern in the data.

Summary: Field Testing in the German Context

Two sets of ready-made machinima were piloted by LP. The two machinima courses provided on its e-platform were entirely web-based

Table 4.1 Students' Responses to Statements on Machinima and Content (German context)

Statement	1	2	3	4	5	Total
1. I enjoy watching machinima in my lessons.	37.10%	43.55%	12.90%	4.84%	1.61%	100%
2. I enjoy making machinima in my lesson.	16.13%	9.68%	12.90%	3.23%	58.06%	100%
3. Short machinima are better to help me learn.	24.19%	46.77%	24.19%	3.23%	1.61%	100%
4. I learn a lot with machinima.	19.35%	51.61%	19.35%	8.06%	1.61%	100%
5. Machinima help me to learn new words.	20.97%	41.94%	25.81%	11.29%	0.00%	100%
6. Machinima help me to understand new grammar.	17.74%	40.32%	30.65%	9.68%	1.61%	100%
7. Machinima help me to improve my listening.	30.65%	35.48%	24.19%	9.68%	0.00%	100%
8. Machinima help me to improve my speaking.	8.06%	27.42%	35.48%	16.13%	12.90%	100%
9. Machinima help me to improve my writing.	9.68%	27.42%	37.10%	11.29%	14.52%	100%
10. Watching machinima is fun but I am not learning anything.	3.23%	17.74%	9.68%	22.58%	46.77%	100%
11. The avatars don't look natural.	5.00%	63.33%	21.67%	5.00%	5.00%	100%
12. I find it difficult to learn a language if the avatars do not show what they feel.	14.52%	51.61%	24.19%	6.45%	3.23%	100%
13. I learn and understand the subject better with machinima.	16.13%	51.61%	20.97%	6.45%	4.84%	100%
14. I will continue learning machinima in the future.	16.67%	48.33%	23.33%	5%	6.67%	100%
15. Machinima help me to learn on my own.	24.59%	47.54%	16.39%	6.56%	4.92%	100%

Note: 1 equals *strongly agree* and 5 equals *strongly disagree*.

and self-contained and did not use a facilitator to interact with the students. They were freely accessible and designed for adult learners of German at the A1 and A2 levels. The A1-level machinima course consisted of three independent self-contained machinima:

1. "In Sport interessiert sein" (see https://youtu.be/IeF6kzoZNSk)
2. "Reisen mit Musik" (see https://youtu.be/b_oviCmXrCw)
3. "Paula feiert Geburtstag" (see https://youtu.be/xJWuG3uKgko)

The machinima used in the first piloting phase were created by a Polish university which used the same machinima for their field testing in Polish. For the LP courses, the Polish dialogues had been overdubbed by German speakers. The activities provided with the machinima on the LP platform followed the same structure as the exercises developed for all the other videos for language learning on the platform; thus, each machinima was provided with a transcript, subtitles, a dictionary and interactive exercises. The most significant difference, however, was that all five machinima were interrelated through a story line that had been designed and filmed by LP as follows:

Film 1: "Conversation With a Waiter" (see https://youtu.be/IBFM920w2R4)
Film 2: "Buying a Painting" (see https://youtu.be/UiPariAw3oU)
Film 3: "In the Gallery Part 1" (see https://youtu.be/6YXlCAGtVp4)
Film 4: "In the Gallery Part 2" (see https://youtu.be/IyHqeD3UIho)
Film 5: "Conversation With Police" (see https://youtu.be/AlxPUO4YFDg)

The storyboard concerned a work of art that had been stolen from a gallery, and the episodes included the police investigation and the pursuit and eventual arrest of the thief. All the participants who had taken part in the machinima courses were asked to complete a questionnaire to determine their likes and dislikes about learning with the technology; 36 responses were received for course 1 and 62 responses for course 2. The gender of the participants varied between 44% males and 56% females in course 1 and 63% males and 37% females for course 2. The age groups ranged between 20 and 50 years, whereas the majority in both courses was between 32 and 36 years old. Sixty-four per cent of the respondents in course 1 and 63% in course 2 were not familiar with 3D environments or computer games such as Minecraft or WoW. None of the respondents in course 1 and 85% in course 2 had never created machinima. Although 33% of the respondents in course one felt 'satisfied' with machinima, 41% were 'sceptical', whereas 31% of the respondents in course two were 'satisfied'. Thirteen per cent were 'motivated', 15% were 'confident' with the learning experience and 13% were 'sceptical'. Despite the positive response, it is noteworthy that the majority of respondents in course 1 (89%) and course 2 (65%) did not consider machinima to be as useful as conventional video-based language learning lessons.

The results of the earlier discussion reported previously relating to the quality of machinima were also reflected in the feedback from the questionnaires. Moreover, some additional comments made in the questionnaires were valuable for further consideration as they addressed the expected quality standards of machinima compared with other videos provided on the LP platform. For a commercial company whose business is selling language courses, it is essential that its products are of a high quality. In this respect, the quality of machinima provided for the course left room for improvement. They had been produced by a machinimatographer who had limited experience of the genre, and this explained why some of the avatar movements were not always smooth and lip movements lacked synchronisation. The content was originally designed for Polish courses and might have fit more appropriately in another context as indicated by Amsterdam's comments (as cited in Johnson & Pettit, 2012, p. 44): "Machinima is a beautiful medium; the question is how to create film that can stand up to the scrutiny of all audiences." However, it was interesting to note that the reactions to the machinima in course two were much more positive, an outcome which may have resulted from the use of better quality machinima that were created by a professional team which had prior experience in real-life video production. Apart from the deployment of a stimulating story line in which each episode ended with a dramatic 'cliffhanger' that left the viewer curious about the next episode, the film team used advanced techniques such as pose animations and lip-synching to overcome the points of critique reported earlier in the participants' comments. In relation to LP's machinima course 1, it is noteworthy that 81% of respondents to the questionnaire in course 2 'enjoyed watching machinima', 71% 'learned a lot with machinima', 63% 'learned new words', 65% 'improved their listening skills', 68% 'understood the subject better with machinima', 65% promised to 'continue learning with machinima' and 72% indicated machinima 'helped them to learn independently'. Overall, according to the results from both courses, conventional videos were the preferred learning tool compared to machinima and hence it cannot be claimed that working with machinima added more value to the learning experience in this context.

Case Study 2: Teaching English for ESP and General English in the Czech Republic

During the field-testing phase, the university partner from the Czech Republic (UCR) piloted several machinima with mechanical and electrical engineering students learning English. The teacher conducting the courses had ten years' teaching experience facilitating different levels of English at grammar school and university levels, including, in particular, considerable expertise in designing and teaching ESP courses. She had developed a significant interest in experimenting with several innovative ways of teaching and enjoyed using web-based materials and tasks in her language lessons. Besides some experience with SL, the teacher had also been involved in distance learning instruction using Moodle as a course management system. Because she had little or no prior experience creating machinima and had never used this form of instruction in her classes, the teacher was provided with ready-made machinima that had been tailored to the needs of the participants in her classes.

The topic of the lesson was *health and safety at work in a technical environment.* The machinimatographer was given instructions on how to film for this particular topic and groups of 50 students at A2–B1 (CEFR) level and 94 students at B1–C1 level of English piloted the machinima. Of the three machinima produced, the video titled "When No Smoking Really Means 'No Smoking'" (see https://youtu.be/xA-jPtJq2dQ) was selected to be examined in this case study.

The machinima described an accident caused by a workman who was smoking a cigarette in an area where smoking was prohibited. His actions later resulted in an explosion at the plant. The aim of the lesson was to practise students' investigative skills, note-taking and writing accident reports and had a particular focus on speaking and writing skills in the target language. While watching the machinima, students took notes of what they observed at the scene. The machinima did not include dialogues, but realistic ambient sounds were used to enhance the atmosphere. No non-player characters (NPCs) controlled by computers were used; instead, avatars manipulated by human users acted in all the scenes, and this made the scenarios appear more realistic. After watching the machinima, students role-played an accident investigation scene in small groups of three in the classroom. One student played the role of a health and safety officer, and two other students acted as witnesses. The health and safety officers prepared a set of questions to interview the witnesses, and responses were recorded and used to write an accident report, while students used their textbooks and vocabulary lists to support them with the interviewing and report writing process. The teacher identified the benefits of using tailor-made machinima compared to other videos downloaded from YouTube, as the machinima focused precisely on the topic she wanted to teach, whereas she criticised the other videos as they often contained irrelevant parts that could easily distract students from the main topic of attention.

Since the machinima did not contain any dialogue, participants encountered several problems adjusting to the language level. In an interview after the class, the teacher commented that working with the machinima appeared to improve her students' engagement and levels of motivation. Another advantage emphasised by the instructor was that the machinima did not affect the students emotionally as the characters involved in the accident were avatars rather than real people.

Effective teaching and learning with machinima depend on the teachers' level of engagement and enthusiasm. Even though the teacher of this group did not want to involve her students in virtual learning, as she feared that she could not afford the investment of extra time envisaged, she valued machinima as they brought a virtual atmosphere into the physical classroom and perceived them as an innovative tool for teaching technical topics as they supported technical thinking.

The findings from students who completed a questionnaire after the lesson indicated that the majority of students encountered the learning experience with machinima as positive. As most of the respondents were familiar with 3D environments or computer games, it is not surprising that the majority considered machinima as useful as traditional videos in the classroom. The students' responses thus reflected the positive impression the teacher had reported about the use of machinima in her lessons.

The teacher taught three groups of 50 students at the beginner level and six groups of 94 students at the advanced level using the machinima, all of which had been created specifically for her classes as part of the field-testing process. Following the course curriculum, which was based on the theme of 'Safety at Work', the machinima "When Smoking Really Means 'No Smoking'" was chosen as it had been tailored exactly to her students' needs. In her classes, the instructor used materials provided for the technical students as part of the curriculum. The machinima, "When Smoking Really Means 'No Smoking'" (see https://youtu.be/xA-jPtJq2dQ) showed an accident caused by a workman smoking a cigarette in an area where smoking was prohibited which subsequently resulted in an explosion. The language focus for this activity was speaking and writing, and the learning objective was to practise accident investigation skills and write an accident report. The students worked in groups of three and were asked to take notes while watching the machinima. They then role-played the accident investigation scene in which one student acted as a health and safety officer and two others were witnesses. The witnesses were interviewed about the accident by the health and safety officer, who asked the following questions:

What happened?
When did the accident happen?
Who was involved in the accident?
Did the worker follow the standard operating procedure?
How did the worker get injured?
Did the workers carry out first aid at the site?
Were there other people who saw the accident?

All the students noted down the answers to the questions and wrote an accident investigation report. Although there were no additional materials to use in this part of the lesson, the students used their textbooks and lists of vocabulary, and they completed accident report activities to support their work with the machinima.

Based on observation and interview data, the teacher underlined the potential advantage of using machinima compared with other videos downloaded from YouTube, as the machinima were focused on the topic she wanted to teach, whereas downloaded videos often contained parts which could not be removed and often distracted students from the topic. The teacher noted anecdotal increases in students' engagement and motivation through the use of machinima. Notably, because the accidents were simulated, they did not affect the students emotionally; this may have been the case had they seen real people involved in a similar accident. The students also liked the practical approach the teacher used in her classes as she gave them different activities for listening, speaking and writing and used role-plays to practise tasks related to writing accident reports, completing forms and observing, witnessing and describing an accident.

Describing Shapes, Further Machinima Piloted by a Czech Teacher at University

Further to the machinima discussed earlier, a new set of machinima were created for the instructors and used to help teach shapes with two groups of learners, one of which was A2 to B1 level and the other was B1 to B2 level. The machinima titled "Looking at Shapes in Buildings" (see https://youtu.be/A2iTb-b_hF8) was mainly designed to practise describing structures and materials. The objective for both groups was to produce a description of the machinima content that used various shapes of buildings and did not include the use of any avatars, voice or text. The teacher organised this session differently from the health and safety sessions as the students worked with tablets and viewed the machinima individually at first, before then investigating several different kinds of buildings and related structures. Following this, students were then asked to choose the shapes they liked best, form small groups and share their preferred shape or object. In their groups, students were then asked to agree on one shape which all group members preferred before then describing their shape or structure to the rest of the class. Following this, the other students had to guess which shape was being described. During the activities, the students were able to use their textbooks and supplementary vocabulary lists to support their descriptions. In another activity, the students were asked to provide a guided tour in which they described the location and contents of a specific building or object and its shape from the machinima.

Creating Machinima With Learners

While there were positive pedagogical implications as a result of involving students in the virtual classroom activities, the teacher feared that the investment required would be too time-consuming and that it would take away valuable learning or teaching time. Although she considered having her students prepare and create their avatars outside the classroom prior to the lesson using a flipped-classroom approach, she decided against it, because she was concerned that only two thirds of the students would have prepared their avatars for the actual lesson. She suggested that those teachers who were able to afford the extra time could attend a course to learn how to make and produce machinima for their specific needs in addition to the materials used within the curriculum; others helped by writing the storyboard according to the topics and tasks needed. Interview data suggested that the teacher viewed machinima as an approach that had the potential to be highly innovative in the language teaching context, particularly in relation to the teaching of technical topics, but there were several accompanying limitations that teachers needed to consider.

Teachers' Focus Group Discussion Report

After the field testing with mechanical and electrical engineering students, six female teachers took part in a focus group discussion, all of whom were teaching ESP/English for Vocational Purposes. Fifty per cent of the teachers were aged between 31 and 36 years old, 18% were 26 and 30, 15% were 41 to 45 and 12% were aged over 51. The majority (67%) had 6 to 10 years' teaching experience; 18% had 11 to 15 and 21+ years' experience, respectively. All the instructors were used to teaching with technology, and they were all familiar with interactive whiteboards. Most of them (84%) used tablets (mobile devices), a dedicated computer lab and video in their lessons, while 67% used Moodle or other VLEs. Although only 12% had experience with 3D environments, they all had become acquainted with using machinima during the last six months. It was noteworthy that all the teachers intended to use machinima for language practice and that 83% wanted to use it for language production and cooperative language learning, whereas 50% intended to use machinima to introduce content into their lessons. Eighteen per cent were interested in using machinima to introduce their subject, 32% wanted to use it as an autonomous activity and 18% wanted to use it as a learning task.

The teachers reported that there were no technical issues when presenting the machinima in the physical classroom. The machinima were used to practise specific vocabulary items and write safety reports, and thus, the main emphasis was placed on speaking and writing skills development. Although not all the teachers had experience with virtual environments, they commented that they would like to use machinima in both physical and virtual classrooms. When asked what advantages or disadvantages machinima had compared with real-life videos, the teachers thought that this depended on the topic and the interests of the students. However, when comparing machinima with real-life videos the biggest disadvantage was perceived as the lack of facial expressions and lip movements from the avatars, as this made it difficult to lip-read what they were saying, particularly for people with special needs. Nevertheless, the teachers considered it an advantage that machinima inspired technical students to engage in creative and imaginative thinking and that the students who liked to work with technology were able to record machinima themselves and manipulate them with mechanical devices in 3D.

Further advantages related to producing or working with machinima were also identified, such as being able to create or have machinima created by a third party that contained a specific focus required by the lesson. The production costs for machinima were considered relatively small compared with shooting real-life videos, especially when filming dangerous scenarios such as a fire, a storm, or an earthquake. As the teachers all used ready-made machinima during the pilot lessons, including ready-made lesson plans, this underlined to them how it was possible to adapt existing materials in a potentially productive way and that this would save them a lot of time preparing their own lesson plans.

It was notable that the teachers valued machinima as they saw in them the potential to overcome communication barriers that might normally be presented by autistic or introverted students. They were also convinced that machinima supported forms of technical thinking that might otherwise be challenging to engage with in 2D spaces. Indeed, almost 95% of respondents agreed or strongly agreed that their students' motivation increased when machinima were used in the language classroom, and 93% indicated agreement or strong agreement that machinima fostered learning. Fifty per cent of the participants agreed that machinima could provide supplemental resources for after-school self-study, but 33% also disagreed with this statement. It was significant that 67% disagreed with the statement that machinima were more effective than other learning materials. Although none of the teachers had ever created a machinima prior to the pilot lessons, 100% agreed that *'being able to shoot your own film according to your needs'* was a significant advantage for teachers. All the teachers *'intend[ed] to use machinima to assist their teaching in the future'*, and the majority (83%) saw the potential in *'using machinima as an autonomous learning resource'* in that *'machinima [could] help their students to understand/grasp the lessons'*. Overall, 100% of teachers indicated that they were all satisfied with the contribution of machinima to their lessons.

Students' Course Evaluation

The entire cohort of students who attended the lessons with machinima were asked to complete a questionnaire after the session. In total, 301 higher education students responded to the questionnaire, although not all participants responded to all questions. The majority (80%) were familiar with 3D environments, computer games, Minecraft, WoW or similar applications, whereas 21% were not. Ninety-five per cent had never created machinima as opposed to

5% who had. Most students did not respond to the question related to technical problems, as it referred to learners using SL in their lessons, which was not the case for the majority of respondents. According to their statements, the majority of learners 'enjoyed watching machinima in their lesson'. A significant number of students (55%) stated that they liked 'short machinima better to help them learn' and a further 44% (164) 'strongly agreed' or 'agreed' with this statement.

The learning experience was considered positive by the majority. Forty-four per cent stated that they were 'happy'; 32% felt 'comfortable'; 27%, 'motivated'; 19%, 'curious' and 'satisfied'. Twenty-seven per cent found it 'hard to say'; 18% felt 'sceptical'; 17% felt 'confused'. It was notable that 73% of the learners considered machinima 'as good as normal videos in the lesson', whereas 27% of learners 'did not agree'. The responses reflected the positive impression teachers had reported about the use of machinima in their lessons.

Teaching English With Idioms and Mystery Stories

As part of this case, another Czech teacher who had taught Czech, English and history at a secondary school from the sixth to ninth grade (13- to 15-year-old students) piloted machinima in her English classes. The teacher had limited knowledge of machinima production and had never produced any; however, she hypothesised that machinima would interest her students, especially those who frequently played computer games from among the cohort.

Arising from interview data, the Czech teacher indicated that her pupils felt attracted to machinima videos as they felt connected to the avatars which were similar to the virtual characters they encountered in their computer games. As machinima were not the typical kind of videos teachers used in their lessons, the machinima helped to raise pupils' interest and motivation in her lessons.

A similar assumption was made by a group of Turkish teachers who piloted machinima in their classes. Provided that the machinima suited the language level and integrated engaging content and characters, feedback from teachers suggested that they could be a source of inspiration for the students. As with other teachers involved in the study, the Czech teacher created her own lesson plans, worksheets and activities for the ready-made machinima she used. She was given a range of machinima to choose from, which she considered a disadvantage, as she had to watch a significant number of videos until she found the most appropriate ones and this was a time-consuming process. She suggested tagging a suitable language proficiency level to each machinima, as this would help teachers decide how the machinima could be integrated more effectively. On the challenges side, the teacher criticised the quality of several machinima as some parts of the dialogues were difficult for learners to understand.

Piloting Machinima: Lesson Samples

In relation to the length of the machinima, the Czech teacher preferred short stories no longer than three minutes in duration which included the use of grammar in context through the use of natural dialogues or songs. When she watched her first machinima, she was surprised that the characters behaved like robots as they had limited movement and few fluent gestures. In contrast, her pupils did not experience any problems with the visual appearance of the avatars as they were similar in quality to the characters in the computer games they played. The teacher used machinima with 16 students in two different language classes which had different language proficiency levels. The interview and observation data showed that she found her experience with machinima challenging; nevertheless, she concluded that the machinima videos 'enhanced her language teaching approach' by providing a significant variety of language input. Several examples of lesson plans are given in the following section to illustrate the approach adopted by the Czech teachers.

Revising Grammar With Animal Idioms

The Czech students were from the 9th grade (15-year-olds) and advanced-level learners of English. The lesson plan focused on revising grammar related to adjectives and comparatives. In this case, the teacher used machinima which included animal idioms. The lesson began with a worksheet which included all the idioms provided in the machinima. The students worked in pairs on a task aimed at discovering the meaning of the idioms on the list. To aid them in this task, students were able to use dictionaries, and they were permitted to provide their explanations in Czech if required. After completing the activity, students worked in groups of four to share their findings with one another. After this, they watched the machinima video, which was stopped after five idioms, prior to a further viewing. The aim of the exercise was to enable the students to compare their ideas with the actual meanings of the idioms. After checking and correcting them, students were asked to identify the seven idioms they liked best. Individually, they then produced sentences in which they used the idioms that they had chosen. Their productions were shared with other members of the class in groups of four, and group members tried to translate the sentences into Czech.

The interview data showed that the teacher believed that her students enjoyed the activities, were interested in the idioms and felt they had learnt a considerable amount of the target language in the process. For her, it was interesting to see the different ideas students had about different meanings. A few sessions later, students were asked to write an essay which included some of the idioms they had learnt to round off the activity.

A Mystery Story Machinima Used in a General English Class

The Czech teacher chose a mystery story, *Midnight Mystery*, to use in the classroom. The machinima had originally been created for English as a Second Language (ESL) classes based on the topic of a burglary. The lesson has been designed to practise words and expressions related to facial descriptions, simple commands and verb tenses. In the first step, the teacher showed a few seconds of the machinima to the class and asked the students to summarise what they had seen. They were asked to read their summaries to each other in pairs. Then, three students were asked to read their summaries aloud to the rest of the class. In a further stage in the process, the students had to predict what would happen next and note their ideas down using two or three sentences. Some pupils read their predictions aloud, and this procedure was repeated until all the machinima had been watched. Towards the end of the process, all the students read their last prediction aloud to the class.

The teacher reported that her students were eager to know what would happen and commented that the predictions were very inspiring. The final predictions were interesting as the students all had similar ideas, and as these were different to the ending of the real story, a great deal of surprise was evident in the group, and this stimulated further learning. All the students appeared to be absorbed by the story and engaged by the process. As a result, the students were asked to

focus their attention on grammatical structures such as the past simple, past continuous, and future *will* forms, and the teacher observed
a noticeable improvement in writing following these activities. The
machinima underpinned the importance of creativity in the lessons,
and this was demonstrated at the end of the session as students will-
ingly provided a title for the stories that captured their involvement.

Survey of Czech Learners' Experience With Machinima

Sixteen students (f = 7; 9 = m) responded to the questionnaire. All
the students were attending a secondary school in the Czech Republic, and all of them equally stated that they were familiar with 3D
immersive environments. None of the students had ever created a
machinima. As indicated in Table 4.2, students were asked to mark
the 15 statements on a scale of 1 to 5 anchored in *strongly agree,
agree, undecided* to *disagree* and *strongly disagree*.

The questionnaire results show that the majority of the students enjoyed watching the machinima (75% 'agreed' and 18.75%
'strongly agreed'); only 6.25% 'disagreed'. All the students stated that
'*machinima helped them to learn new words*' (44% 'strongly agreed'
and 56.25% 'agreed'). Everyone agreed and one student strongly
agreed that machinima 'helped them to learn grammar'. All but one
agreed or strongly agreed that '*short machinima help to learn better*'. Seventy-five per cent of participants disagreed with the statement that '*machinima helped to improve speaking*'. It can be assumed
that the teacher on this course focused on listening and writing skills
in her lesson with machinima rather than on speaking skills. Results
were less convincing with respect to whether students '*learn and
understand the subject better with machinima*', a statement to which
62% 'agreed' and 37% 'disagreed'. It is remarkable that the majority
of students believed that they could '*learn from machinima – apart
from being fun*' and that '*machinima foster autonomous learning*',
which 75% 'agreed' and 19% 'strongly agreed' with, whereas only one
student 'disagreed' with the statement that '*machinima help students
to learn on their own*'. Fifty-six per cent of the participants 'agreed'
that '*the avatars don't look natural*' and 31% 'strongly agreed' with
this statement, whereas 16% 'disagreed'. Forty-four per cent 'agreed'
and 19% even 'strongly agreed' that '*they find it difficult to learn a
language if the avatars do not show what they feel*'; 31% 'disagreed'
and 6% 'strongly disagreed' with this statement. Students were not as

Table 4.2 Students' Responses to Statements on Machinima and Content (Czech context)

Statement	1	2	3	4	5	Total
1. I enjoy watching machinima in my lessons.	18.75%	75%	0%	6.25%	0%	100%
2. I enjoy making machinima in my lessons.	This cohort did not create their own machinima and therefore did not respond.					0
3. Short machinima are better to help me learn.	37.5%	56.25%	0%	6.25%	0%	100%
4. I learn a lot with machinima.	16%	62.5%	0%	25%	0%	100%
5. Machinima help me to learn new words.	44%	56.25%	0%	0%	0%	100%
6. Machinima help me to understand new grammar.	6.25%	93.75%	0%	0%	0%	100%
7. Machinima help me to improve my listening.	6.75%	50%	0%	16%	0%	100%
8. Machinima help me to improve my speaking.	6.25%	16%	6.25%	75%	0%	100%
9. Machinima help me to improve my writing.	16%	56.25%	0%	31.25%	0%	100%
10. Watching machinima is fun, but I am not learning anything.	0%	16%	6.25%	69%	16%	100%
11. The avatars don't look natural	31.25%	56.25%	0%	16%	0%	100%
12. I find it difficult to learn a language if the avatars do not show what they feel.	18.75%	44%	0%	31.25%	6.25%	100%
13. I learn and understand the subject better with machinima.	0%	62.5%	0%	37.5%	0%	100%
14. I will continue learning with machinima in the future.	16.25%	16%	50%	25%	6.25%	100%
15. machinima help me to learn on my own.	18.75%	75%	0%	6.25%	0%	100%

Note: 1 equals *strongly agree* and 5 equals *strongly disagree.*

clear about whether they wanted to continue learning with machinima in the future, taking into account that they had been exposed to learning with machinima in one lesson only.

Students were asked about their learning experience with machinima. The majority (69%) reported that they felt 'comfortable' with learning in the medium, 44% were 'curious', 37% were 'satisfied', 25% felt 'happy', 19% felt 'motivated' and 16% felt 'excited', whereas 19% felt 'neutral' and only 6% felt 'confident'. It is remarkable that 31% felt 'confused', 25% felt 'anxious' but only 6% felt 'bored' or 'disengaged' with the machinima format. The questionnaire data showed that the students who learned with machinima were satisfied and motivated, and this reflected their teacher's assessment of their progress. Students were also asked to what extent they considered machinima to be as effective as real videos, to which 69% responded positively and 31% negatively. The latter group added some noteworthy comments that expanded on their response, identifying the problems they encountered with machinima in their lessons:

> The sound quality was not good.
> The graphics were poor.
> The characters in the machinima did not speak well.
> The avatars don't look as natural as in real videos.

Whereas a minority of students did not see any difference between using machinima and real-life videos, the majority saw some major advantages in its use:

> Machinima are more engaging to watch than normal videos.
> Machinima are fun to watch.
> I can learn a lot with machinima.
> Machinima help me to practise listening skills.
> The machinima helped me to understand grammar and learn new words.

Summary: Field Testing in the Czech Context

Arising from the field testing conducted by the university partner in the UCR which piloted several machinima with mechanical and electrical engineering students learning English, questionnaire data and teachers' feedback revealed that the sessions carried out with machinima were successful overall. Students enjoyed the novelty of using machinima in the language classroom and according to the teacher's lesson plans, it was possible to adopt a flexible approach in which there were different foci in the lessons, depending on the specific skills that were required. Although one teacher remarked on the extra work involved in setting up the machinima-based lessons, teachers were not expected to be experts in the field or to invest significant amounts of extra time and effort.

Case Study 3: Understanding Mathematics With Machinima and CLIL in the Netherlands

The following case study illustrates how a Dutch CLIL teacher, who taught mathematics to 13- and 16-year-old students in English at a secondary school in the Netherlands, integrated machinima in his lessons. Even though the instructor was willing to use innovative technologies in his teaching, such as integrating the use of tablets and 3D immersive environments, he firmly indicated that he had no intention of creating his own machinima, as this was considered too time-consuming an investment for the potential return envisaged at the start of his pilot project.

The male teacher was a CLIL specialist who had been teaching mathematics in English for 9 years. He taught 13-year-old students of mixed gender who had limited or beginner-level English proficiency. During the first eight weeks of the school year, he spoke both English and Dutch with his pupils; after that, he switched to an immersive English-only approach. According to the teacher, this approach worked well as pupils learned English quickly and effectively. In addition, he also taught third-grade students aged 16 who were studying for the Cambridge Advanced or First Certificate examinations at the end of their respective academic years. Prior to his involvement in the machinima pilot testing, the teacher used interactive websites like Socrative, Yahoo and ClassDojo in his lessons and therefore had developed satisfactory levels of confidence with digital tools. Based on this experience, he used the application ClassDojo as it helped him to keep track of his students' activities and homework, as well as to motivate them to speak English. The teacher used an iPad to check student contributions on the web and to award students points as they were eager to receive feedback on their work and demonstrate engagement. The teacher encouraged his students to bring their own digital devices to the classroom as the school did not provide tablets or computers. Though he was interested in creating 3D animations (see Figure 4.10) and understood the potential of working with computers, he had never used an immersive environment such as SL to create machinima for an actual learning context.

Implementing the use of machinima in his CLIL classroom was an interesting experiment for the teacher as he often encountered students who had problems visualising 3D objects typically used in mathematics. The teacher used machinima in his lesson to explain Pythagoras's Theorem, engaging his students to draw and calculate the length and space of diagonals, a task which he reported is quite challenging for students. While this task is typically challenging to demonstrate on a blackboard in real life, machinima allow for modifications and animations so that students are made aware of the changes when the perspective is changed, a point that is essential for the students' understanding. Accordingly, the animated shapes provided in the machinima were easier for the students to comprehend.

Prior to showing the machinima, the teacher asked the students to look at a worksheet (see Figures 4.7 and 4.9) and take notes in order to make sure that they understood the vocabulary and content.

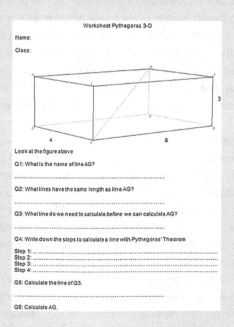

Figure 4.7 Worksheet for Teaching Pythagoras in 3D

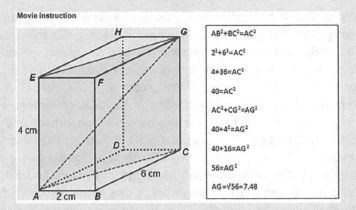

Figure 4.8 The Pythagoras Model

A second step was to view the machinima, which explained how to calculate a space diagonal (see Figure 4.8). The machinima was titled "Space Diagonal" (see https://youtu.be/WR_TGdbVv44). Following that students had to complete an exercise to check their understanding. In order to examine the effectiveness of the approach, the same topic was discussed in two classes using an experimental design. Test results indicated that the experimental group, which used machinima, achieved higher end-of-year tests than the control group, which had not used the video-based medium. The results were especially noteworthy because the group taught without machinima had typically scored higher in their end-of-year tests in other subjects. As a consequence, the teacher felt encouraged to reuse the machinima in future lessons and classes and to conduct further research on the topic.

Twelve of the 16 students in the teacher's class, five females and seven males, responded to the questionnaire. All the 13-year-old students attended a secondary CLIL school in the Netherlands. All but one student stated that they had been familiar with 3D environments and computer games such as Minecraft or WoW prior to the course, although none of them had ever created any machinima. Students were asked to state their opinion on a 5-point Likert scale in relation to the 15 statements shown in Table 4.3.

The results reflect that it was challenging for the participants who had little or no experience with machinima to describe their perspective based only on one specific lesson. Hence, statement 2, '*I enjoy making machinima*', could imply that the students might have had

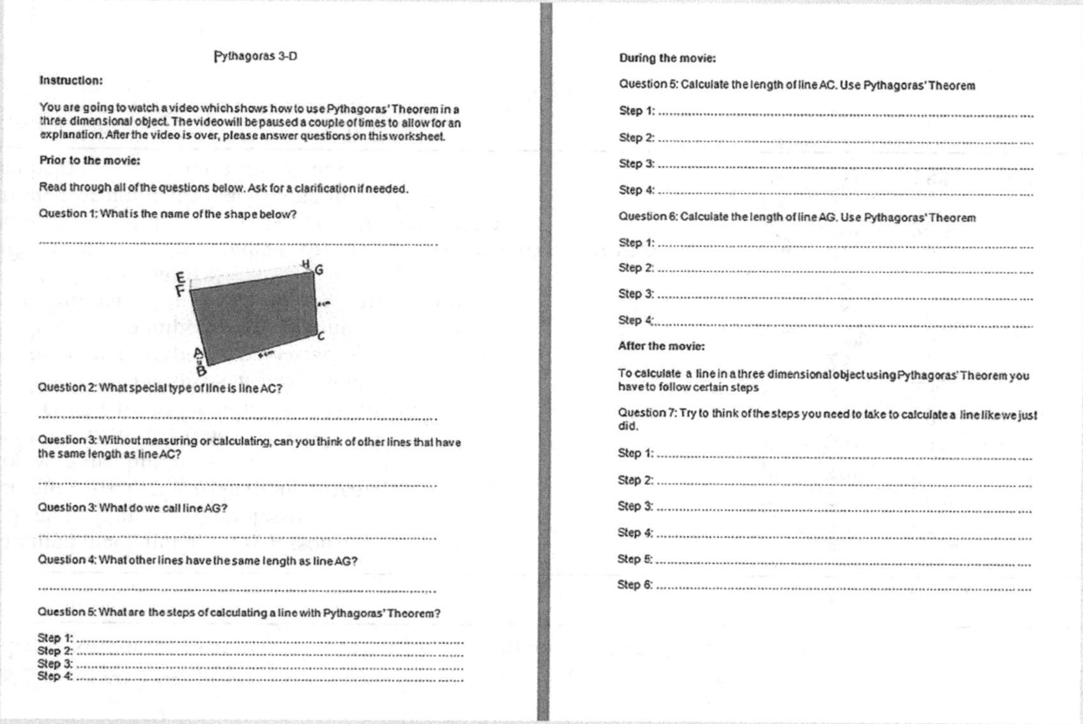

Pythagoras 3-D

Instruction:

You are going to watch a video which shows how to use Pythagoras' Theorem in a three dimensional object. The video will be paused a couple of times to allow for an explanation. After the video is over, please answer questions on this worksheet.

Prior to the movie:

Read through all of the questions below. Ask for a clarification if needed.

Question 1: What is the name of the shape below?

....

Question 2: What special type of line is line AC?

....

Question 3: Without measuring or calculating, can you think of other lines that have the same length as line AC?

....

Question 3: What do we call line AG?

....

Question 4: What other lines have the same length as line AG?

....

Question 5: What are the steps of calculating a line with Pythagoras' Theorem?

Step 1: ....
Step 2: ....
Step 3: ....
Step 4: ....

During the movie:

Question 5: Calculate the length of line AC. Use Pythagoras' Theorem

Step 1: ....
Step 2: ....
Step 3: ....
Step 4: ....

Question 6: Calculate the length of line AG. Use Pythagoras' Theorem

Step 1: ....
Step 2: ....
Step 3: ....
Step 4: ....

After the movie:

To calculate a line in a three dimensional object using Pythagoras' Theorem you have to follow certain steps

Question 7: Try to think of the steps you need to take to calculate a line like we just did.

Step 1: ....
Step 2: ....
Step 3: ....
Step 4: ....
Step 5: ....
Step 6: ....

Figure 4.9 Task Sheets Before, During and After Watching the Machinima

Table 4.3 Students' Responses to Statements About Machinima and Content (Dutch context)

Statement	1	2	3	4	5	Total
1. I enjoy watching machinima in my lessons.	25%	67%	8%	0%	0%	100%
2. I enjoy making machinima in my lessons.	0%	27%	55%	18%	0%	100%
3. Short machinima are better to help me learn.	8%	75%	8%	8%	0%	100%
4. I learn a lot with machinima.	8%	50%	25%	17%	0%	100%
5. Machinima help me to learn new words.	0%	33%	33%	33%	0%	100%
6. Machinima help me to understand new grammar.	0%	50%	8%	42%	0%	100%
7. Machinima help me to improve my listening.	0%	50%	25%	25%	0%	100%
8. Machinima help me to improve my speaking.	0%	25%	17%	58%	0%	100%
9. Machinima help me to improve my writing.	8%	8%	8%	67%	8%	100%
10. Watching machinima is fun, but I am not learning anything.	8%	8%	8%	58%	17%	100%
11. The avatars don't look natural.	18%	18%	36%	27%	0%	100%
12. I find it difficult to learn a language if the avatars do not show what they feel.	9%	27%	36%	9%	18%	100%
13. I learn and understand the subject better with machinima.	0%	70%	20%	10%	0%	100%
14. I will continue learning with machinima in the future.	9%	55%	18%	9%	9%	100%
15. Machinima help me to learn on my own.	18%	55%	18%	0%	9%	100%

Note: 1 equals *strongly agree* and 5 equals *strongly disagree*.

some experience in gaming and recording machinima outside the classroom. The positive results relating to the effect that the integration of machinima had on students' motivation was quite significant and supported the teacher's impression. Hence, the majority 'agreed' (25%) or 'strongly agreed' (67%) that they '*enjoy watching machinima in the lesson*' and 70% 'agreed' that they '*learn and understand the subject better with machinima*', while more than 50% stated that they '*learn a lot with machinima*'. Statement 11, '*The avatars don't look natural*', and statement 12, '*I find it difficult to learn a language if the avatars do not show what they feel*', were not applicable for this group of learners to answer because the machinima used in the lesson did not include any avatars, voice or text. Students were asked how they felt about their learning experience with machinima. Sixty per cent felt 'motivated', 30%, 'comfortable'; 20%, 'curious'; 10%, 'confident'; 10%, 'happy'; 10%, 'excited'; and 10%, 'frustrated'; and 20% marked it as 'hard to say'. The question, '*Is machinima as good as normal video in the lesson?*' was answered in the affirmative by 80% and in the negative by 20%. Moreover, students wrote that the lesson with machinima was simpler and clearer than without, that it looked more professional and that it explained the problem well.

Summary: Field Testing in the Dutch Context

In the mathematics classes described earlier, the instructor had always experienced explaining Pythagoras's Theorem to his students as challenging, as they typically encountered difficulties in visualising the calculation of space presented on a 1D blackboard. Due to the 3D affordances of machinima, the video-based medium emerged as a viable alternative that potentially enabled the instructor to create and modify animations in order to make students aware of changes in perspectives and therefore to understand key scientific principles. The instructor's machinima were created by Mathland (Techland Grid) in accordance with his instructions. Prior to showing the machinima to students, he asked them to look at a worksheet and take notes as the text was in English, and he wanted to make sure that vocabulary and content were understood. After watching the machinima students had to complete another exercise to check their understanding. The same course content was used without machinima for teaching another class with 16-year-old students. Performance tests taken by both groups revealed that the machinima group was more successful than the group that had not used machinima. According to the teacher, the use of machinima in combination with the extra materials helped students to visualise and therefore understand the theorem in greater depth. Twelve of the 16 students in the instructor's class responded to the questionnaire given to them after the lesson. Arising from this, in summary, the learners in the course enjoyed the experience with machinima, felt motivated by the innovative teaching approach and learned a great deal of relevant language-related content.

Case Study 4: Piloting Machinima With Learners of Turkish

The Turkish project participants created five machinima that were utilised as complementary course materials in addition to the units used in their course books for A1 level users of Turkish (see Figures 4.10–4.13).

Five teachers piloted a series of ready-made machinima in their classes, whereas one teacher created machinima with her students and one teacher trainee reported his experience of creating machinima in SL with a group of four other trainees. The number of participants in the seven courses varied between 4 and 24 students per course (a combined total of 98 students). The research aimed to find out whether and how the use of machinima could enhance language learning.

Use of Machinima in the Classroom

Most of the machinima implemented were ready-made and used to support the units and dialogues found in the textbooks used in the course.

Figure 4.10 Film 1: "Conversation With a Waiter" (see https://youtu.be/p68 AEk6bVL4)

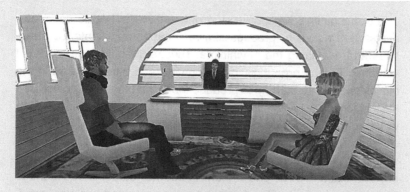

Figure 4.11 Film 2: "Buying a Painting" (see https://youtu.be/M56IUoRsTeo)

Figure 4.12 Film 3: "In the Gallery Part 1" (see https://youtu.be/467hhrz14TM)

Figure 4.13 Film 4: "In the Gallery Part 2" (see https://youtu.be/nUHZ15y83d4)

One teacher reported that several of his students did not take the session seriously because they regarded the machinima as a video game. This concern was also shared by another teacher who argued that compared with real-life videos, machinima could not be taken seriously.

The machinima were utilised in different ways. In one case, students were asked to produce similar phrases and sentence structures after watching the machinima. Thus, students had a model of authentic Turkish pronunciation, intonation and phrases used in the machinima before starting to produce their own phrases. Others used their machinima to practise grammar and vocabulary. One teacher, who had created her machinima using her own lesson plan, had her students watch the video and guess the ending or write a background story to the machinima. She preferred using her machinima in the physical classroom as she wanted to see her students' reactions to it while watching the film. Another teacher provided her own activities with the machinima and did not follow a ready-made lesson plan, which she did not consider as useful, because some details were missing in the ready-made materials or lesson plans. She preferred interactive machinima, where the students were able to make their own decisions in the learning process. She liked to use machinima for speaking and listening activities or as an activity to conclude the lesson with. Although using her own activities, when teaching with machinima, one teacher thought that the ready-made lesson plans that accompanied the machinima were very useful. Some teachers used both the ready-made lesson plans as well as their own activities or adapted ready-made lesson plans according to their needs and students' demands. Although the majority of teachers were quite positive about the use of machinima, one teacher did not think that ready-made lesson plans were useful as they were not compatible with his own 'personalised' lesson activities.

On the other hand, another teacher preferred using machinima in-world as she reported this was more effective. The most significant advantage of using machinima was seen in its novelty, especially when students were bored with the traditional videos. A teacher trainee, who had his students create their own machinima involving the learners in the process, reported that it was sometimes difficult to see the purpose of the machinima and contextualise a specific topic to be filmed. He preferred short machinima, which actively involved the students and included activities students could practise their language with by note-taking, responding to questions or completing the story. In his view, the use of machinima helped students in their learning progress as long as they exchanged ideas and structures and practised the language they experienced in the machinima by communicating with others.

Teacher Trainees Creating Their Own Machinima

A group of four teacher trainees worked collaboratively to create a machinima for language teachers in SL. One of them used the machinima in a private language club and reported that the audience was enthralled by the product. This was not surprising as the trainee shared ownership of the product and communicated the content enthusiastically, whereas other teachers, who used ready-made machinima tended to be more critical and were less successful in persuading others of their value.

As the teacher trainees did not have the opportunity to teach with the machinima in their own classes, they were not sure about the genre of machinima to be used. However, they thought that machinima would mostly appeal to young learners because they would enjoy the animations. They strongly believed that contemporary students enjoyed watching videos and therefore machinima videos would attract their attention. This cohort of language teacher trainees in their final year of training were very motivated to continue creating machinima.

Lack of Gestures in Machinima

The lack of facial expressions and gestures was criticised by the majority of teachers who used the machinima in this case study. Mimicking and realistic gestures were considered an important part of communication, especially for language learners, but were missing in all of the machinima piloted. This feature was considered to be a requirement for future improvements. One teacher stated that non-verbal clues are an essential part of communication as, for example, body language is needed to clearly convey intentions. As the avatars in the piloted machinima had little variety and sophistication with respect to mimicking real-life gestures and movements, the teacher concluded that real-life videos were better than machinima for pedagogical purposes at this point in time.

Machinima Convey Cultural Differences

There was a consensus of opinion among the piloting teachers that cultural differences could be appropriately conveyed via machinima, especially after one teacher in the group asked her Erasmus students to create a new video production following discussion of a machinima which compared similarities and differences between the students' own cultures. According to this teacher, it was simpler to encourage students to create new machinima to demonstrate such differences than to produce a real-life video. Another example of conveying cultural differences through machinima was given by a teacher who had created machinima to show the cultural differences between the reactions of parents when their son and daughter talked about getting married. The machinima conveyed the underlying values of Turkish culture and gave opportunities to the other students to explain their own cultural point of view. According to the teacher's comments, the machinima enabled cultural differences to emerge as different avatars were used by adding visual clues to the scenarios and actions. However, a minority of teachers felt that the scenes in the machinima were artificial and therefore that only real videos could convey the feeling of real contexts and real-life situations suitable for conveying cultural issues.

Advantages of Using Machinima

According to one of the piloting teachers, lessons could become too traditional without the use of new technologies such as machinima, and as a result, students might easily lose motivation or disengage from classroom learning. He saw significant advantages in working with machinima as a form of pedagogy as the videos could be created to include a particular focus on a broad range of topics relevant to his lessons. A more traditional teacher argued that his students did not learn much with the ready-made machinima he piloted, and he had to convince his students to change their minds about the value of machinima in learning as they were frustrated that things did not work the way they had expected. The teacher saw the main disadvantages of the ready-made machinima relating to their artificiality and believed that only real videos could convey the feelings associated with a real context. For another teacher, who liked using both machinima and real-life videos, the ready-made machinima were more suitable than having to create them herself and this saved time. However, she recognised the advantage of using machinima compared with real-life videos as they could easily be designed and created according to what was needed in her course.

One teacher reported that machinima helped her students to learn more effectively because they were more interested in the subject matter and felt more motivated than in the lessons without machinima.

Although one of the teachers commented that she did not see much difference between the use of machinima and real-life videos, she reported that short films were more likely to attract students rather than longer ones as her students easily lost motivation in situations when content took a long time to be communicated. Thus, she saw great potential in machinima compared with real-life videos in that they could be created instantly for specific purposes or topics in a lesson, and in this respect, machinima were considered an effective learning tool as they contributed to learning in context. Indeed, one teacher praised the variety of machinima added to her lesson as it encouraged her students' creativity. According to one of the other piloting teachers, the machinima were effective for revision and con-solidation purposes and students benefitted from the scaffolding they provided in the classroom-based learning process. From her experi-ence, the machinima helped her students to learn more effectively as they provided more opportunities for language input than in the classes without machinima. Consequently, her students were able to listen to 'real' language and to work on pronunciation in authentic contexts.

Post-Piloting Questionnaire Evaluation

A post-pilot questionnaire was completed by 57 learners (56% male and 44% female). The majority of learners (62%) were aged between 12 and 21 years old, 14% were between 22 and 26 years old and 23% were older than 26 years. Eighty-eight per cent of the learn-ers came from higher education, whereas 12% came from secondary schools. Students were asked how they learnt about machinima, and the majority of responders (69%) reported being familiar with 3D envi-ronments or computer games, while 31% claimed they were not. The majority of learners (82%) had not created machinima yet, whereas 18% had. In terms of operating in a virtual environment, only a few learners (19%) had had prior experience of working with 3D immer-sive environments like SL. The most significant challenge encoun-tered was 'moving avatars' by 33%. In terms of how they felt about their learning experience with machinima, 37% of learners stated that they were motivated by learning with machinima, whereas the same number felt disengaged. Thirty per cent felt 'very satisfied'; 26%, 'comfortable'; 23%, 'curious'; 21%, 'excited'; 19% 'satisfied'; 11% 'con-fident'; and 5%, 'anxious'. Twenty-six per cent indicated that it was difficult to say what they felt. Eighteen per cent felt 'confused'; 12%, 'sceptical'; 11%, 'frustrated'; 7%, 'scared'; and 4%, 'disappointed'. Learners were of two minds about whether machinima was as good as traditional video in lessons as 55% responded 'no' and 45% more positively with 'yes' to this question. This diversity of responses was also reflected in the responses to 15 statements learners agreed or disagreed to (see Table 4.4).

The majority of learners agreed (32% 'strongly agreed' and 30% 'agreed') that they enjoyed watching machinima and 13% were 'undecided', whereas 16% 'strongly disagreed' and 9% 'disagreed' with this statement.

The statement '*I enjoy making machinima in my lessons*' was not relevant for the majority of the learners as they had not been previously exposed to ready-made machinima in their Turkish lessons. Most 'agreed' (31%) or 'strongly agreed' (25%) with the statement '*Short machinima are better to help me learn*', although 18% 'strongly disagreed' and 11% 'disagreed', whereas 16% were 'undecided'. There was more disagreement (12% 'strongly disagreed', 25% 'disagreed') than agreement with the statement '*I learn a lot with machinima*', to which only 16% 'strongly agreed' and 18% 'agreed' and 20% were 'undecided'. However, it was significant that 21% 'strongly agreed' and 46% 'agreed' that '*machinima help them to learn new words*'. Only 7% 'disagreed' and 19% 'strongly disagreed', 7% of the learners were 'undecided'. Sixteen per cent 'strongly agreed' and 25% 'agreed' that '*machinima help them to understand new grammar*', while almost the same number of learners 'disagreed' (23%) or 'strongly disagreed' (18%) with this statement; 19% were 'undecided'. It was significant that the majority of learners 'strongly agreed' (44%) and 36% 'agreed' that '*machinima help[ed] them to improve their listening*'. Seven per cent 'strongly disagreed' and 11% 'disagreed' with this statement, and one learner was 'undecided'. A similarly high level of positive responses was achieved with the statement '*Machinima help me to improve my speaking*' to which 40% 'agreed', 24% 'strongly agreed', 9% were 'undecided', 16% 'disagreed' and 11% 'strongly disagreed'. With regard to writing skills achieved through machinima, the statement '*Machinima help me to improve my writing*' was 'strongly disagreed' with by 36% and 'disagreed' with by 26%. Twenty-one per cent were 'undecided', whereas 7% 'agreed' and 11% 'strongly agreed' with the statement. It was noteworthy that the majority 'disagreed' (32%) or 'strongly disagreed' (23%) with the statement '*Watching machinima*

Table 4.4 Students' Responses to Statements on Machinima and Content (Turkish context)

Statement	1	2	3	4	5	Total
1. I enjoy watching machinima in lessons.	32.4%	30.36%	12.50%	8.93%	16.07%	100%
2. I enjoy making machinima in my lessons.	18.52%	16.67%	18.52%	18.52%	27.78%	100%
3. Short machinima are better to help me learn.	24.56%	31.58%	15.79%	10.53%	17.54%	100%
4. I learn a lot with machinima.	16.07%	17.86%	15.79%	10.53%	17.54%	100%
5. Machinima help me learn new words.	21.05%	45.61%	7.02%	7.02%	19.30%	100%
6. Machinima help me to understand new grammar.	15.79%	24.56%	19.30%	22.81%	17.54%	100%
7. Machinima help me to improve my listening.	43.64%	36.36%	1.82%	10.91%	7.27%	100%
8. Machinima help me to improve my speaking.	24.56%	40.35%	8.77%	15.79%	10.53%	100%
9. Machinima help me to improve my writing.	10.53%	7.02%	21.05%	26.32%	35.09%	100%
10. Watching machinima is fun but I am not learning anything.	21.43%	10.71%	12.50%	32.14%	23.21%	100%
11. The avatars don't look natural.	42.11%	15.79%	14.04%	19.30%	8.77%	100%
12. I find it difficult to learn a language if the avatars do not show what they feel.	25.00%	33.93%	16.07%	12.50%	12.50%	100%
13. I learn and understand the subject better with machinima.	19.30%	19.30%	21.05%	21.05%	19.30%	100%
14. I will continue learning with machinima in the future.	14.29%	21.43%	8.93%	8.93%	28.57%	100%
15. Machinima help me to learn on my own.	14.55%	27.27%	16.36%	16.36%	29.09%	100%

Note: 1 equals *strongly agree* and 5 equals *strongly disagree.*

is fun, but I am not learning anything'. Twenty-one per cent 'strongly agreed' and 11% 'agreed' with the statement; 12% were 'undecided'. Most learners 'agreed' (42% 'strongly agreed', 16% 'agreed') with the statement *'The avatars don't look natural'*, 14% were 'undecided', 19% 'disagreed' and 9% 'strongly disagreed'.

With regard to using machinima in language learning, it was noteworthy that 25% of the learners 'strongly agreed' and 34% 'agreed' with the statement that it is *'difficult to learn a language if the avatars do not show what they feel'*, 16% were 'undecided', 12% 'disagreed' and the same number of learners 'strongly disagreed' with this statement. 19% of the learners 'strongly agreed' and an equal number 'strongly disagreed', that they *'learn and understand the subject better with machinima'*, whereas 21% 'disagreed 'and 19% 'agreed', 21% were 'undecided'.

Twenty-nine per cent of the students 'strongly disagreed' and 9% 'disagreed' that *'they will continue learning with machinima in the future'*; 27% were 'undecided', whereas 21% 'agreed' and 14% 'strongly agreed' to continue learning with machinima in the future. About half of the participants 'agreed' (27% 'agreed', 14% 'strongly agreed'), that machinima *'help[ed] them to learn on their own'*, while 16% 'disagreed' and 29% 'strongly disagreed'. Slightly fewer learners intend to *'continue learning with machinima in the future'* (21% 'agreed' and 14% 'strongly agreed'). Twenty-seven per cent were 'undecided', 29% 'strongly disagreed' to continue with machinima and 9% 'disagreed'.

From the questionnaire results, it was interesting to see that learning with machinima seemed less popular among some of the learners than had been assumed by their teachers according to the teachers' questionnaires and focus group discussions. As only 61% of the learners completed the questionnaire, a lower response rate could account for this outcome, as could the fact that a larger number of students who were more sceptical about its potential responded to the questionnaire whereas others who were more positive did not.

Summary: Field Testing in the Turkish Context

The majority of teachers observed throughout the pilot studies indicated that the use of machinima videos enhanced their language teaching in a positive way, and they noted positive changes in the short-term motivational levels of their students. Several teachers were convinced that machinima added to the quality of language learning by capturing students' attention and this made the lessons more effective. They claimed that as long as machinima interested the students, they were helpful for them and added to the quality of language learning because the new technology, new materials and new concepts appeared to affect motivation in a positive way.

Not all teachers shared these generally positive views about machinima, however. As one teacher remarked, machinima could not in their present state contribute to the quality of language learning, although they may be able to add some variety to lessons. Indeed, machinima were viewed as contributing a 'wow factor' (Bax, 2011b), and teachers were concerned that following the rise in students' initial interest, their motivation might decrease after they had been used to working with the medium for a more significant time.

Case Study 5: Using Machinima in a Military University in Poland

In the final case study, three teachers were involved in field-testing machinima at a university in Poland at the beginner and intermediate levels. The participants were soldiers, both officers and non-commissioned, between the ages of 25 and 50, and the machinima were integrated into a course curriculum related to revising Polish grammar. One teacher used machinima with a group of 15 military students at the A1 level. Her aim was to use machinima in the classroom to investigate how to bridge the gap between a traditional approach to learning and one which integrated innovative digital technologies in the process.

The teacher reported that ready-made lesson plans along with the machinima were particularly useful for teachers who were not familiar with the medium as this provided guidelines on how to implement machinima in a language session. She saw a significant advantage in creating machinima as they could be produced at low cost and demonstrated a capacity to be innovative for students. On the other hand, she reported that it was a disadvantage that high specification technical equipment was needed; for example, a good computer with a good graphics card was necessary to create machinima of good quality.

Another teacher of Polish used machinima with two intermediate-level groups of fourteen 25- to 50-year-old soldiers (officers and non-commissioned officers). This teacher agreed that cultural differences could be conveyed via machinima, such as looking at different locations in-world or discussing different kinds of clothes. It was interesting that this teacher reported that a number of her students described the movements of the characters in SL and the facial expressions as 'non-natural', 'strange' and 'stiff' and considered language learning with machinima as disengaging for learners.

The most important use of machinima for this teacher was to encourage her students to listen and repeat the dialogues in the target language. She regarded mimicking and the use of gestures as very important, as when used appropriately, the machinima could take on the characteristics of a real-life video. In her lessons, the teacher used a variety of methods to trigger students' interest and engage them in the topic. Screenshots of example exercises can be seen in Figures 4.14 and 4.17 which included participants from an Erasmus group (aged 20–25) teaching Polish for beginners.

Following the course curriculum, the first two machinima were used to present new grammar structures and to encourage students to create their own dialogues. The teacher used cloze exercises with the machinima, and the students created their own texts and used the voice-over technique to create new dialogues for the existing machinima. For the first session with "Ona ma urodziny" (see

Figure 4.14 "Co to jest" (see https://youtu.be/OXlYXZ_VqAs)

Figure 4.15 "Interesuję się sportem" (see https://youtu.be/rDgNL4Ghbk0)

Figure 4.16 "Ona ma urodziny" (see https://youtu.be/6e1jZBTADTk)

Figure 4.17 "Moja podróż z muzyką" (see https://youtu.be/pfXAbjRBdck)

Figure 4.16), the teacher needed 45 minutes. For the session with "Interesuję się sportem", 90 minutes was needed (see Figure 4.15).

The teacher also used machinima with her military officers' group (aged 30 to 40) during an intensive Polish course for beginners (see Figure 4.17). One of the other Polish teachers presented machinima to two groups of 14 intermediate-level soldiers. The main practice skills the teacher applied included watching the scenes and encouraging students to observe the way characters talked in the target language and then to create their own dialogues. The teacher did not have any ready-made lesson plan as she considered machinima to be supporting material for her language courses rather than a main tool for teaching languages. The teacher, who had used the machinima in her English class to recycle conditional phrases as part of the curriculum, reported that her students found the videos more suitable to younger children and preferred real-life videos.

Post-Piloting Students' Survey

Thirty-nine students took part in a post-pilot questionnaire (m = 37; f = 2). Forty-four per cent of the students were aged between 37 and 50 years old, 28% of students were between 27 and 31 years old and 26% were between 32 and 36 years old. The majority of the students (63%) were not familiar with 3D environments, whereas 37% reported some form of prior experience. None of the students had previously created their own machinima.

Seventy-one per cent of the students considered machinima to be 'less effective than watching traditional videos' in their lessons, whereas 29% thought machinima was 'just as good as traditional video'. The responses about the learning experience with machinima corresponded with the teachers' assessments of how their students felt about machinima, and hence, it was no surprise that 38% were 'disappointed', 26% felt 'bored', 23% found it 'hard to say' and the same number of students were 'sceptical'. Eighteen per cent felt 'happy'; 15%, 'satisfied'; 13%, 'confused'; 10%, 'comfortable' and 'frustrated', respectively. Only 8% indicated that they *were motivated* by using machinima in their lessons.

Half of the participants '*enjoyed watching machinima in their lessons*', and half of them did not. More participants disagreed that *they learn a lot with machinima* than those agreeing to the statement. Thirty-four per cent 'agreed' and 13%' strongly agreed' that '*short machinima are better to help me learn*'; 13% 'disagreed' and the same number 'strongly disagreed' with this statement. Thirty-three per cent 'agreed' and 8% 'strongly agreed' that '*machinima help[ed] them to learn new words*', whereas 28% 'disagreed' and 10% 'strongly disagreed' with this statement; 21% were 'undecided'. More people 'disagreed' than 'agreed' that '*machinima help[ed] me to learn new grammar*'. On the other hand, more people 'agreed' than 'disagreed' that '*machinima help to improve listening and speaking*'. The majority 'disagreed' that '*machinima help to improve their writing*'. An equal number of people 'agreed' and 'disagreed' with the statement '*Watching machinima is fun, but I am not learning anything*'. As already stated in the teachers' feedback, a significant majority of students 'agreed' that '*the avatars don't look natural*'. The majority of students stated that '*they will not continue to learn with machinima in future*'. However, 30% of the students 'agreed' and 8% 'strongly agreed' that '*they understand the subject better with machinima*', whereas 22% of the students 'disagreed' and 16% 'strongly disagreed' with this statement, and 24% were 'undecided'. Thirty-four per cent of the students 'agreed' and 11% 'strongly agreed' that they '*find it difficult to learn a language if the avatars do not show what they feel*', whereas 13% 'disagreed' and 11% 'strongly disagreed' and 32% of the students were 'undecided.' Thirty-two per cent of the students 'agreed' and the same number of students 'disagreed' with the statement '*Machinima help me to learn on my own*'.

Evaluation of Post-Pilot Questionnaires for Teachers

In addition to the focus group discussions, 11 teachers who had used machinima in the classroom from universities in Turkey, the Czech Republic and Poland gave their feedback following field testing. The participants were all female, with 75% aged between 26 to 45 years of age; the remaining 25% were over 51 years old. Their teaching experience ranged from 1 to 5 years (33%), 6 to 10 years (33%) and 21+ years (25%).

In terms of prior experience with learning technologies, the majority of teachers already used video in their lessons (75%). Fifty per cent of the teachers used interactive whiteboards, and the same number of teachers used the computer lab. Thirty-three per cent used Moodle or other VLEs, and only 16% had used SL or 3D environments. The majority of teachers had been using technology in their lessons for between 1 and 5 years (56%), others (36%) had been using technology for 6 to 10 years and one teacher for more than 20 years. The time range teachers had been using machinima for varied from those who had just started to others who had used them for a couple of months to one year.

The language taught in lessons was Polish in the majority of cases, while the other courses used English as the medium of instruction. The major focus was on languages for specific purposes (64%), a smaller percentage focused on general language learning (18%) and international students (8%); 9% responded with 'other'. In the context of CLIL classes, the teachers taught a variety of English for mechanical engineering, history and physics and Polish and English for military content.

All the teachers implemented machinima for language practice. Fifty-five per cent used it for cooperative language learning and 45% for language production. Thirty-six per cent of the teachers used their machinima for introducing content. Very few responders (18%) used the machinima as an autonomous activity, and even fewer (9%) used it as a learning task or introduction to a subject. Only one teacher had recorded her own machinima and reported that the main technical issues she had related to connecting to SL, finding appropriate locations and acquiring permission to film there.

In relation to learning with machinima, teachers were asked how far they agreed or disagreed with the following statements on a 5-point Likert scale (1 = *strongly agree* to 5 = *strongly disagree*). Sixty per cent 'agreed' and 30% 'strongly agreed' '*that machinima fosters learning*'. Fifty-five per cent 'agreed' and 36% 'strongly agreed' that their '*students' motivation increases when using machinima*'. Only one teacher disagreed with this statement. Seventy per cent believed that '*machinima provides a self-study after school*'; 10% were 'undecided' and 20% 'disagreed' with this statement. Eighty-two per cent of the teachers 'agreed' and 9% 'strongly agreed' that '*machinima help students to understand and grasp the lessons*'. Seventy per cent of the teachers 'agreed' and 20% 'strongly agreed' that '*they are satisfied with the contribution of machinima to their lessons and intend to use machinima to assist their teaching in the future*'. Seventy-three per cent 'agreed' and 18% 'disagreed' that they '*intend to use machinima as autonomous learning resource*'. Sixty-four per cent of the teachers 'disagreed' with the statement that '*students get sidetracked by machinima, because it is more entertaining than educating*', whereas 18% 'agreed' with it or were 'undecided' about the statement.

Another interesting result was that 55% 'disagreed' with the statement that '*body language is missing in the avatars and this disturbs students*', whereas only one teacher 'strongly agreed' and another 'agreed' to this statement. Twenty-seven per cent were 'undecided'. It is notable that 45% of the teachers 'disagreed' and one 'strongly disagreed' '*that machinima is more effective than other learning materials*', to which only 18% 'agreed', whereas 27% of the teachers were 'undecided'.

Summary: Field Testing in the Polish Context

The questionnaire results from both teachers and learners demonstrated that a significant number of learners did not always react positively to the machinima they were exposed to in language learning contexts. The majority of students preferred using real-life videos to machinima. With this particular group of participants, it is significant to note that compared to the field-testing evaluations from the other groups reported earlier, a significant majority felt disappointed, disengaged and lacking in motivation to use the machinima in language learning contexts. In order to investigate the causes of this sceptical attitude towards machinima, further research will need to be carried out to answer questions such as

- Are adults the most effective target group to use machinima with?
- Why did the content of the lessons not appeal to the students?
- To what extent did the quality of the videos influence their response?
- Would a different set of machinima have made any difference?
- Did the teacher's attitude influence the students' acceptance of machinima in any way?
- How different would their reactions be to comparative uses of real-life videos?
- Would the students' attitude towards avatars and machinima be different if they were involved in creating their own machinima?

Summary

Several pilot studies of machinima have been reported in this chapter based on field testing in Turkey, the Netherlands, the UCR, Poland and Germany. The research was based on the question, In what ways can machinima enhance language learning? The evaluation of the questionnaire results in the various piloting institutions, ranging from the commercial sector to adult education and university students, demonstrate a diversity of opinions in this respect. The question of whether students learn more effectively with machinima is complex and depends on many factors. As these diverse case studies have shown, a majority of teachers were enthusiastic about teaching with machinima. The main difference between video and machinima is that the characters often lack facial expressions and natural gestures, a fact that was criticised by a majority of teachers and learners. All teachers involved in the questionnaire used ready-made machinima focused on a specific topic or grammar point. Most teachers had only recently discovered machinima and were reluctant to create their own, either because of the lack of necessary skills or time constraints.

It was interesting to observe, however, that not all ready-made machinima fulfilled everybody's interests or requirements. Indeed, according to teachers' and learners' feedback the most effective and rewarding machinima were those that involved the learners in the production process as the group of English teacher trainees from the Turkish context discovered, when they created machinima for language teaching in SL. They worked collaboratively, involving everybody in the production process, either as part of the production team, filming or acting, for example. For the learners, the process of achievement was more important than the final product. Interviews with the teachers also confirmed this point. Engaging learners in contributing to any stage of the production process, whether it was writing a script, recording dialogue or rehearsing it until all the participants were satisfied, was the most rewarding aspect of the process. Furthermore, observation of the learner's linguistic performance through machinima indicated that they provide opportunities to notice and reflect on their language learning habits and behaviour. One participant, for example, reported that she had learnt to control her speaking time after reflecting on her performance throughout the machinima production process. This appears to confirm Dreher and Dreher's (2009, p. 449) point, that machinima offer learners an "opportunity for critical reflection", by repeatedly reviewing their performances "to permit a deeper level of reflection upon what has been done and how to improve what has been learned".

As some teachers mentioned in their feedback, making machinima can be very time-consuming, especially when they are not familiar with 3D environments and challenging if there is a lack of technical support. Older computers, poor graphic cards or a lack of bandwidth can be barriers that prevent teachers from creating machinima. Hence, the use of ready-made machinima may be the best solution for the majority of teachers at this point in its development, which was the approach followed by the groups of Czech, Turkish and Polish teachers. Nevertheless, according to focus group reports, there was some controversial discussion about whether it was advantageous to use ready-made machinima which included materials and lesson plans. Several teachers stated that ready-made machinima and material saved them time and effort with respect to preparing their lessons, whereas others argued that the materials did not fit with their course objectives. Creating their own machinima was considered too demanding with regard to the ICT skills, equipment and the level of institutional support that was required (Schneider, 2014a). Indeed, several teachers argued that there were numerous good-quality machinima on the web to choose from so there was no need to invest significant time in designing and creating their own. However, several teachers reasoned that it was equally time-consuming to watch many example machinima before being able to identify a suitable one that had the required language level and focus they required. Another sceptical view was expressed by more traditional teachers, who argued that students did not learn much with the ready-made machinima as they preferred real-life videos. It was an interesting finding that a group of Polish participants exposed to some ready-made machinima in their English lesson were not motivated by the machinima and found the graphics more relevant to children than to adult learning environments. This attitude towards machinima provoked many questions that cannot be resolved here, and further research is required about the reasons for the negative responses focusing on whether it derived from the content, the role of the teacher or the relevance of the machinima to different target groups.

In spite of the mostly positive rating of the machinima used, some concerns were highlighted with regard to the artificial and unrealistic nature of the avatars as a result of missing facial expressions and gestures. This constraint derived from existing technical limitations and may be overcome in the future as the technology develops. Nevertheless, it was also experienced as a major challenge by students involved in the field testing as the questionnaire data revealed. In some cases, poor sound quality and graphics capabilities added to the critical assessment of the machinima.

However, when technical obstacles can be overcome, learning with and through machinima may be highly motivating (Schneider, 2014a). Regardless of the critical comments received from the participants, the majority of the teachers across each of these cases were convinced that their learners were attracted by the novelty of using machinima in the language classroom and had fewer problems adapting to the use of avatars given that they were used to manipulating virtual characters in their computer games (Jauregi et al., 2011). The majority of teachers valued the machinima they piloted as they inspired their students to actively participate and engage in the lessons. Examples of good practice can be seen in the outcome of the MOOT course, to which we turn in the following chapters, as this demonstrated how teachers who immersed themselves in virtual worlds were able to produce several machinima for their specific teaching contexts.

The success of the machinima was based on teachers' assessment of students' progress and the suitability of the machinima for language learning. Surveys of students' evaluation of the piloted lessons with machinima were also collected and resulted in 726 responses. It is noteworthy that 75% of the students felt comfortable about the learning experience, although the majority preferred using traditional language learning videos to machinima. No matter whether traditional videos or machinima are used in a lesson, the activities performed in the classroom may be the same; the major difference is the creation process that students engage in and with when producing machinima. The creation of machinima is also often seen as an opportunity for artistic expression in this respect (Harwood, 2014; Vandagriff & Nitsche, 2009) and Johnson and Pettit (2012) similarly regard machinima as a piece of art, that "like a good film, begins with a good story, but must be crafted as visually and aurally stimulating for its viewers" (p. 41).

5 Evaluating a Machinima CALL Teacher Education Course

Introduction

As we have seen in the preceding chapters, the video-based instructional project at the centre of this book aimed to investigate language teaching in virtual worlds using machinima and make it easier for instructors to access the pedagogies, technologies and materials required to use the medium effectively in 3D immersive environments. The five case studies presented in Chapter 4 also included trainee teacher and learner perspectives on the process of using 'ready-made' machinima, as well as self-created examples, within the context of a project-based approach, sometimes involving CLIL. A MOOT was designed to enable CALL language teachers, particularly those from a CLIL background, who already had some pedagogical background and relevant teaching experience but were not familiar with virtual worlds, to create and use machinima in a variety of situations and to understand the potential benefits and challenges of the video-based medium. The training course was based on a two-stage approach involving, first, the creation and then field testing of the machinima and, second, the identification of guidelines for their possible use in the language classroom, both of which we explored in Chapter 4

Previous research has identified the educational potential for language learners to utilise machinima and become involved in the process of producing machinima in virtual worlds as this may boost their confidence, creativity, motivation and sense of autonomy while also supporting their language skills development in communicating in the target language (Nowak, 2015; Schneider, 2014a). The research presented in this chapter is focused specifically on the trainee teachers' perspective on the role of machinima as a tool for reflection, assessment and feedback and examines their participation in the CALL training course, as this addresses a gap in the research on the subject (Myers, 2014).

The course was designed to run over two iterations. The findings arising from the first phase iteration were used to redesign the second iteration based on several key recommendations. The first part of the chapter explores the first iteration, while the second iteration is the subject of the latter part. A framework arising from the trainees' participation in the CALL teacher education course is outlined in Chapter 6, alongside recommendations and implications arising from the research project as a whole.

Methods Used for the Evaluation

A mixed-methods approach was chosen to evaluate both iterations of the CALL teacher education course (Creswell, 2014). Data were collected utilising both quantitative and qualitative methods and involved the use of questionnaires, interviews, focus groups, interactions in an asynchronous learning platform (Moodle) and observation (Boellstorff, 2008; Cohen et al., 2007; Mawer, 2014) during the creation and use of machinima by an international group of language teachers. It was essential to observe how teachers immersed themselves in a virtual world, engaged in creating machinima and became comfortable filming and editing their video productions and supplementary language teaching resources. The researchers who conducted the observation were also part of the teacher training course facilitating team, and this added an ethnographic dimension to the research. Two of the most important questions guiding the research process were, What value did the teachers perceive in creating and using machinima in their language teaching? and If positive, how would they apply the newly acquired knowledge and skills in their lesson planning and teaching activities?

The First Iteration

Course Aims and Structure

The substantive goal of the CALL training course was to enable each trainee to produce (at least) one example machinima by the end of the five-week course and share it with the entire group of trainees to stimulate a process of critical peer reflection and feedback. The learning objectives for the five-week course are shown in Table 5.1.

The first iteration of the course adopted a blended learning approach based on the use of the Moodle learning management platform for discussions in which learning resources and materials were available to course participants for download. Several discussion fora were established to enable the trainee teachers to engage in asynchronous communication and peer reflections and exchange feedback through the sharing of completed tasks. The 3D immersive world of SL was used for practical work such as developing in-world skills and for filming machinima, whereas the videoconferencing application, Adobe Connect, was used as a platform for live, synchronous workshop sessions in which the trainees were

Table 5.1 Weekly Overview of the CALL Teacher Education Course

Week 1	*Pedagogical rationale for using machinima* Aim: Become familiar with the virtual world of SL and consider how and why teachers could use machinima in their teaching and learning.
Week 2	*Technical skills and avatars* Aim: Learn to dress avatars, change avatars, mix and match avatar clothing, work with gestures and animations, use a holodeck and control light in the 3D immersive world environment.
Week 3	*Navigation skills* Aim: Learn to move and navigate in SL, develop basic camera control skills and use related navigational tools such as the mini-map.
Week 4	*Finding locations* Aim: Find appropriate places and locations to film, request permissions, create landmarks and become skilled in the use of storyboards.
Week 5	*Editing* Aim: Learn basic film, editing and sharing techniques and how to evaluate machinima.

able to present materials and/or results, exchange tips and ideas, take part in focused discussions and ask for clarification where appropriate. The facilitator of the training course used the latter platform mainly for providing instructions, feedback and presenting results to the trainees.

The first two weeks of the training course were designed to provide the trainee teachers with the opportunity to acquaint themselves with the immersive environment of SL. In the following three weeks participants were tasked with examining in more depth how to design and critique existing language teaching machinima and finally create their own examples in the medium. It was intended that the 'curriculum framework' for the machinima teacher training course would be modified after the first iteration based on the trainees' and observers' feedback and their experiences of the course format. Successful participants were given the incentive of receiving a 'Certificate of Completion' at the end of the course, as is typically the case in MOOCs, if they completed the required attendance and task requirements on time.

Teachers' Experience and Expectations

The course participants were from the Czech Republic, Italy, Spain, Turkey and Portugal and consisted of language teachers, teacher trainees and a science teacher. They combined a significant mix of skills and experience, which meant that some participants had to learn basic SL navigation skills first, whereas participants who had already developed them could start recording and acquiring film footage for their machinima productions. A minority of the participants were able to quickly absorb the technical skills required for SL, whereas the majority required more significant periods and practice, or even struggled throughout the course, in order to do so. Of the 12 participants and five mentors who originally enrolled in the first iteration of the course, seven completed the requirements. These successful participants (whose names have been anonymised) had the following background and experience:

A **male science teacher (P1 Fernando)** who was working in a Portuguese middle school and had more than 20 years of teaching experience. He had no experience with SL or in making machinima, but he had produced and used videos in his chemistry and physics lessons. His motivation to participate in the course was to make his lessons more interesting to his students and to discover new ways of explaining complex processes in a 3D visual format that they could easily understand.

A **female Spanish teacher (P2 Carmen)** who ran a small business in Spain and who had been involved in education in virtual worlds for the past five years. She aimed to learn from other teachers' experiences on the course and hoped that her challenges in using English for communication in the course could be overcome with the help of peers who could speak Spanish.

A **female English teacher (P3 Lucia)**, originally from France, who was teaching young children at a primary school in Italy. She had already had some experience with SL and had used the 3D immersive world of OpenSimulator over the past three years. She was also familiar with filmmaking, although not with making machinima, and at the time of the training course, she was running a 3D project with her young students in which she hoped to include machinima as a central feature.

A **female Turkish teacher trainee (P4 Fatma)**, from a university in Turkey, who was originally part of the mentoring team for the CALL teacher education course but then decided to switch roles and participate as a trainee as she felt she still needed more instruction to improve her machinima production skills.

A **female Czech teacher (P5 Barbora)** who was working in the field of applied language studies at a university in the Czech Republic, teaching ESP to mechanical and technical engineers. She hoped to create machinima related to the field of engineering. She had limited experience with SL and no experience with filming or film editing but was keen to extend her knowledge to work with video-based learning. At the time of the CALL teacher education course, she intended to produce machinima for and with her students and, with some practice, introduce colleagues to the skills necessary for making machinima.

A female Italian teacher of Spanish (P6 Francesca) who was working on her PhD in literature and ICT and wanted to enhance her digital skills. While she had a strong interest in utilising the potential of SL, she had no previous experience of using immersive environments for teaching and learning.

A female Italian teacher of English and Italian as Foreign Language (P7 Paola) who specialised in teaching students with special needs in a secondary school in Italy. She had been teaching in public schools for 20 years at all levels and was experienced in designing courses and teaching in SL. Her motivation to participate in the CALL teacher education course was to learn more about the potential of machinima as a tool for learner creativity.

At the start of the course, the participants identified a diverse range of individual expectations, including the following aims:

Find new ways to engage students.

Experience new approaches for learning and co-creating with the students.

Find alternative ways to improve learner collaboration.

Meet other teachers from languages and other disciplinary backgrounds who were interested in experimenting with video-based instructional approaches.

Acquire the skills to make effective machinima".

Learn new technical and pedagogical skills.

Discover how to make machinima and integrate them in the classroom.

Create machinima that are related to the field of engineering.

Provide authentic tasks for students.

Use 3D virtual worlds like Second Life in teaching and introduce students to different aspects of English-speaking countries in a potentially engaging and motivating format.

The main concerns identified by participants prior to the beginning of the course related to (1) the potential of the machinima creation process to require significant amounts of preparation time and (2) the creation of inhibiting technical challenges.

The Use of Discussion Fora

Several discussion fora were established on Moodle to aid communication among the trainees, the course facilitators and mentors and these were accessible throughout the course: the *Announcements* forum, a *General* chat forum, a *Mentors* forum and a *Problems* forum. All the teacher-led synchronous sessions in SL or Adobe Connect were recorded and uploaded to the *Announcements* forum as well as other important announcements. The *General* forum was established for more personal exchange and informal discussion, the *Mentors* forum provided a dedicated space for questions and exchanges between mentors and trainees and the *Problems* forum enabled trainees to address issues they encountered during the weekly training sessions and to ask for facilitator and/or mentor support when required.

Furthermore, two to four discussion fora were provided each week, where trainees were asked to share the machinima they had created, provide feedback to each other or discuss the pedagogical implications of their work. The *Announcements* forum was established to enable the project team to disseminate important information to the course participants. The announcements were mainly posted by the facilitators; the trainees did not have relevant privileges to make their own contributions. Although it could be argued that trainees might also have important information to disseminate, this area of responsibility was left to the discretion of facilitators to avoid message overload (Prendergast, 2000). Thirty announcements were posted in total in this forum including all live-session recordings, which were edited and uploaded to the forum immediately after the actual session, so that the trainees who had missed live sessions could revisit them later if required. In addition to the weekly recordings, other announcements were posted to inform participants about the time and place of meetings and whether these were going to be held in Adobe Connect or SL. The forum also served as a reminder for tasks waiting to be completed, such as completing any required readings, for example. The points raised in the announcements usually referred to issues that had arisen during the live sessions, such as how to use camera controls or instructions for Apple users as they differed from PC commands. Arrangements for groups collaborating on the same topic were also posted in this forum so that all the trainees could check who they were collaborating with. Other posts included information relating to changes to the course programme or scheduled replacements for an absent facilitator.

The second forum was intended for mentors. The motivation to invite mentors from a group of trainee teachers arose following an interview held by a project researcher with some trainees who had created several machinima in a drama course at a Turkish university. In order to inform the trainees about the concept of mentors and introduce them to the course, the *Mentors* forum was established. At the outset, the facilitator welcomed the four mentors and explained the key aspects and expectations of their role and how they could support the trainees with their machinima and lesson plan development. While the use of mentors was an important development, it was apparent, however, that the mentors also required ongoing technical skills development themselves (Meskill et al., 2006). Three mentors were unable to continue after two weeks, and one further member of the mentoring team changed roles to become a participant in order to create her own machinima. The mentors who had previously been involved in making machinima in their drama course explained that they had been given different roles in their machinima production teams and therefore did not have the expertise in all the skills required arising from the first iteration of the course. No interaction took place in this forum during the course. Moreover, the *Problems* forum did not receive any postings related to pedagogical matters as concerns were mainly related to issues of a technical nature.

The *General* forum had originally been established for trainees to share their thoughts on any topic of relevance to them as participants in the course in order to aid bonding between the members in the group. While it was expected that the trainees might use the forum for casual conversation on topics such as the weather, holidays, weekend activities or other topics of small talk, not all the trainees contributed to the forum, and those who did posted issues related to the development of their first machinima or queries about technical problems. The trainees were thus given the opportunity to decide which forum to post to rather than be directed to a particular one as specified by the facilitators (Blancette, 2012).

The discussion in the *General* forum reflected the trainees' interactions throughout the course and provided insights into their expectations of filmmaking prior to the course. It was observed that those trainees who were already quite experienced with virtual worlds or real-life film production interacted more with each other than with those who were inexperienced with the environment of immersive worlds. However, it was encouraging to see how trainees' mutual support mechanisms developed during the required levels of trust, openness and non-judgemental flexibility required (Monsour, 2003), and this was evident in the footage they deposited in Dropbox, a free online file-sharing application, which enabled members of the group to use video 'off-cuts' produced by others in their own film productions. Moreover, using Dropbox in this way also enabled trainees to comment on each other's first machinima productions in a supportive atmosphere, ask questions and receive feedback (Hubbard & Levy, 2006). The feedback provided was always constructive and supportive, including useful tips, especially for Apple users, as all the instructions on the course were mainly designed for students using the Windows operating systems. It is notable that the trainees who were active participants in the *General* forum were also those who appeared to be most active in the other discussion fora.

Based on an analysis of interactions, it is clear that the facilitator interacted with all the trainees in the forum, as is required for the smooth running of an online class, and instant feedback was provided throughout the course across all fora. This was a small group with four very active participants, and therefore, the feedback and interaction between the facilitators and trainees was an important dimension that contributed to enriching the quality of the contributions as a whole (Miller & Conrad, 2009). In online contexts where active discussions are the norm, message overload can quickly occur and inhibit some trainees from taking part (Schneider, 2003, 2014a). In such cases, individual messages to acknowledge and encourage trainees to participate may best be posted privately, although this presents challenges in that private correspondence cannot be evaluated later (Schneider, 2004).

An analysis of feedback and online tracking data in the VLE revealed that most trainees did not take the opportunity to view the recordings of the live course training sessions which they had missed. Only one enthusiastic trainee who attended almost every live session watched each of the recordings. The majority of the trainees did not regularly check the instructions on Moodle or watch the videos and practise the weekly tasks prior to the actual live sessions. As a consequence, some of the instructions disseminated during the live sessions were not clearly understood by the trainees and, as a result, required several iterations of additional explanation and extra time from course facilitators to reinforce them. Trainees were expected to watch demonstration video clips on Moodle to prepare them for their participation in the virtual environment and to help them to apply their knowledge during the live sessions, such as moving, sitting and using the arrow keys and camera controls, among other functions related to manipulating their avatars. Participants' lack of expertise contributed to the slow pace of achievement in general. More advanced trainees, however, appeared to face other problems such as intermittent audio or Internet lag due to outdated or insufficient technical equipment or bandwidth that delayed the film production process. Confronted with such challenges it was invaluable that the course was led by several facilitators whose role it was to mentor individual trainees through specific technical problems; in this case, three facilitators were regularly available, and this number was found to be optimum for the size of the group as a whole.

As mentioned earlier, most interaction and participation on Moodle took place in the *General* forum and the *Sharing and Feedback* forum. However, during the course, several groups were specifically formed to work together, and in order to facilitate this level of collaboration, they had to arrange suitable times to meet, act or film each other. Working in small groups on film production fostered group interactions and amplified mutual support, and it was observed that this resulted in increased levels of motivation and course completion by the trainees (Kozinets,

2010; Miller & Conrad, 2009; Wheeler, 2005). Throughout this process, the tone of contributions and feedback was very positive as the following qualitative comments from the trainees' first machinima productions demonstrated:

> I love the trailer! It is brilliant! You manage to get such a sense of tension in your machinima!
>
> Wow, this is great! I loved it. Thanks for giving the insight about making machinima in Minecraft, I had no clue that it was so expensive. I can imagine that your students were thrilled as this is THEIR WORLD.

Indeed, it was remarkable to observe how sensitive some participants' reactions were to well-intended feedback and how careful and explicit they needed to be when communicating in an asynchronous learning environment using only text-based interaction, as the following extract between a trainee (T1) and facilitator (F1) shows:

T1: Thank you for your nice comments.

F1: Would you like me to record my speaking part and send it to you? Would it be useful to try to fit it in?

T1: Is the sound in my video problematic? Sorry, but I could not understand why you have offered me this . . .

F1: The sound is fine. I was just thinking of practising a new technique, adding audio later! It is not necessary at all. I was just thinking about the problems that you have had with voice. Your video is great.

T1: We have already used the technique that you have mentioned – voice over – in our drama project last term. We added the voice later. If you want to have a look here is the link.

The same trainee's (T1) reaction to peer (PE1) feedback was also evident in the next extract:

PE1: The video is great, congratulations! We should really figure out how to hide the HUD [head-up display] in Apple computers. It is a shame that we still see the speech thingy above our heads.

T1: Thank you for your feedback. Is there a way of hiding that speech thingy above our heads? I do not know, so if you have any suggestion, I would love to hear ☺

As the trainee had not been able to learn about the problem raised during the course, he or she was willing to follow the peer's advice and suggestions.

Blending Asynchronous With Synchronous Learning

Throughout the course, a minimum of two and a maximum of four discussion fora were made available to the trainees each week on Moodle to aid reflection and the exchange of ideas and tasks and to provide opportunities for peer support and feedback (Hubbard & Levy, 2006). In addition, two synchronous sessions were made available each week, one in Adobe Connect and one in SL. Adobe Connect sessions were used for presentations, instructions on how to use the Moodle platform and to share discussions on the pedagogy for using machinima in the language classroom. The sessions in the virtual world of SL gave participants hands-on practice with respect to filming, and facilitators also offered extra training sessions to those who needed more practice or had missed a session. In the live sessions, learners were always accompanied by a facilitator, participating observer and a technical support assistant.

Initial Meeting

The initial kick-off meeting for the first iteration of the CALL teacher education course took place in Adobe Connect's videoconferencing system with two of the six participants attending the first session. All those present in the live online meeting had little or no experience in the immersive world of SL. The facilitator explained the course structure and where to find tasks and post responses in the various discussion fora. Even though all sessions were recorded and hence could all be revisited by trainees who had been absent, only a few participants made use of this opportunity according to tracking data. The course overview stated that sharing knowledge was a core requirement of participation and that the discussion fora were open for use throughout the entire duration of the course. The minority of trainees interpreted this liberally so that they responded to tasks as and when required without following a specific schedule. Facilitators also explained that there would be weekly meetings in SL for all activities demonstrated in Moodle in order to provide an opportunity for trainees to practise their in-world skills. As the course structure, expectations and meeting schedules were discussed during the initial kick-off meeting, it was impossible for trainees who were not in attendance to schedule suitable times for live meetings. During the kick-off meeting, several example machinima were shared with participants in order to facilitate their use in language teaching and to prepare for the first task, which involved consideration of the question, Why use machinima?

Production Time

The facilitators addressed several queries during the kick-off meeting, such as how long does it take to produce a machinima and what quality of machinima is required for the completion of the course. The project team shared their experience with regard to machinima production time, stating that practice helped the speed of the production process and that the more experienced a filmmaker was, the quicker he or she would be able to produce machinima videos.

Quality of Machinima

With respect to the question of the quality of machinima, focus group data identified that participants involved in video production often did not mind about the quality of the finished productions. Interviews with facilitators indicated that machinima do not have to be high quality as long as they could adequately convey the learning outcome that motivated its production. Nevertheless, it was also stated that quality does accrue more significance when machinima from other authors are being used (Peachey, Gillen, Livingstone, & Smith-Robbins, 2011). One participant identified how teenage students were motivated by any productions that involved movement and that learners would tolerate poor video quality overall as long as the audio quality was sufficient to enable comprehension. While another trainee reported how the low visual quality of machinima she produced held the attention of her learners as they included lots of engaging or 'fun' elements, such as actors falling off a sledge and avatars bumping into each other or slipping on ice, her students appreciated that their teacher had created the machinima for them and thus demonstrated her own fallibility rather than projecting the image of an 'all-knowing expert' distanced from the process of learning. A similar experience was made by a third trainee who identified how her students were more interested in the content than the overall quality of the machinima when they knew that they had been produced by their own instructor for their unique teaching context.

The Use of Machinima in the Classroom

The discussion about the use of machinima in the classroom, which was initiated at the kick-off meeting, was extended and developed in the asynchronous discussion forum. Trainees were asked to watch and comment on a machinima created by English language learners, and in the ensuing discussion, all the course participants highlighted the advantages of using machinima in language teaching. It was evident, as one trainee suggested, that "[a]ll students were more engaged in watching a grammar-based machinima than by listening to a traditional grammar-based lesson". The same trainee pointed out that students working in-world and producing machinima demonstrated more empathy and confidence, became less shy and dared to do things they would not have done in the physical classroom (Schneider, 2014a). A similar experience was made by several other trainees who reported that shy students and special need learners completely changed their ability to engage with one another and with the learning material in a virtual environment (Smith, 2010). As reported by several research studies, it was noteworthy to observe how these learners visibly engaged more in the learning experience (De Jong Derrington, 2013), even to the extent that they took the lead in activities on several occasions, which they had not previously done in a physical classroom. The immersive experience gave them the opportunity to overcome what Suler (2005) has referred to as the 'online disinhibition effect', which describes a relaxing of perceived restrictions on behaviour in online mediated environments that would not normally be observed in face-to-face interaction.

One reason for this change in behaviour stems from machinima's use of filmed role-plays which provide opportunities to engage learners in a process of reflection on and evaluation of their own performance (Schneider, 2014a). One of the trainees helped us understand this process in more depth, as she compared virtual worlds to a stage with in-built opportunities that her students would never have access to in a traditional physical classroom. In her opinion, machinima could also be used by teachers within a flipped-classroom model, thus allowing learners to watch their own video creations prior to making them a vehicle for in-class discussion and further activities as Peachey et al. (2011) imply. According to the trainee, teaching with machinima

> can be an opportunity to develop passive skills such as listening with the help of pictures/videos/virtual flashcards. In a world full of video stimuli and digital devices, our students may feel at ease. It is a way to involve them to act/create/speak/write as well, beyond the traditional classroom.

It was evident that this trainee had reflected on how her training could be used to stimulate further activities once her initial training with machinima had been completed:

> I have a clear idea of the way I will use machinima as soon as my training is over. We are already running a project in the OpenSim virtual world managed by the research bureau of the Italian Department of Education. They have already worked on the texts and we will start with role plays. The kids are used to working in teams, through e-learning platforms and in a 3D environment. Despite their young age, they are fast-learners and quite creative. I would like them to organise and use the instrument to prepare a learning environment about dreamtime legends, through storytelling. A good way to make them work as a team, to solve problems together and to do something they would never have done in the classroom or on a real stage.

Similar to the experience of this trainee, several others highlighted the importance of involving learners in the process of machinima production to help team-building processes and encourage learners to engage in creating their own end product (Shrestha & Harrison, 2019). Another trainee developed this further when she suggested that the virtual environment also helped learners to get out of the "dull classroom settings and arrange their own learning working at their pace". She saw a lot of opportunities for her own teaching in future, such as practising job interviews through role-plays or using machinima to introduce her English students to British culture. Another trainee, who was fascinated by a machinima used in the course, speculated about how this kind of scenario could also be applied to other subjects than languages, indicating that "the engagement in the task at hand was the key to make machinima effective as a teaching/learning tool".

Interaction and Filming in SL

The sessions in SL were designed to be interactive and to provide the trainees with opportunities to familiarise themselves with their avatar, in particular to develop their in-world identity by changing clothes and outfits, making themselves invisible or setting scenes for filming and undertaking different roles. There was a collegial and supportive atmosphere throughout the course, and high levels of peer support were evident as indicated by observation and the qualitative data. Those trainees who were already familiar with SL shot videos or made photographs of their new outfits and/or locations which they had visited and shared them with the wider cohort.

Three of the trainees on the course were using computers with Apple operating systems, and they experienced problems hiding and viewing the user interface when filming. The facilitator and one of the participants posted instructions on Moodle to help the Apple users to find keyboard shortcuts to overcome these challenges. This resulted in a discussion which culminated in the recommendation that all participants should download such applications as the SL viewer in English rather than in their mother tongue to avoid further misunderstandings; this provided the CALL training course with a common language.

End-of-Course Machinima Productions

Whereas several of the trainees had produced only one machinima by the end of the course, others produced several videos which they continuously improved during the course according to the feedback received (e.g., they received feedback such as setting the correct frame or increasing/decreasing the volume of the speakers, adding different angles, hiding the mouse pointer or adding credits). Feedback from peers and facilitators aimed to be constructive and positive comments were received from all of the participants.

During the final session of the course, the completed versions of all trainees' machinima were watched and evaluated in the group. Several examples of screenshots from the videos are shown in Figures 5.1 to 5.5.

Figure 5.1 shows a scene from a machinima involving a scenario in which a couple order a meal. The waitress and female guest were acted by facilitators to provide learners with the opportunity to concentrate on filming, manipulating the camera controls and shooting different angles. The result was a complex final version of the machinima which incorporated several different perspectives and scenes. Trainees commented on the ambient background music and the director's attention to detail. The male actor, one of the course participants, was praised for his performance, and the machinima was judged as highly engaging following peer review.

Figure 5.2 shows a screenshot from a machinima created by a female trainee who was already experienced in film editing. She was skilled at making clothes and objects in SL with her pupils and had created her

Figure 5.1 A Restaurant Scene From a Trainee's Machinima

Figure 5.2 "Unexpected Roommates Parts 1 and 2"

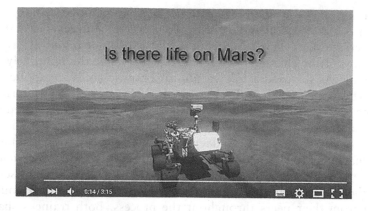

Figure 5.3 "Life on Mars" Machinima

Figure 5.4 "Complaining: Act 1 Scenes 1 & 2"

Figure 5.5 "Listen or Not Listen"

avatar's clothes for a hotel scene in the machinima titled "Unexpected Room Mates Parts 1 and 2". She used several different animations to re-create the avatars' authentic facial expressions, and as seen in close-ups of the character in Figure 5.2, this made the film lively and engaging. As she used a free version of Fraps, a software application used widely in virtual worlds to record screen activity, the watermark can be seen at the top of the screenshot. She initially experienced several problems with the quality of audio in the machinima, but she was able to solve these using Audacity wand as a voice-over technique. The machinima were produced in collaboration with another female trainee who also worked on the same scenario with a different script, and they received positive comments about the script and pronunciation from their peers throughout the process. Both trainees shared video resources and helped and supported each other; this relationship exemplified the collaborative aspects of the learning and production process, which is fundamental when making machinima in immersive environments.

Another trainee, who was new to SL and machinima production at the start of the CALL training course, was eager to experiment throughout its duration. He was very enthusiastic about virtual worlds and was keen on learning more advanced techniques such as the use of green screens, and he was successful at 'mashing' green-screen footage from Minecraft with SL. He brought a deep knowledge of film editing to the course, which helped with his machinima productions (see Figure 5.3). Peers praised his varied mix of animations, his use of real-life pictures including National Aeronautics and Space Administration footage in his "Life on Mars" machinima, and as a consequence, his video productions were dynamic, educational, realistic and easy to understand for his students. It was considered good practice to present difficult content this way. Based on his technical knowledge, he proved to be a valuable peer mentor for other trainees on the course, frequently sharing footage and providing feedback to improve other machinima.

Figure 5.4 shows a machinima which demonstrated the range of advanced technical skills possessed by the trainees. This trainee used facial expressions to create an ambient atmosphere and captions to show what the avatar was thinking using two languages, Italian and English. Peer feedback on these productions was highly complimentary. Nevertheless, the trainee who produced it had to overcome several challenges related to audio as well as balancing filming and acting in the production at the same time.

The author of Figure 5.5 produced a script for filming based on an appeal to young people about the dangers of listening to music too loudly to raise awareness about the potential for damaging their hearing as a result of headsets. The machinima involved several scenes, including dialogues with a receptionist in a doctor's surgery and an interview with a doctor about the medical consequences of hearing loss. Throughout the machinima, captions were used to emphasise the dangers of noise.

Feedback and Focus Group Discussion

During the final course session, all the trainees were asked to provide feedback about their experience, machinima production schedule and the time they had spent on the course, as well as their use of recordings and future use of machinima in their teaching and learning environments. For trainees new to SL, feedback suggested that they enjoyed the experience overall, but several encountered technical problems using the Apple operating system for machinima production and applying the instructions for using Camtasia Studio as a screen-recording application in this environment, given that most instructions on Moodle were for Windows users. Several suggested that they expected to create machinima collaboratively but this was not always possible. The facilitator explained that trainees in the course were expected to learn and demonstrate the skills they had gained, which included scriptwriting, filming and editing the footage to create a machinima, in order to experience and acquire a first-hand understanding of the collaborative machinima production process.

Timing

All the trainees agreed that there was a lot of learning materials and too many resources to be covered within the scope of a five-week course. The fourth week was considered rather too dense; in particular, the trainees that were new to SL found it difficult to follow towards the end of the course. Their qualitative feedback suggested that the first two weeks passed slowly, especially for those who were already experienced in SL. Therefore, it was easier at the beginning but became increasingly more difficult and demanding towards the end, especially when the trainees had their professional and personal commitments running alongside the course as this placed parallel demands on their time. For several of the trainees, there was too little time devoted to actual machinima production. Even though four groups of trainees had been identified to work together on a machinima production, the others worked individually, and this resulted in fewer trainees being available to act as film extras such that several participants had to manage everything by themselves. As the aim of the course was to create machinima, there was too little time allotted during the five weeks to cope with the tasks, considering the trainees had other work commitments as in-service teachers. Consequently, the majority of trainees suggested that at least six weeks were necessary to run the course in future, whereas others suggested seven to eight weeks would be more appropriate for an online training course of this type. According to interviews with the facilitators, a course duration

of longer than six weeks may lead to higher rates of dropout. Nevertheless, the consensus across the facilitators, mentors and trainees based on
their qualitative feedback was that more time was needed to practise
machinima production prior to the final filming process.

Balance Between Synchronous and Asynchronous Learning

Exit interviews asked trainees about the balance of the training sessions
they attended in terms of content. While the trainees all considered that
the sessions were well balanced and appreciated the extra time given by the
facilitators when needed to support them, the time allocated for participation in the live sessions established prior to the beginning of the course
did not suit all participants. As a result, the facilitator arranged extra sessions for participants who had missed a session or had problems attending at the required time. It was suggested that future training courses
should be sensitive to different time zones when working with international groups of trainees and to arrange the best time for all students to
participate or arrange several different meetings in which priority was
given to different groups of participants on a rotating basis. However,
with the addition of an extra week, the six-week format was considered
sufficient to complete the course effectively. Time spent on the course
varied between one trainee spending every night in-world, socialising,
experimenting, filming and trying out different things to the majority
who spent much less time trying to cope with time management.

Pedagogy Covered During the Course

Observation indicated that the pedagogical tasks created by the course
designers led to a lack of trainee engagement in the discussion forums.
Several participants stated that they were more concerned with learning
the technical rather than pedagogical skills required for video-based teaching (e.g., how they could obtain footage, look for locations, find props
or where to acquire title animations and music for their machinima).
Thus, the main goal for the majority of trainees was to learn to create
machinima rather than to consider relevant pedagogical learning theories
during their first engagement with the topic.

With regard to the pedagogy required to use machinima in the physical classroom, the trainees devised numerous strategies, such as inserting
questions into the video and leaving space for students to respond in or
adapting activities typically used alongside real-life videos in the classroom (Peachey et al., 2011). Observation of their activities underlined
that participants were often so engrossed in developing their own ideas
that they neglected to share more of them in relevant forums. Devising
strategies to permit more effective sharing across the group is one area
for future development.

Future Use of Machinima

Three of the six trainees were already using their machinima creations in their physical classrooms during the course. Technical problems relating to the creation of effective dubbing techniques, however, were consistently cited as a hindrance to further progress in classroom integration. Another trainee added that acquiring consent from parents to use machinima, which was typically viewed as a form of game playing rather than a standard language learning activity, was also perceived as a potential challenge to acceptance. As an interview with machinima expert Myers (2014) suggested in this respect, "[i]t is important that people not involved in machinima and virtual learning understand that playing is learning". Teachers need to be sensitive to the contexts in which they are working adapt where appropriate to the expectations from students, parents and administrators, particularly if test-based outcomes are important. When filming in the physical classroom it is often problematic to obtain parents' permission for filming. In a virtual environment, such problems do not occur, as it is only the avatar that is being filmed rather than the individual child.

Lessons Learnt

Language Used for the Training

One of the trainees had severe communication problems as she did not speak English to a sufficiently high standard and hence did not understand instructions from the moderators on the course. Even though peers who spoke her mother tongue tried to assist her with the instructions, it was not always possible to assist her to fully understand advanced technical vocabulary. It was suggested in response that the course should be offered in several languages. However, when working with international groups, it is essential to use one language as a lingua franca; in this case, English was used as the medium of instruction.

Supplementary Material

The training or filming time in SL was often extended to two or more hours due to technical issues, a perceived lack of skills or trainees not being adequately prepared for the session in advance. For example, it took significant time for a restaurant scenario in one machinima to be established (see Figure 5.2), because the trainees were not prepared and dialogue had not been adequately scripted. As this type of problem can recur, it is necessary in the future for machinima courses to prepare several dialogues in reserve for the participants to choose from. Related to this, checking props and scripts prior to filming was essential to save valuable time prior to course instruction; as a consequence, a 'flipped' format may be considered in future in which preparation is required by the trainees before attending the relevant training session.

Setting Clear Course Requirements

It is essential that the course curriculum is clear about expectations, such as how many weekly tasks trainees require to receive a *Certificate of Completion* at the end of the course. As a result of a lack of clarity in the CALL course, not all participants responded to all the tasks; nevertheless, all of them produced a machinima.

A significant amount of time was spent familiarising trainees with basic virtual world skills, and too little time was left for scripting, filming and editing, even though an extra week was added to the course to provide them with the time and opportunity to complete their machinima. It was suggested that the course should be extended to six weeks in the next iteration and start in week 3 with scripting and filming. An orientation course prior to the actual course to familiarise trainees with virtual world skills would be ideal so that they could focus on making machinima rather than on basic technical skills training during the course.

End-of-Course Evaluation

The trainees were asked at the beginning of the first iteration of the course to assess their virtual world skills before entering. It was intended that this information would provide the facilitator with an overview of trainees' skills so that they could adjust the course programme accordingly. Trainees were asked to revisit their original self-assessments at the conclusion of the course and respond to the following ten questions as shown in Table 5.2. Of the seven course participants, five responded.

Several trainees commented further on the areas they still needed support in. As a result of their lack of confidence in the areas addressed

Table 5.2 Qualitative Exit Survey Responses

1. How to do you feel about your own skills of using Second Life?	*Fernando:* I feel quite confident about my general skills in Second Life. I just have some trouble about inventory management and building objects. *Carmen:* I had experienced previously. *Lucia:* I have been using virtual world for three years, Second Life has some functions and rules that are a little different from OpenSim but it was ok. No specific problem. *Fatma:* Still incomplete, so I need to learn much more. *Francesca:* I am enthusiastic and I want to improve.

2. Do you feel confident to create a simple Machinima?	*Eduardo:* Yes, I have done quite a few machinima and I'm in the process of doing more. *Carmen:* Yes. *Lucia:* Yes even if filming and to postproduction are time demanding, really time demanding. *Fatma:* Yes, certainly *Francesca:* Not sure yet. I need collaboration
3. Did you make a Machinima for use in class?	*Fernando:* The Machinima done by me, so far, will be used in an eTwinning project. *Fatma:* I will. *Susan:* I have made one with my group for the sake of drama class and one more during this course. *Francesca:* I'd like to support a friend of mine, difficulty in explaining his job to teenagers.
4. Would you include your students in making future Machinima?	*Fernando:* Certainly. In fact, I'm doing just that at the moment. *Carmen:* Yes. *Lucia:* Sure, that was my first intent. *Fatma:* I would like to involve my students in this extraordinary experience.
5. Did the course meet your expectations? If yes, in what way?	*Fernando:* Yes, I now feel I have every tool and knowledge to carry on doing Machinima on my own, and with help from other teachers and students. *Carmen:* Yes. *Lucia:* Yes, it did. I must confess I thought that the group Machinima work would have ended up in a single movie but that is fine that we all develop our skills and ideas individually. *Fatma:* Yes, thanks to this course I have seen much more examples of Machinima and new technics such as Minecraft Machinima *Francesca:* Yes, it did. Being a total beginner now I understand what it is and include create a simple Machinima.
6. What could be improved in the training course?	*Fernando:* In the course itself, nothing. I just had issues with Moodle, particularly with the management of tasks to do. Online sites like Coursera do it brilliantly. *Carmen:* Translate the videos into other languages. *Lucia:* Maybe curb the Second Life adaptation training time. If working groups are set, that is better if all the members agree to work together. *Francesca:* Smaller groups work better.
7. Did you face any challenges (i.e. time/ language/ technological)? If yes, what were they?	*Fernando:* Just language challenges, when it came to collaborative tasks. *Carmen:* Language. *Lucia:* Time both for the creation of videos and the appointments to meet or film. *Fatma:* Sometimes I have had problems in time but it is not so much important. The most challenging one for me was technical problems especially the voice problems. *Francesca:* Learning technology in real time.

(*Continued*)

Table 5.2 (Continued)

8. How might you use Machinima in the future?	*Fernando:* To involve students in improving communicative skills. *Carmen:* Yes. *Lucia:* In OpenSim with my students both to film Dreamtime legends, tutorials and exercises. *Fatma:* I am planning to apply a function based syllabus so with Machinima, I can create countless contest and give functions of language to my students. *Francesca:* Many ideas – mainly deliver difficult issues.
9. Any additional comments you would like to make?	*Fernando:* I'd like to thank Carol, Christel and Heike for all the support and brilliant work done in making this course. *Carmen:* Very satisfied with the tutors, they were always available. *Lucia:* Thanks for everything, I am still working on it and this time I will surely use OpenSim. That is a pity that this forum will be closed after one month. Having contact with former and future learners builds up a community and helps to grow. *Fatma:* It was a good experience for me, thank you everyone so much. *Francesca:* The importance of patience tutoring. My tutors are angels, as it is difficult. If they hadn't been so patient, I would have given up Second Life.
10. Would you recommend this course to others?	*Fernando:* Yes, and I have done that as well. I think the course teaches skills central to teaching in the 21st Century. *Carmen:* Yes it is very rewarding. *Lucia:* Yes, I have already done it. *Fatma:* Absolutely yes. Also I am so happy that I did not give up the course. As our instructor says, we should always update ourselves together with world standards not only our context. *Francesca:* Yes, I do. It's serious and professional.

earlier, these participants strove to take part in the second iteration of the training course to gain more confidence. The fact that some trainees still had queries about several of the key terms used during the course led to the suggestion to establish a wiki glossary in the next iteration to enable participants to add terms they were not sure about, which, in turn, could be explained by peers or facilitators.

Research Results and Conclusion

The machinima produced during the first iteration of the CALL teacher education course provided significant insights into the practicalities of teaching with machinima as a type of video-based instruction and supports recent research on its potential to foster creativity (Shrestha &

Harrison, 2019). Trainees learned how to create machinima from scratch and to develop ideas to use them in their professional background. One participant used his machinima immediately after the course in his physics classes and involved his students in creating more, integrating Minecraft and 'mashing' it with green-screen techniques. All the trainees were eager to identify opportunities to apply the newly acquired skills in their everyday teaching. It was notable that all the initial course expectations had been met, particularly about establishing an environment for creativity to thrive. Fostering a creative environment was seen as crucial by the majority of trainees on the CALL course.

Even though one trainee had been unable to create machinima related to her special interest in the field of engineering, she felt confident that she had acquired enough skills during the course to produce new machinima according to her specific needs within the school curriculum in the future. As the final assessment demonstrated, all the trainees were highly satisfied with the course, even those who were already skilled in the use of virtual environments and filming when prior to entering the course, as they claimed that there was something new for everybody to learn.

At the beginning of the research, it was anticipated that the process of creating machinima collaboratively in a virtual learning space could motivate learners to interact while also improving their language and digital skills (Ushioda, 2011). In addition to the digital skills acquired during the course, language fluency was promoted by rehearsing for the role-plays the machinima were based on, where texts had to be re-read several times until the filming team was satisfied with their shots (Tsou, 2011). This was a remarkable side effect for non-native speakers on the course as they could assess and reflect on their own performance and improve their intonation and pronunciation through the use of voice-over recordings.

Those involved in the production process demonstrated what can be achieved by making machinima for specific purposes, either for a public announcement, practising typical dialogues at a restaurant or providing complaints and showing how machinima can be prepared with or without captions depending on how teachers want to use them in their classroom. It was observed that those participants new to the virtual environment were eager to immerse in this virtual environment and keen to try out new things, were engaging enthusiastically in exploring new places and scenarios to film, were supporting each other by sharing footage and were giving tips and feedback (Carroll & Cameron, 2005; Catak, 2010).

Arising from these positive findings, the first iteration of the course was utilised to identify several areas for improvements in order to further develop the effectiveness of the community of practice approach: adapting relevant technical and pedagogical materials, formulating clearer requirements and expectations and making changes to the schedule, duration and timing of course meetings.

The Second Iteration of the CALL Teacher Education Course

This section of the chapter explores data arising from the second iteration of the machinima open online training course. The course aimed to incorporate several lessons learnt which resulted in an extension to the duration of the course, the addition of a pre-course orientation week, clearer instructions on course requirements and more targeted course information, as well as instructions on how to disseminate pre-course questionnaires and self-assessments to participants (see Appendix IV).

The course was scheduled for six weeks from the outset and given an extra week for completion, making it a total of seven weeks for the entire course (see Appendix III). Additionally, a pre-course orientation week was offered to allow novices to SL sufficient time to practise basic virtual worlds skills, such as walking, flying, sitting, dressing, speaking and changing their avatar. This included two 90-minute live sessions in SL. Arising from these sessions, the facilitator also offered extra time to help trainees to practise in small groups or on a one-to-one basis as required and to consider the pedagogical aspects of machinima integration.

Aims and Purposes of the Research

The data collection instruments used to collect data from the second iteration of the course were the same as for the pilot, including qualitative methods such as interviews, focus group discussions, observations of interactions on the Moodle platform, participating observations of live sessions in Adobe Connect and/or in SL, as well as quantitative methods, such as the evaluation of participant self-assessments and questionnaires. The research was based on observational participation to investigate the ways in which machinima contributed to language teaching and whether participants' original expectations of the course had been met. Furthermore, the research aimed to discover if the teacher trainees immersed in the virtual environment had been able to learn the techno-pedagogical skills necessary to create machinima and to identify the ways in which this knowledge could be applied in their everyday classroom teaching at the end of the course. Another core aspect of the second iteration was to discover if the quality of machinima mattered to the trainee teachers and their learners and how machinima compared with traditional video-based learning approaches that they may have previously encountered.

Course Participation

Twenty-two participants registered on the course; nine teachers participated in total as three of the original group withdrew towards the end for a variety of personal reasons. One participant who had already taken part in the first course also struggled during the second iteration because of time constraints and did not complete all the requirements. Due to significant work commitments of several participants, the facilitator offered to provide extra sessions in the evenings and/or at weekends. The trainees were given the options to follow either a 'facilitated' course or a 'self-directed' version which had been developed to provide the participants with greater flexibility. Due to course expectations, trainees who wanted to receive a *Certificate of Completion* were required to achieve a completion rate of 80% with respect to the tasks; as a result, there was noticeably more interaction among the participants in the second iteration than in the pilot course. Although several participants did most of their work towards the end of the course, they managed the tasks effectively and produced a wide variety of machinima, as well as some significant reflective insights into the process of teaching with machinima. Based on observation and interview data, it was clear that the trainees remained enthusiastic for the entire duration of the course and displayed high levels of personal motivation throughout as a result of the dialogical approach fostered by the course (Wegerif, 2013).

Teachers' Backgrounds and Virtual World Experience

An international group of teachers from Bulgaria, Italy, Spain, Poland, Sweden and the UK took part in the training. All but two were language teachers by profession, and there was a significant mix of skills and experiences in using virtual worlds and/or filming. The nine teachers were all female and the age of the group ranged between 51+ (55%), 46 to 50 (22%) and 36 to 40 (22%). The participants worked in higher education (44%), schools (22%) and vocational schools (22%). Sixty-seven per cent used Moodle or other VLE in their classroom, 44% used interactive whiteboards (IWBs) and video and 33% used tablets or mobile devices and computer labs, whereas only 11% used the virtual world of SL or other similar 3D environments for teaching and learning. The time span in which the participants had been using learning technologies ranged from five to ten years or more in the majority of cases. The subjects they taught included English (five teachers); the other subjects were chemistry and physics, English and media, critical thinking, education for security didactics, instructing in a marine ecology lab and Spanish as a Foreign Language. Given this diverse range of subjects, participants provided a wide range of reasons for undertaking the teacher training course on machinima as these extracts from the qualitative data indicate:

> I'm interested in learning more about virtual world techniques.
> I want to help my students to learn my subject in a motivating and engaging way.
> I am studying new ICT tools in my PhD.

More ways of using technology in my teaching and classroom.

I would like to incorporate a Second Life character in my online courses. So far, I have used Voki and other devices, but I think Second Life will improve the quality of the materials I prepare for students or, at least, it'll make them more interesting.

Using 3D environments to support student engagement and participation.

The reasons given in the pre-course questionnaire corresponded reliably to the information given in the focus group discussion on Adobe Connect. In the questionnaire, 67% responded that they were already familiar with virtual worlds; 56% claimed that they had never made a machinima or used them in their teaching, whereas 44% stated that they had created machinima and 44% had used machinima in their previous teaching.

When asked about the purpose for creating machinima, 67% intended to use machinima to introduce content, 44% to introduce a subject and for cooperative language learning and 33% wanted to use machinima for language production and as learning tasks, whereas 22% intended to use machinima as an autonomous activity or for language practice.

In introductions provided during the Moodle course, the trainees gave more detailed background information about themselves and their motivations for undertaking the course as follows:

An English teacher (P1 Sarah) who was not familiar with SL but saw considerable potential in using the medium to teach her language classes. As the course took place during the school examination period, she encountered several challenges connecting to the live sessions. In the interview data, she indicated that watching the recordings of the training sessions did not offer her the same experience as being an active participant during the live course. Consequently, she participated in a series of extra hour classes offered by the facilitator which were aimed to help her practice outside the scheduled course sessions.

A Spanish teacher from Valencia (P2 Pilar) who had previously taught rhetoric and linguistics in SL and therefore was already familiar with immersive environments. She had already created several machinima but wanted to improve her technical and pedagogical skills by undertaking the course.

An English teacher working in a secondary school in Poland (P3 Gabriella) who had had very little previous experience in SL but was interested in discovering how she could use the format of machinima in her everyday teaching. Throughout the course, she experienced significant technical challenges using immersive environments due to her lack of prior technical skills.

- A **research group instructor and supervisor working in Sweden (P4 Astrid)** who taught mostly PhD and master's students in laboratory skills. Although she was familiar with SL, she did not feel confident using it and wanted to learn more about the immersive environment, especially since she had never created any previous machinima.
- A **teacher in a vocational school for catering and tourism in Italy (P5 Anna)** who had been teaching for 21 years in primary schools but was not very familiar with SL. She was nevertheless curious about new approaches to language teaching that would help her to innovate in the language classroom and considered the video-based techniques associated with machinima as a potential source of interest to her language students.
- A **teacher of English at a university in Bulgaria (P6 Mila)** who wanted to acquire new ideas and skills to improve his language teaching. She considered herself a lifelong learner and wanted to experience what it was like to participate in an online training course as a participant as well as use the medium for training purposes.
- A **filmmaker and secondary school teacher (P7 Angela)** who was working as a media film enrichment coordinator with 11- to 13-year-old students in an after-school setting to develop student-led media content for the school's website. She had been involved in real-life filmmaking and won an award for a short film she made in 1988. She saw the machinima training course as a learning opportunity which would enable her to observe the facilitator's style of delivery. She was already skilled in SL but had not yet created machinima.
- An **English teacher, originally from Turkey (P8 Adin)**, who was living in London during the course. She taught English to migrants in small groups or one-to-one sessions. She was new to the virtual world of SL and enjoyed the time she spent in-world whenever she had the opportunity.
- A **female Italian teacher of Spanish (P9 Francesca)** who was working on her PhD in literature and ICT and wanted to enhance her digital skills. While she had a strong interest in utilising the potential of SL, she had no previous experience of using immersive environments for teaching and learning.
- A **female teacher of Czech (P10 Svetlana)** who was working at a military university in Poland. She was an experienced teacher with many years of working in schools and higher education, and she had several years' experience with digital technologies in learning, video production and virtual worlds.

Course Expectations

All the trainees shared their expectations about the course in the initial kick-off meeting which took place in Adobe Connect and in their responses to the pre-course questionnaire. The following are excerpts from the qualitative data reflecting the participants' motivation for undertaking the course:

> Improving skills with respect to making machinima.
> Practicing recording and editing short videos.
> Improving knowledge on Second Life.
> Find a motivating way to engage students through machinima.
> Becoming confident in assisting others.
> Becoming familiar with machinima to make lessons more enjoyable for kids.
> Get students into Second Life for 1:1 lessons.
> Learning new skills.
> Meet students from different countries and interact with them.
> Introduce students to different aspects of English speaking countries via Second Life in an interesting and engaging way.
> Prepare videos for the students that will be more engaging.
> Keep students motivated enough to be willing to cooperate and participate in different activities that will most certainly help them to boost their English level.
> Meet people who are interested in creating machinima for educational purposes.

Participants' hopes and concerns about the training in the pre-course questionnaire are evident in the following excerpts:

> The course might be too time consuming.
> Not to be able to complete the course, not enough time to carry on with it.
> To complete the course and learn how to incorporate Second Life in teaching.
> Working with partners of different nationalities can become quite challenging, especially when both parties don't have English as their mother tongue. This has happened quite often in eTwinning projects and some EUN Academy online courses. People often misunderstand what others are saying and that can become quite troublesome in peer evaluated tasks.

At the end of both courses, trainees' expectations were mapped against the outcomes of the course.

Self-Assessment Questionnaire

The self-assessment questionnaire (see Appendix II) was disseminated to participants five days prior to the beginning of the second iteration of the course and was designed to collect data relevant to their current knowledge and skills. The responses helped the facilitators to adjust the training sessions according to participants' needs. Ninety per cent of participants responded to the 'can do' statements contained in the questionnaire. The responses indicated that participants entered the course with a significant range of skills related to the use of immersive environments. All the skills referred to in the self-assessment questionnaire were either prerequisites of the training course or, if the trainees were not familiar with them, part of the intended training course.

Terminology in SL

Based on the self-assessment data, the majority of the trainees were 'already familiar' with the terminology used in the virtual world of SL or were 'not sure', whereas only a few 'did not understand' some of the terms at all. Table 5.3 shows trainees' responses to the statement '*I understand the following terms*'.

Only a few participants, 11%, did not understand the terms *landmark*, *rez* (12%) or *screencasting*; 22 % were not familiar with the terms *SLURL*, *sandbox*, *lag* or *holodeck*. Only 11% marked 'a little sure' about the term *avatar*, whereas 89% 'fully understood' the term. Twenty-two per cent were 'a little sure' about the term *sandbox*, whereas 56% 'fully understood' the term. Sixty-seven per cent of the responders were 'a little sure' whether they understood the term *viewer*, whereas 33% 'fully understood' the term. Thirty-three per cent marked that they were 'a little sure' about the terms *holodeck*, *lag* and *landmark*, whereas 57% indicated that they 'fully understand' these terms. Forty-four per

Table 5.3 Self-Assessment Terminology

Categories/Statements	Not at all	A Little	Very Well	Total	Mean
1. Viewer	00.00	66.67	33.33	100	2.33
2. Avatar	00.00	11.11	88.89	100	2.89
3. Landmark	11.11	33.33	55.56	100	2.44
4. SLURL	22.22	55.56	22.22	100	2.00
5. Rez	12.50	50.00	37.50	100	2.25
6. Inventory	00.00	44.44	55.56	100	2.56
7. Sandbox	22.22	22.22	55.56	100	2.33
8. Lag	22.22	33.33	44.44	100	2.22
9. Holodeck	22.22	33.33	44.44	100	2.22
10. Screencasting	11.11	44.44	44.44	100	2.33

cent were 'a little sure' about the terms *screencasting*, which 44% 'fully understood'; *inventory*, which 56% 'fully understood'; and *rez*, which 38% 'fully understood'.

Tasks in SL

Ninety-five per cent of the participants completed the section on 'can-do' statements, which included the skills required to be mastered by the end of the training course. The data (see Table 5.4) indicate that there were several skills that trainees were already familiar with. It was noticeable that the majority of trainees were already familiar with basic skills in the virtual world but not with skills related to film-making, such as taking video footage or using screencasting software such as Fraps or Camtasia Studio.

Table 5.4 Self-Assessment 'Can Do' Statements

Categories/ Statements	Not at all	A Little	Fairly Well	Very Well	Total	Mean
1. Use camera controls	25.00	00.00	25.00	50.00	100	3.00
2. Set the window size	62.50	00.00	12.50	25.00	100	2.00
3. Set appropriate lighting	62.50	00.00	12.50	25.00	100	2.00
4. Hide the user interface	62.50	12.50	00.00	25.00	100	1.88
5. Use screen recording	62.50	12.50	00.00	25.00	100	1.88
6. Add a new landmark	25.00	00.00	55.56	50.00	100	2.56
7. Navigate to landmarks	25.00	00.00	55.56	62.50	100	2.33
8. Add an inventory object	25.00	12.50	44.44	62.50	100	2.22
9. Rez an inventory object	25.00	25.00	44.44	37.50	100	2.22
10. Read in notecard	37.50	12.50	44.44	50.00	100	2.33
11. Use the mini-map	37.50	25.00	12.50	25.00	100	2.25
12. Use the world map	37.50	37.50	12.50	12.50	100	2.00
13. Alter avatar appearance	12.50	12.50	25.00	50.00	100	3.13
14. Use the search facility	12.50	25.00	25.00	37.50	100	2.88
15. Rez and clear a holodeck	50.00	12.50	12.50	25.00	100	2.13

Categories/ Statements	Not at all	A Little	Fairly Well	Very Well	Total	Mean
16. Take & save a snapshot	12.50	12.50	25.00	50.00	100	3.13
17. Use text chat	12.50	00.00	37.50	50.00	100	3.25
18. Walk, run and fly	12.50	00.00	25.00	62.50	100	3.38
19. Use voice chat	12.50	12.50	25.00	50.00	100	3.13
20. Use instant messenger	25.00	0.00	12.50	62.50	100	3.13
21. Befriend someone	12.50	0.00	50.00	37.50	100	3.13
22. Accept friend invitation	25.00	0.00	12.50	62.50	100	3.13
23. Teleport	12.50	0.00	25.00	62.50	100	3.38
24. Accept teleport invitation	25.00	12.50	0.00	62.50	100	3.00
25. Use audio streaming	25.00	0.00	25.00	50.00	100	3.00
26. View a slideshow	37.50	25.00	12.50	25.00	100	2.25
27. View a video stream	57.14	0.00	14.29	28.57	100	2.14
28. Add a landmark	25.00	0.00	25.00	50.00	100	3.00

Fifty per cent of participants reported that they could use 'text chat' very well, 37.5% could use it fairly well and 12.5% could not do this at all or 'walk', 'run' and 'fly'; use 'voice chat'; 'befriend someone'; 'teleport' to a location; 'change an avatar's appearance and clothing'; use the 'search' facility to find people, places and objects; or 'take a snapshot from Second Life and save it onto the computer's hard drive'. Twenty-five per cent could not 'send an instant message', 'accept a friendship invitation', 'accept an invitation from someone to teleport to their location', 'switch audio streaming on and off', 'add a new landmark to the inventory',' navigate to an existing landmark which is in the inventory', 'add an object in the inventory',' rez an object from the inventory' or 'use camera controls'. These skills were marked by all other participants, with 50% reporting that they could do them very well and 63% fairly well.

Of participants, 37.5% could not 'view a slideshow on a projection screen', 25% could do this a little, 12.5% could do this fairly well and 25% could do this very well. Among participants, 37.5% could not 'read a notecard and add it to the inventory', 12.5% could do that a little, whereas 50% could do this very well. 37.5% could not 'use the mini-map'; 25%, a little; 12.5% could 'read the mini-map' fairly well; and 25%, very well.

Of participants, 37.5% could not 'use the world map'; 37.5% could do this a little; 25% could do this either fairly or very well. Fifty per cent could not 'rez and clear a holodeck', 12.5% could do this a little and 12.5%, fairly well, whereas 25% could do this very well. It was noticeable that 62.5% were not familiar with 'taking video footage and screencast software' and 'hiding the User Interface (UI)', whereas 25% could do this very well. Furthermore, 62% were not familiar with 'setting the window size for machinima' and 'setting appropriate light for taking footage', which 12.5% could do fairly well and 25% could do very well.

What Do I Know About Machinima?

In this section of the questionnaire trainees' skills related to making machinima prior to the training course were explored (see Table 5.5). The assessment results showed that 37.5% already knew very well how to 'import media into Camtasia' or other similar video-editing applications and how to 'add media to the timeline', whereas 12.5% claimed that they were a little sure and 50% reported knowing nothing about it. Thirty-seven per cent knew how to 'add media to the timeline' very well, while 12.5% were a little sure about and 50% did not know at all. Among participants, 37.5% did not know how to 'split media', 'how to control audio' and 'how to add transitions', whereas 37% knew about it and 25% were a little sure. Forty-two per cent did not know how to 'add callouts', whereas 14.2% were a little sure, but 42% knew how to do this very well.

Table 5.5 What Do I Know About Machinima?

Categories/Statements	Not at all	A Little	Quite Well	Very Well	Total	Mean
1. Import media to editor	50.00	12.50	0.00	37.50	100	2.25
2. Add media to timeline	50.00	12.50	0.00	37.50	100	2.25
3. Split media	37.50	25.00	0.00	37.50	100	2.38
4. Control audio	37.50	25.00	0.00	37.50	100	2.38
5. Add transitions	37.50	25.00	00.00	37.50	100	2.38
6. Add callouts	42.86	14.29	0.00	42.86	100	2.43
7. Use Audacity to create	62.50	00.00	12.50	25.00	100	2.00
8. Add music/sound effects	62.50	00.00	00.00	37.50	100	2.13
9. Add title and credits	62.50	0.00	12.50	25.00	100	2.00
10. Publish a video	25.00	25.00	00.00	50.00	100	2.75
11. Upload video to host	25.00	25.00	00.00	50.00	100	2.75
12. Share video	25.00	25.00	00.00	50.00	100	2.75

The use of the application Audacity to 'create audio files', 'how to add music', 'audio and sound effects' or 'add titles and credits' was not known to 62%; however, the use of Audacity was well known by 25%, how to 'add music' and 'sound effects' by 37% and how to 'add titles and credits' by 25%. Fifty per cent knew how to 'publish a video', how to 'upload a video' to a video host and how to 'share a video', which 25% were a little sure about and 25% did not know at all. The results suggest that the majority of participants needed to learn or improve their skills related to film editing, which are crucial in the context of teaching with machinima.

Course Structure

The second iteration of the CALL training course also aimed to enable the trainee teachers to develop simple machinima adapted to their learners' needs. From the lessons learnt during the pilot testing, several changes were made to the design of the new course regarding the duration and length of the modules, the layout of the tasks and organisation of the discussion fora. In addition, more interviews and focus group discussions were established in the second iteration which took into account questions that had arisen during the pilot testing. As a result of trainees' contributions to Moodle, a timetable of all live meetings was also clearly displayed in the VLE, and an additional week was added to the schedule alongside some extra individual sessions in the virtual world to provide additional opportunities for familiarisation (see Table 5.6).

The pilot course was considered too short in duration to manage all the course requirements on time; therefore, an extra week was added to the second iteration to extend its duration. In addition, a one-week orientation

Table 5.6 Schedule of Time and Place of Live Online Meetings

WEEK	DATE/TIME	PLATFORM
1	Wednesday 27 May	Second Life
	Tuesday 2 June	Adobe Connect
2	Wednesday 3 June	Second Life
	Tuesday 9 June	Second Life
3	Wednesday 10 June	Second Life
	Tuesday 16 June	Adobe Connect
4	Wednesday 17 June	Second Life
	Tuesday 23 June	Adobe Connect
5	Wednesday 24 June	Second Life
	Tuesday 30 June	Second Life
6	Wednesday 1 July	Adobe Connect
	Friday 3 July	Second Life
7	Tuesday 7 July	Adobe Connect

course which included two live practice sessions was offered a week prior to the beginning of the second training course. Despite the addition of the extra week to help participants who were unfamiliar with the virtual world environment, only a few participants were able to take advantage of it.

Arising from the experience with the pilot course, more time was allocated to the trainees' machinima production process. In addition to the tasks provided in the pilot training, several more tasks were combined with the weekly modules. The additional activities included several reflective tasks on pedagogy and teaching with machinima, as well as a 500-word written reflection at the end of the course. Another difference from the pilot course was that participants started to create their first examples of screencasting in week 2 and began writing their lesson plan and storyboard in week 3 in a process that consciously sought to engage the trainees earlier in the creative process. Furthermore, it was clearly stated at the beginning of the course that the trainees were required to complete 80% of the tasks in the second course to receive a *Certificate of Completion* at the end. Even though the course was scheduled for six weeks instead of five, an extra week was added so that the trainees had enough time to complete their machinima and finish any of their outstanding machinima production tasks.

Pre-Course Orientation in SL

The first part of the pre-course orientation in the virtual world was aimed at familiarising the trainees with how to move in-world, and an obstacle course was established on EduNation Island in SL to accomplish this. The second part of the session was held on the Virtual Ability Orientation Island (VAI), which provided an orientation which enabled the trainees to complete several activities, such as adjusting lighting (Figure 5.6)

Figure 5.6 Experimenting With Different Light Effects

catching butterflies, trying out dancing, practising sitting on a chair (Figure 5.7) and interacting with automated bots using text chat (Figure 5.8).

On the second pre-course orientation session, several trainees learnt how to receive and accept items and use objects. Moreover, the participants then had the opportunity to change their clothes in Boutique Renoir on EduNation and in addition to change their mesh avatar into a classic avatar, which enabled lip movement when speaking (Figure 5.9).

As a result of these activities, the trainees had had the opportunity to experiment with new accessories such as hair and dresses, and they learnt how to save their new outfits and to navigate their avatars in several different spaces.

Figure 5.7 Dancing, Flying, Running, Sitting on VAI Island

Figure 5.8 Catching Butterflies

Figure 5.9 Boutique Renoir on EduNation

Weekly Modules

Compared with the pilot course, the module descriptions for each week of the second iteration were more elaborate. There was one additional objective in most weeks, such as considering some of the pedagogies related to teaching in a virtual world. However, the learning activities and discussion fora remained the same in that they were organised slightly differently as there was one folder with topic-related headers for the discussions each week (see Figure 5.10), whereas in the pilot training course, there was a new folder for each discussion.

In contrast to the pilot course, different topics and responses to tasks were included in the *Discussions* folder which had one corresponding thread for each topic. The thread "Why use machinima" led to 32 replies, the thread "Introduce yourselves" led to 53 replies and "Getting used to Second life" attracted 18 replies.

Resources and Organisation of Fora

The folder containing *Course Resources* was placed prominently on the homepage of the Moodle VLE and was frequently updated during the lifetime of the course. The *Resources* contained the *Course Overview* document, a wiki with a *Glossary* of key terms used during the course, useful tips and a space for brainstorming about machinima-related ideas. A few trainees were unfamiliar with the format of the wiki and this led to many random contributions which were often placed in the incorrect

Week 1 Discussions

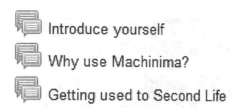

Introduce yourself

Why use Machinima?

Getting used to Second Life

Figure 5.10 Week 1 Discussion Fora on Moodle on MOOTI

location. The consent form for the participating observation as well as PowerPoint presentations on task-based learning and Bloom's Taxonomy (Bloom, Engelhart, Furst, Hill, & Krathwohl, 1956) were also part of the *Resources*. The course fora in the second iteration were kept in the same format as in the pilot, *Announcements*, *Problems* and *General Chat*. The only difference to the pilot course was that the instructions and functions of the fora were displayed prominently for the participants to read prior to entering.

As in the pilot, the *Announcements* area was only accessible for facilitators to post in. Twenty-seven posts were submitted in total, including those related to uploads of session recordings, information about events, reminders of tasks and deadlines, lists of film groups with links to the Google documents and changes in the meeting schedule or additional sessions, as well as various tips for filming and editing machinima. The *Problems* forum was used appropriately by two trainees who submitted queries about an incorrect link for the venue of the final session and specific live recordings that could not be found. In the second iteration, the *General Chat* forum was mainly used to circulate tutorials relating to technical issues such as enlarging the size of an 'emote HUD', the use of WASD keys to navigate in the virtual world, a fix for shortcuts, and tutorials describing how to create green-screen productions. Other threads included information describing the appearance of African avatars (Figure 5.11).

Compared with the pilot course the *General Chat* discussion forum was used appropriately in the teacher training course to share ideas and topics which were not related to tasks discussed in the weekly fora.

Mentors

In contrast to the pilot course, no extra forum was opened for the mentors in the second course. The two mentors on the course, one of whom

Figure 5.11 Demonstration of Avatars Available for Filming

had previously won an award for her own machinima following the MachinEVO 2015 training events and another who had been a participant on the pilot course, were both well known to the facilitating team and were introduced in the *Announcements* area.

Only one discussions folder was established for each week of the course and this included an explanation of the tasks and topics for each particular week. The *Discussions* folder in week 1, for example, read: "This forum is where you will respond to all of the week1 tasks. Please look for my message with the topic heading and reply to that". The tasks in the *Discussions* folder were the same as in the pilot course: Introduce yourselves (53 posts), Getting used to Second Life (18 posts), and Why use Machinima (32 posts).

The *Introductions* forum was very interactive with all but one trainee posting a biography, and most introductions triggered further comments or questions from the wider group. The tone in these discussions was very supportive, as the following response demonstrates:

> Hello everyone, I'm Astrid and I live close to Kalmar, south east of Sweden. I'm working at [a university in Sweden] but not teaching. I have been working in a research group in Marine Ecology and instructing PhD and master students in laboratory skills. Lately I have taken some university courses in Second Life, and I think it is a fantastic way to implement distance learning. I'm still not so experienced and want to learn more. I have never made any machinima, and I am very excited to get the opportunity to try that out.
>
> Welcome Astrid. It's nice to see a fellow scientist in a language course! Me? Biochemistry degree from the Lisbon University! The video project was a real life changer for me, as I learned a great deal about the use of video as a teaching/learning tool. So, now I use SL to get in touch with both scientific and educational communities, as well as a way to make instructional machinima and get my students involved in the subjects I teach; Physics and Chemistry. Come visit us at EduNation.
>
> Hi Fernando, seems like I can get some inspiration from you finding communities in SL. I thought SL and machinima could be used in other subjects than language teaching. I got to know about the video project through my English teacher at [university] and got really interested in trying to make machinimas. Unfortunately, I have had a lot of computer problems, but I hope I have solved most of them now.

The trainee developed the issue with Astrid's computer further and started a new discussion threat titled "Computer problems? Try using an old fossil like my laptop!"

> Hi Astrid,
> Let me just give you a taste of what teaching/learning can be in a near future, especially for us, life science teachers/researchers.

Check this High Fidelity (SL2!) preview from last month: https://youtu.be/F6zft3usvd0?t=25m38s

Oh, and by the way, this old laptop of mine (6–7yrs) has as many problems as you can imagine (or more!), but it's not going to stop me from trying to take the most of this course.

I'm here to have fun!

The participants who were not teaching languages discovered the potential of machinima for their own subjects. It was interesting that two participants added two new threads to week 1 titled "Discussions: Fixing the levels of knowledge in a second language" which accrued no responses and "bilingualism" which led to three responses. The trainees used the forum for their research on bilingualism, which would have been more appropriate in the *General Chat* area as it was neither topic- nor task-related. All the trainees' introductions received appreciative comments from peers and facilitators, and several different languages were used for interaction in the related discussion.

Getting Used to SL

Not all trainees responded to the forum with personal introductions (there were 18 posts in total); however, the most remarkable experiences with SL involved opportunities for trainees to meet other teachers and establish professional and personal relations. Pilar, for example, felt motivated as a result of her involvement in the virtual world, describing it "as an effective way to learn a lot of things you would never think you could do". Sarah believed that 3D technology added important supplemental information to the lessons, whereas others were inspired by the amount of work invested in the architecture and landscaping of the virtual world to provide it with an authentic feel. Fernando reported that he often spent several hours examining buildings and visiting the International Space Museum, where he discovered interesting resources related to the subject he was teaching. Gabriella enjoyed visiting several islands in SL and meeting people to interact with. She felt inspired by the creative ideas and the futuristic design of the buildings and facilities and enjoyed meeting other teachers from other countries to network with. She considered the immersive environment inspirational for learning and teaching. By gaining further skills in SL, Gabriella hoped to motivate her students to learn how to use the environment for language learning. Mila had visited virtual worlds several times in the past, but without making any progress beyond the first island she had landed on. She appreciated the help she acquired during the second training course and reported how this newfound knowledge had helped her to appreciate the authenticity of the immersive environment for teaching and learning.

Astrid reported that she felt a strong personal attachment to her avatar. She had never thought of her avatar as a puppet but rather as an extension of her own physical identity; hence, this close identification led her to explore her own feelings of insecurity and fear, particularly when she travelled to different locations in SL and experienced being attacked by griefers. Although she was highly conscious of belonging to a virtual environment, the more she invested in her avatar's virtual identity, the more she felt emotionally closer to her avatar and wanted to protect her from harm.

Angela, who had been a distance learner in SL for approximately 18 months at the start of the research, reported how the virtual world enabled her to create synergies between her social and learning activities and how her "most engaging activity" involved "owning a number of breedable virtual world cats, meeting other Second Life residents . . . going to auctions and developing her own collection of seal point Siamese cats". In her view, "play, relaxation and socialising are important to the experience of learning". Her interest in cats inspired her to "log on more often to Second Life, learn more about the environment, the behaviours and commerce of its residents and also to develop a personal network for [her] continued engagement with the Second Life community". Angela perceived her machinima project as "the start of a new Second Life collaborative experience", which was inspiring, but also challenging, as it required consistent effort, the investment of time and practice.

Why Use Machinima?

In the next task, participants were asked to listen to an interview from a prominent advocate of virtual worlds in language learning and share their thoughts about using machinima in the classroom. Although not all participants responded, 32 entries were posted to the forum. As an example, Sarah had used podcasts in her school projects, some of which included radio programmes with inter-school interviews, and thought that SL could add a new dimension to her projects. Her views were supported by Pilar, who stated that machinima helped students discover, understand, use and practise new words they had visualised in the machinima:

> When groups of learners are involved in the detailed planning of their activities, in order to achieve their learning outcomes, the collaboration usually involves a repetitive process of checking what the learning outcomes are, negotiating how best to achieve them and evaluating the results against the original plan. After all that work, it's difficult to forget a learning experience, and retention is part of the journey to making progress.

One of the mentors suggested changing the title of the forum to *Why not use Machinima?*

> From personal experience while emerging into this process, I can only think of positive reasons to incorporate this technique into teaching. Language learners need meaningful tasks to inspire them; to encourage productivity and language use; to apply their existing knowledge for a purpose; to activate existing skills and cultivate new ones; to bring out their full potential; and to engage in meaningful preparation and presentation of what they have grasped.

The mentor indicated that she saw "the process of machinima-making (involving the educator or the learner) as an ideal way to help learners understand how to take control of their own learning".

Moreover, Adin was convinced that the process of making machinima helped learners to improve their communication skills by planning, sharing roles and co-presenting with their peers. The recordings of this process could also be used for reflection and constructive feedback. Additionally, Astrid argued that reflections on learners' spoken texts will help students to improve their language fluency and pronunciation. Astrid saw a significant advantage when creating machinima, in that students need to collaborate, solve problems and take responsibility for their own work. Astrid also indicated that machinima could be used in other subjects as the medium offers opportunities for learning about a variety of real-world activities, such as providing safety instructions and creating authentic scenarios for training in risk-free emergency situations. Astrid suggested that there would be a reversal in skill sets between teachers and learners in that learners who were used to computers and gaming environments would, in turn, inspire teachers by creating machinima which demonstrate their pedagogical value.

For Anna, who taught in a vocational school, machinima provided a range of valuable pedagogical resources for ESP. Using machinima, she argued, would provide resources to recreate authentic learning contexts that could help both teachers and learners to relate to the immersive spaces in which they were working. Mila questioned whether students' language performance during the process of machinima creation could adequately be assessed through observation only. Several other participants argued that the levels of learner engagement and attention triggered by the use of machinima would compensate for challenges presented by the investment of time and financial resources required to produce them. Over time, it was postulated that familiarity with the format would help to make the process of machinima creation easier and less time-consuming (Rainbow & Schneider, 2014). It was generally agreed by the majority of the participants that machinima were valuable for project-based pedagogy, as the process was collaborative and focused on developing communication and problem-solving skills, which, in turn, promoted forms of incidental learning related to cooperation and intercultural understanding.

Interviews with Corrigan (2014) highlighted that the use of machinima in pedagogical contexts such as language learning was not aimed at achieving technical proficiency as a central outcome but at creating and using machinima as a learning tool, regardless of imperfections. When created in a thoughtful and structured fashion, the machinima productions were dramatic and captivating and caught the attention of the students and encouraged them to learn grammar in new and interesting ways. Gabriella considered SL as an optimal environment to potentially enhance language learning as it enabled learners to practise new skills, express their ideas, take responsibility and improve their ICT literacy (Schneider, 2014a).

Advantages of Using Machinima: Trainees' Perspectives

The introduction to week 2 of the training course was more detailed and had an additional objective compared to the pilot course thus giving the trainee teachers opportunities to plan task-based and project-based learning involving machinima. An additional task was to share machinima ideas on a collaborative wiki platform. The group discussion was initiated by a video depicting an interview with Meissl-Egghart (2014) in which she shared her ideas about making machinima. Meissl-Egghart considered machinima a great opportunity for trainee teachers to express their creativity. As Astrid explored further, creating machinima involved a process of incorporating different tasks and responsibilities, including writing storyboards, rehearsals, taking up different roles and practising language skills; the machinima production could then be used to analyse the language performance, pronunciation, intonation and intercultural encounters of the student and could be repeated, whether in the classroom, individually, in small groups or at home (Schneider, 2014a). Astrid argued that the potential advantage of machinima is that they allow students to document their use of language and performance and thus could also be used as evidence in a student's language portfolio. Mila further suggested in this respect that the portfolio could then be utilised as a document to show to potential employers to aid employability.

Pilar highlighted the importance of motivation when using machinima. She reported how creating machinima could trigger students' interest and, as Sarah further suggested, provide students with creative methods to engage them in real-world communicative processes of re-creating or simulating authentic situations in a safe environment (Falconer, 2011).

Inspired by Ellis' (2003) work on task-based approaches, Sarah explained further that

> by providing the students with a 'real' (or at least realistic) situation, not only would they have to figure out the language they need to use but they also have to work out how to say it, how to behave in a particular context and, in short, how to solve the problem or task at hand.

Sarah, Anna and Adin identified new opportunities for collaboration and social interaction through virtual worlds as it allowed students the chance to interact with each other, while also offering a safe space in which they could explore different aspects of their identity in an anonymous environment. In addition, Astrid suggested that machinima offered a way for trainees to visualise the context in which language is used.

Discussions on the Practical Application of Machinima

First Machinima Productions

The trainees were asked to post their first machinima ideas in the course wiki in week 2; this was early in the course and not all of them had developed concrete ideas at that time. This changed in week 3 when the trainees started their filming project, began to develop lesson plans and write storyboards. There was a lot of interaction especially when the trainees produced their first machinima and shared it with their peers in the group. This process resulted in mutual feedback involving the communication of a significant number of tips and suggestions from peers, mentors and facilitators. For example, one of the actors encountered a technical issue due to his computer's graphics card which did not manage to render an object properly. The film cameraman had not realised that there was a technical issue; he had assumed that the interviewee had chosen the object for his interview. In spite of that, the creator of the machinima was very proud of her first production, and the feedback was very supportive as the following sample from the dialogue exchange demonstrates:

Great :-)	A successful machinima! Transitions, music, camera panning – there is a little bit of everything there, very well done.
Did you use Camtasia?	There is a narrow black line down each side of the screen, if you filmed at 1280X720 and made it in Camtasia those black bars should not be there. It is something to watch for next time. I am pleased you added a title :-) If you

want to, you can pull out the size of the box to fill the screen, that is something you could play with on the next one. A great first attempt! (Rainbow, 2015)

Everyone was highly engaged in the discussions, which included discussion on technical and filming-related content.

Observations During the Live Online Sessions

SL

Apart from individual tutorials or group meetings, 12 live sessions took place in the immersive environment of SL during the course. The attendance participation level was consistently high and sessions involved participants, facilitators and mentors. The training sessions actively gave participants the opportunity to practise a wide range of relevant skills that had been introduced on Moodle, such as sending instant messages to peers or calling them in a private chat, navigating their environment, identifying places or changing locations. The activities encouraged collaboration and helped to create an atmosphere conducive to bonding between the trainees. Trainees reported that there was a considerable amount to be learnt for those who were new to immersive environments, as well as more experienced teachers. It was noticeable how trainees enjoyed the practical sessions, and their enthusiasm was particularly evident when they acquired skills for creating different scenarios, using holodecks and going shopping in Boutique Renoir to use their inventories with new clothes and outfits for their avatars (see Figure 5.12).

Figure 5.12 Rezzing Boutique Renoir in the Sandbox on EduNation

One of the highlights of these activities was visiting the MOSP, a location which had been specifically designed for making machinima using different scenes such as Stonehenge, a watermill, a graveyard, a snow scene, a lighthouse and other ready-made scenes. As none of the participants had previously visited the MOSP, they were intrigued by the realistic nature of the potential teaching resources available and several trainees revisited promising locations to practise light settings or search for suitable film scenarios.

During the SL sessions, it was important to have technical support from mentors and facilitators in place to deal with technical problems by opening a private chat to guide participants through sound issues, finding appropriate locations to film or other challenges they were confronted with. A few participants reported that they were struggling with the process of film editing. While they had been guided through relevant sessions on editing, they felt isolated in the final phase of the process as they had to film and create their own machinima. The course was a supportive environment because facilitators were very patient. Other more inexperienced trainees argued that it was challenging to know what kind of equipment they required for filming. The facilitator had hoped that participants would be able to progress faster on these tasks. However, it was apparent, based on observation of the trainees, that their greatest challenge concerned identifying ideas for filming. Trainees often took a long time to find inspiration for their stories, taking time to reflect on what the film might look like and what it could be used for. It was not therefore the filmmaking technique related to producing machinima that troubled some trainees; it was rather their ambition to produce valuable machinima that were directly related to their current pedagogical context that other teachers and learners could potentially find useful that troubled them most. Angela, for example, learnt several filmmaking techniques during the course, and although she had had many ideas, some of her ideas were too ambitious and had to be curtailed as a result.

Although group arrangements had been made for filming teams, it was difficult for some participants to identify common ground given the complex decisions involved, and therefore, each trainee decided to make their own video for pragmatics reasons. The largest barrier to completing machinima was the editing process, and trainees considered this to be a special skill that required specific training. The facilitator offered a demonstration of editing in the screen recording software Camtasia, which was screencasted in Adobe Connect, to show how footage could be cut and joined and how captions, sound and music could be added. By the end of the course, only one group had worked collaboratively in a team to produce a machinima, supported by one of the mentors, as others worked individually to fulfil the clear vision of what they wanted to create.

Adobe Connect

The first and the final live sessions in the training course were held in the videoconferencing application Adobe Connect. In this environment, it was easy to visualise live instructions in addition to the instructional machinima provided on the Moodle platform. Adobe Connect was used to share content about the course and the structure of the Moodle platform and to explain where to post tasks, find resources and other relevant information. Consequently, the initial kick-off meeting was one of the six dedicated live sessions in the second iteration of the training course held in Adobe Connect. It began with nine trainees in addition to the course coordinator, the facilitator, an observer and technical support. After a round of brief introductions, trainees shared their expectations with the group. The facilitator explained the course structure in Moodle via a screencast and confirmed the agreed time for further meetings. She concluded the session by showing the group several example machinima and reflected on how they could be used in classroom teaching contexts.

Two days per week were scheduled for the live sessions (Tuesdays and Wednesdays), which was not an ideal option for the training as there were no days between the sessions for reflection. During the course, the live sessions in Adobe Connect were used by the facilitator to discuss the pedagogical implications of using machinima and to provide the trainees with a clear idea of how machinima could be adopted in their classrooms.

As an example, the facilitator demonstrated how Edward Lear's nonsense poem "The Owl and the Pussycat" could be used in English teaching. This session was interactive as the instructor involved the trainees in the several tasks related to the poem, such as identifying adjectives that described the owl or the cat, adding prepositions to the text or writing a diary entry. Further activities included a role-play, in which one trainee had to identify reasons why he or she did not want to take the boat trip and other activities as mentioned, such as rewriting the poem, changing the nouns and creating a new video from the new poem, as well as using media to produce it. Participants could then design a set of evaluation criteria and evaluate each other's work. These activities were based on skills from every level of Bloom et al.'s (1956) taxonomy from the lowest level of knowledge to the highest level of critical analysis. Although the sessions were interactive, it was noticeable that none of the trainees used their voice in the immersive world, and all interaction took place in the form of text messaging. The Adobe Connect sessions were most suitable for demonstrations, explanations and discussions. Consequently, trainees' storyboards and ideas for making machinima and lesson plans had a forum for further discussion and questioning. In all, the Adobe Connect discussions participants preferred to use the text chat instead of voice as a result (see Figure 5.13).

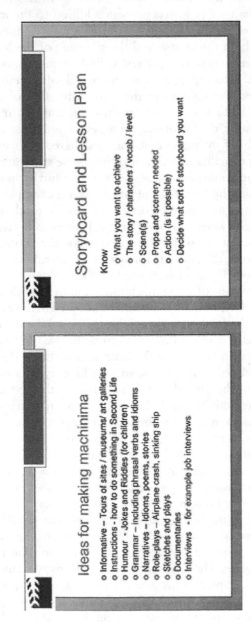

Figure 5.13 Ideas for Making Machinima and Thoughts on Storyboard and Lesson Plan

The Adobe sessions were well attended by the trainees, and they were less distracted by the environment provided by SL, and hence, collaborative groups were established more easily. Participants were asked to reflect on the purpose of their machinima and whether the machinima were going to be used more than once. Trainees were guided to explore the potential of virtual worlds, where to find suitable locations and acquire permission to film if necessary and to identify props and characters as needed, prior to putting their ideas into practice.

Final Machinima Presentations

The final session was attended by four trainee teachers as well as the course organiser, the facilitator, the observer, the training evaluator and one of the mentors. During the session, the final machinima were shared and evaluated. While watching the machinima, the trainees were asked to consider various aspects of the video, such as the costumes, dialogues, props, sets, acting, music and sound effects, mood, period and variety and whether the machinima were realistic. Gabriella and Adin had worked on their machinima together and the titles of their collaborative video productions were "Chilling, "Planning the Long Weekend", and "Going Places". They decided to share "Going Places Dialogue 1" (see Figure 5.14).

Title: "Going Places"
Length of recording: 4:38 minutes

The machinima was intended to be used in a lesson prior to the school holiday, as all students were expected to contribute to create authentic

Figure 5.14 Scene "From Going Places"

scenes related to a swimming pool, visiting holiday destinations and other holiday-related activities. The producers also wanted to focus on vocabulary and grammar about the future, such as *going to*, *present continuous*, *will* and *should*. Several authentic dialogues drawing on specific vocabulary for interaction when visiting places or planning to go to places were central to the machinima. The following points summarise the discussion about the machinima produced on this theme:

- Several trainees particularly liked the background noise such as the sound of holidaymakers shouting and waves breaking on the beach which added to the authenticity of the setting.
- The camera angles in the machinima supported the images extremely well.
- Observers would have liked to have seen some close-ups of the avatars' faces.
- Adding pictures of the locations and key monuments, such as a picture of Big Ben and St. Paul's Cathedral and the Houses of Parliament, would have added an extra dimension of authenticity to the locations used in the scenes.
- Several trainees argued that by not providing pictures students could be inspired to discover more about the locations mentioned in addition to what they already knew and search for more information.
- There are several different approaches to try: teachers could either adopt a transmission-based approach or provide the video and encourage students to think and research independently by asking them, 'What did you hear about?' 'What did you find out?' and 'What do you know about the places?'

The creators of the machinima were very satisfied with their production and the new skills that they had learned.

Title: "Lab Safety HKU Lab"
Length of recording: 3:24 minutes

This machinima (see Figure 5.15) focused on safety procedures in a science lab. The trainee (Astrid) reported that in some scenes it was impossible to use the footage she had taken, because she had problems with objects floating around her invisible avatar and this prevented filming. As a consequence, she had to use some footage other trainees had taken of the scene. She experienced the recording process as challenging overall, as there were many problems with camera control. Astrid was planning to use the machinima in her capacity as a lab engineer to help PhD and master's students in the lab, teaching them to use instruments and learning to follow health and safety instructions. Astrid reported that machinima could be used in a much wider array of fields than merely

Figure 5.15 "In the Laboratory"

language learning. She found the experience on the course inspiring and saw few limitations in using the virtual environment to create authentic environments. While the technology fuelled her imagination and creativity, she felt limited only by her own technical skills with respect to immersive environments. Comments she received suggested that the costumes used for the lab were professionally presented, but the gestures used in the first part of the machinima were not appropriate; this was later changed during the film.

Title: "Prepositions"
Length: 2:42 minutes

A machinima produced on prepositions was regarded as an evocative, fascinating film (see Figure 5.16). In the original script, each of the children had one line to speak, but this was later changed as the machinimatographer was not satisfied with the avatars' facial movements and as the quality of graphics in the machinima was lower than what students were used to in standard videos. The aim of the machinima was to stimulate students to think about a variety of film structures and to inspire them to make their own machinima. Students were encouraged to view examples of short films and to develop their own ideas for machinima productions by reflecting on the main structure of the films and considering the camera movement, lighting and editing processes. The intention was to provide a moving diagram of an existing film that concentrated on facial expressions rather than words. Angela titled her machinima "Prepositions" even though she was not a language teacher, but she thought that

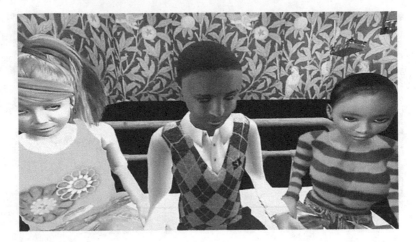

Figure 5.16 "Prepositions"

language teachers could use the machinima to practice prepositional structures. It was also suggested that the machinima could be used for character descriptions relating to behaviour and motives, such as 'why students were unhappy or sad'.

Focus Group Discussion: Benefits and Challenges

Following the creation of the machinima, the trainees participated in a focus group discussion. Several benefits and challenges with respect to machinima production were identified by the participants.

Gabriella was fascinated by the immersive environment of SL and all the places to visit. She thoroughly enjoyed the experience, and the course introduced her to the environment and how it worked. She was also amazed at the various ways the avatars could be utilised for different occasions but her most significant challenge related to the use of the cameras for filming, which she felt she had not mastered yet. She thought that her computer was partly to blame for this and was convinced that better equipment would have helped her to make better quality machinima. She also reported that she has successfully used her machinima in her lessons, which her students enjoyed. She wanted to establish a team of people who would work on dialogues, which she would use in her classes in future, and the current course materials were not good enough in her view. She saw significant potential in machinima as a form of complementary material to help students get more practice and improve their language skills.

For another trainee (Adin), the course helped her to be part of the teacher-oriented community of practice. She learned a great deal during her training, but she also reported that she found it quite challenging at the same time, especially in the first few weeks during the orientation phase when she was struggling to move her avatar. For the researcher who evaluated the sessions, it was fascinating to observe the degree of culture shock experienced by Adin, and it was particularly novel how she was able to share her feelings in the virtual world with fewer inhibitions (De Jong Derrington, 2013).

A third participant called Astrid had already attended several courses in SL prior to the machinima training course, but she had not become fully aware of how to navigate using her avatar. The challenge she encountered was to find a programme for screencasting, how to use it and how to film as she intended to continue working in the virtual world making machinima following the completion of the training course. In the future, she plans to use the Lab in SL to produce machinima and to promote machinima at her university to trigger more interest by involving the person responsible for biology courses. She considered the training course a highlight in her continuing professional development, particularly as she felt close to her avatar and was able to observe the emotional impact it had on her.

Trainee Angela highlighted the importance of the first day of the training course as significant because of the film set where she had to make her first machinima. She emphasised how important it was that the course team had developed a well-structured series of activities that supported the trainees. While Angela considered the time given for reading to be too short, and although she tried to master as much as she could in terms of machinima production, she neglected many of the readings. The readings were nevertheless thorough and provided a foundation that could help her introduce machinima-based practice into her own work. She thought it was helpful that the weekly lesson plans were made available to trainees in advance, as it helped her to prepare for the session. By following other people's learning process, it reinforced her learning, and she benefitted from the collaborative nature of the learning process. Angela was motivated as a result to take her students into virtual worlds. Prior to the course, she had been trying to find the right platform and had considered the use of OpenSimulator given some interest in her school for using the environment for the teaching of Spanish and French. Uppermost in her mind was the need to master a platform for students which would harness their creativity and allow them to work at their own pace. Angela was especially glad to belong to a community of practice which developed on the training course as it provided the support to encourage and develop teachers who were new to immersive environments.

It was evident overall that the trainees became more confident during the course in making machinima, and one of the most positive outcomes was that they wanted to keep in touch with the community following completion. The facilitators suggested that they could join communities and networks connected with machinima on Facebook and other channels concerned with virtual learning like the Euroversity association or attending annual virtual conferences like SLanguages or Virtual Worlds of Best Practice (VWBP), among others.

Feedback

Course feedback was collected from the final course survey (see Appendix VII), the focus group discussion in Adobe Connect, the discussion forum in Moodle and via self-assessment.

Moodle Discussion Forum

At the end of the course, Astrid reported what she felt about the knowledge she gained during the course and added,

> I feel like I have a new mission in life; spread the word to my colleagues about the possibilities there are in using SL and machinima in teaching in higher education. But first I need to do some fabulous filming and editing to illustrate it.

Gabriella believed that using machinima could help improve the quality of her teaching and she saw significant potential in the advantages of having students create their own machinima. She reported that machinima produced by learners allowed them to identify their strengths and weaknesses in learning and improve their language skills. Like Astrid some of the other trainees were also intrigued by the possibilities virtual worlds had to offer outside their ordinary language classroom. They were so enthusiastic and full of ideas when the course finished and there was also a great community feeling after having worked intensively together for seven weeks. One highlight was that several participants had become so enthusiastic about making machinima that they registered on EduNation in the virtual world to become residents.

Advantages of Using Machinima in the Future

Several trainees who had had no opportunity to use the machinima created in their classroom provided ideas about how the machinima could be used in future. Some already had concrete ideas, such as Svetlana, who wanted to implement a task-based approach with machinima in her CLIL lessons in future, teaching security-related issues. She hoped to motivate her students and trigger their interest with machinima. Moreover, Gabriella wanted to use machinima to present new language structures, to practise vocabulary and grammar and to use SL as a tool for learner collaboration. She reported that virtual environments could easily be adapted to cater to most language classroom activities and saw machinima as a tool with significant potential for language learners to practise pronunciation and improve their language fluency by listening to their voice recordings:

> Second Life creates a wonderful opportunity for shy students to open up and express their ideas more freely. I believe the students may also learn to act more responsibly, knowing the nature of legal issues related to it. On the whole, it's a great tool for improving students' media and ICT literacy.

The notion that introverted learners are more able to communicate in virtual environments as identified by Gabriella, was supported by data arising from interviews with Myers, Nowak and Schneider, as well as the research of De Jong Derrington (2013). It was noticeable that two participants who appeared as fairly introverted at the beginning of the course and who considered withdrawing after a few sessions became outspoken and more engaged during the course and successfully continued until the end.

Final Course Feedback Survey

The trainees were given the same feedback questions they had responded to prior to the course in the concluding session of the CALL training course (see Table 5.7). Six trainees responded and were asked to reflect

Table 5.7 Final Course Feedback Survey

Statements	Strongly Agree	Agree	Disagree	Strongly Disagree
1. The training goals of the training were stated clearly in the invitation.	100%	0%	0%	0%
2. I was given all the logins and support needed for the training well on time.	100%	0%	0%	0%
3. Support was provided to help prior to the start of the training.	83.33%	0%	0%	16.67%
4. The goals of the training were clearly defined and well displayed.	83.33%	16.67%	0%	0%

(Continued)

Table 5.7 (Continued)

Statements	Strongly Agree	Agree	Disagree	Strongly Disagree
5. Each learning unit stated the objectives clearly.	83.33%	16.67%	0%	0%
6. There were sufficient opportunities for interactive communication.	100%	0%	0%	0%
7. The format of the course allowed me to get to know other participants on the course.	50%	50%	0%	0%
8. The materials for the training given on the course were very helpful.	83.33%	16.67%	0%	0%
9. The training was too technical and difficult to understand.	16.67%	16.67%	16,67%	50%
10. The training experience will be useful for my language teaching.	100%	0%	0%	0%
11. The materials provided were the appropriate level for me.	83.33%	16.67%	0%	0%
12. The schedule for the training provided was sufficient to cover all the proposed activities.	83.33%	16.67%	0%	0%
13. The sessions were well balanced as regards to input and activities.	83.33%	16.67%	0%	0%
14. The schedule was very tight and it was difficult to manage all the tasks and materials.	16.67%	0%	83,33%	0%
15. The materials provided for the course were good quality.	83.33%	16.67%	0%	0%
16. The training was appropriate for my level of learning.	66.67%	33.33%	0%	0%
17. The units taught lasted for about the right amount of time.	50%	33.33 %	0%	16.67%

Statements	Strongly Agree	Agree	Disagree	Strongly Disagree
18. I learned a lot about producing machinima and feel confident in producing my own machinima.	50%	50%	0%	0%
19. I am still struggling with producing machinima.	0%	0%	83.33%	16.67%
20. The course facilitator was knowledgeable about training in 3D worlds and making machinima.	100%	0%	0%	0%
21. The course facilitator encouraged active participation.	100%	0%	0%	0%
22. The facilitator responded to all questions in a comprehensive way	100%	0%	0%	0%
23. The facilitator used a variety of training methods.	60%	40%	0%	0%
24. The facilitator gave sufficient instructions for homework.	83.33%	16.67%	0%	0%

on their initial interest in the course. A sample of their feedback is provided follows:

> To gain some unusual skills.
> I think SL is a fantastic resource for teaching and getting the chance to learn making and using machinima sounded like a great opportunity to learn more.
> I love making animations and I always wanted my students to use them in class.
> I wanted to know how to make machinima.
> To be familiar with the virtual world.
> Because I want to motivate my students.

Even though the responses deviate slightly from the ones given at the beginning of the course, the results do not show any significant difference. However, the final course questionnaire also included additional questions about the course content and its delivery. The trainees were asked to mark 24 statements on a 4-point Likert scale to indicate whether they 'strongly agreed', 'agreed', 'disagreed' or 'strongly disagreed'.

The responses reflect the trainees' satisfaction with the course content, timing and facilitation as well as their achievements during the course. Apart from the two responses to statement 9, which indicated that the training was too technical and too difficult, everyone had learnt to produce machinima and felt confident in producing their own videos.

Research Results and Conclusion

The research results demonstrate that the initial aim to identify whether the trainee teachers on the course understood the value of creating and using machinima in their professional environment and were able to apply their newly acquired skills to their everyday teaching had been achieved. Furthermore, the initial course expectations were mapped against teachers' feedback during and after the training. These were mainly concerned with learning new skills, enhancing language learning with machinima, triggering interest and motivation in the classroom through machinima, designing machinima for special interest groups, working collaboratively and stimulating learners' passion for learning, all of which have been achieved. Teachers who had a special focus on teaching languages for specific purposes or CLIL considered the production of machinima as useful, as they complemented existing course materials in a motivating way. A machinima created for health and safety, for example, was regarded as particularly valuable as its content was focused exactly on what students were supposed to learn in the course curriculum. It is noteworthy that CLIL teachers, in particular, were intrigued by the affordances of learning in 3D environments, in which situations or simulations could be practised and filmed, as this was not possible in a physical learning environment.

The training sessions revealed that trainees with little knowledge of virtual worlds found it more difficult to adapt to creating machinima as they were confronted with a steep learning curve. However, those participants who already had some experience in virtual worlds, filmmaking or video editing immediately became enthusiastic about the virtual environment and identified its potential for filming, teaching and learning. A positive course outcome was the sense of community developed during the training through collaborative engagement in the process of creating machinima. As a consequence, participants were eager to continue working in virtual environments and actively involve their learners in the process of creating machinima in future lessons. The process of achievement resulting from producing machinima, being part of the team, either filming or playing a role, for example, was considered as more important than the end product, as the experience of active participation, engagement and collaboration, which learners frequently recalled, was essential for their learning to take place (Falconer, 2011).

Video quality was discussed and identified as a major challenge of current levels of technology, and it was concluded that the quality of machinima was not considered as important for teachers and students as the process in which they were able to engage. Feedback from the teaching contexts in which machinima had been used demonstrates that as long as teachers are enthusiastic about their creations students usually appreciate the effort involved, especially if there is a heightened sense of engagement or teachers make mistakes that demonstrate their vulnerability.

Technical challenges can be discouraging in terms of the machinima creating process, especially if there is a lack of technical support, when there are sound problems or a lack of internet bandwidth. However, the trainees who committed to immersing themselves in the virtual worlds demonstrated resilience and were able to find solutions, regardless of any technical obstacles. As the second teacher training course finished at the end of term for most schools, not every teacher had the opportunity to implement their machinima or in-world courses creating machinima in their teaching. Further research is needed to investigate through follow-up sessions how teachers implemented what they learned in their teaching and what effect this had on students' learning. There is a lot of evidence in the research that teachers would find machinima useful in their teaching if they were easier to produce. As virtual worlds become easier places to master, especially, for example, when it is possible in future to enter the virtual world via a browser window rather than through external software, this will make the machinima making process more viable for classroom teachers.

6 Afterword
Implications for Project-Based Teaching and Creativity

Introduction

This book has explored the role of video-based technologies to promote language teacher and language learner creativity. It has specifically examined the potential of this technology by looking closely at the role of machinima, which we have defined as the creation of digital video recordings inside 3D immersive environments (Morozov, 2008), to facilitate opportunities for authentic language learning within a collaborative project-based framework (Alan & Stoller, 2005). Having reviewed the wider research context and examined the role of task- and project-based language learning approaches in the opening chapters, the second half of the book explored empirical findings arising from a large, multinational research project on the subject of machinima and video-based language teaching which took place across several education sectors (adult lifelong learning, higher education, vocational education and schools education) in five countries (the Czech Republic, Germany, Poland, Turkey and the UK) and involved a variety of participants (teachers, teacher trainers and trainees, curriculum designers and educational leaders). Using machinima as the focus, we then explored the implications for CALL teacher education via an online teacher training course that was offered over two iterations. Accordingly, we have not merely examined the potential of a new approach to language teaching with digital technologies but have sought to understand how a framework for effective online CALL teacher education can be developed to foster the techno-pedagogical skills required by teachers (Slaouti & Motteram, 2006; Torsani, 2016).

Background and Context

Through its investigation of machinima as a potentially innovative form of language teaching using video-based instructional approaches, this book has sought to engage teachers, learners, course and materials designers and educational policymakers in a discussion about effective forms of creative language teaching and learning fit for the digital age

(Beetham & Sharpe, 2019). While the approach that we explored was sensitive to the array of opportunities presented by digital technologies, we were also aware of the pitfalls and challenges that accompany them in teaching and learning contexts. In this respect, the book has sought to contribute to the debate about the future of creative forms of language education in an age increasingly dominated by performance testing, the quantification of learner and teacher performance through analytics and, more broadly, neoliberal policies, which construct education as more narrowly focused on an employability and training agenda rather than a holistic view of education that promotes curiosity, individual growth, critical enquiry and personal development (Giroux, 2014). In exploring new approaches to language learning in this context, this book's research focus has been on adopting a *critical* and *historical* perspective on digital education, as well as identifying appropriate methodologies to research digital innovations in teaching and learning, in a balanced way that is neither susceptible to overly optimistic hype or pessimistic determinism. This approach owes more to critical digital pedagogy (Stommel, 2014) and post-humanism (Pennycook, 2018) than to calls to 'normalise' (Bax, 2011a) or evangelise technology usage. Indeed, as Pennycook suggests, countering calls to 'normalise' technology, "posthumanism raises significant questions for applied linguistics in terms of our understandings of language, humans, objects and agency" (p. 6), including, in particular, the need to be vigilant about the impact of technologies on communication and our physical and mental enhancement.

To explore these complex issues, the book specifically examined the community of practice (CoP) that formed around a multinational project on video-based learning that was its point of origin (Thomas & Schneider, 2018) and explored how it sought to advance alternative forms of language teacher creativity that engage trainee teachers dialogically in techno-pedagogical skills development (Wegerif, 2013). Arising from the project, the book specifically investigated the theory and practice of technology-mediated project-based language learning (Gonzales-Lloret & Ortega, 2014; Seedhouse & Almutairi, 2009) as an instructional approach, and this was illustrated by several case studies in which authentic language teaching approaches were developed with machinima by CALL trainee teachers.

The originality of the machinima project derived from its investigation of the medium of user-generated digital video production as a vehicle for constructivist and experiential forms of teaching and learning based on collaboration and creativity, in which several commonly and less commonly taught European languages (e.g., English, Dutch, German, Polish and Turkish), were taught alongside other skills such as team building and digital literacy (Morozov, 2008). The book analysed original data arising from two iterations of an online CALL teacher training course developed to train in-service teachers with limited ICT knowledge to design, create and integrate machinima-based lessons in their language classrooms, as well as data from the process of extensive field testing of machinima involving teachers and learners. Several beneficiary groups were at the centre of the research: practitioners, in terms of the development of teacher training materials; students in relation to new learning resources; curriculum developers in relation to a new video-based foreign language pedagogy; CALL and digital education researchers, in that it was the first to synthesise research on the topic and use it as a lens through which to analyse new data sets from naturally occurring classroom environments; and national and European policymakers who are concerned with the role of languages and technology across the school and post-compulsory education spectrum.

Against this background, foreign language learning in schools, colleges and higher education has been at the forefront of debates about the intrinsic value of learning. In recent years, it has been criticised with increasing regularity and evidence of this can be seen in the closure of university language centres and departments across the UK as the study of foreign languages is increasingly perceived as a 'luxury subject' rather than one that 'makes a profit' or enhances 'employability'. The increasing marketisation and privatisation of education along neoliberal lines with its emphasis on instrumental knowledge, turning educational institutions into job training centres, and the heavy financial burdens placed on students and teachers may all be reasons which have collectively contributed to making students less willing to risk studying subjects that do not appear to have an immediate return on investment or clear career path (Flavin, 2017). In the case of teachers, the emergence of increased accountability measures, the burden of administration and standardised testing have likewise impacted negatively on their ability to embrace unfamiliar or 'risky' pedagogies and creative practices that do not focus on raising examination scores.

On the other hand, this critique of the study of languages, in particular, and the arts and humanities, in general, has given rise to a robust defence, precisely because graduates in these fields are more likely to have the flexibility and transferable skills that enable them to move between highly skilled jobs in different countries. While persuasive this line of argument has often ignored a defence which advocates the intrinsic value of a humanities education in terms of immeasurable, qualitative factors such as the value of community, or the value of citizenship, personal fulfilment or contribution to the 'public good' (Flavin, 2017). Although innovation in language learning and teaching has been promised in order to attract students, move the discipline forward and engage students in creative forms of learning, the economic defence of language education outlined earlier merely risks pandering to the arguments of those who seek to marginalise or dispense with it altogether. Indeed, this instrumental defence has led in many instances to conservative pedagogies that are still largely behaviourist in orientation rather than progressive in design (Lacasa et al., 2012). The pedagogies associated with MOOCs are one example of this trend. While MOOCs were identified as 'revolutionary' during the initial phase of their emergence and promotion in 2012, this form of online learning has typically been based on behaviourist principles in that knowledge is mostly transferred from educator to student and little is done to stimulate deeper forms of interactivity, experimentation and collaboration, a task that is, in fact, very difficult when thousands or even hundreds of thousands of geographically dispersed learners are involved at the same time. As education has moved towards an audit culture in which standardised testing, promoting 'teaching to the test', has become an integral driver, language education in formal contexts, governed by examination results and league tables, has led to pedagogical approaches that are still based on memorisation and rote learning; indeed, in such a climate, it is not surprising that teachers and administrators may have become more 'risk-averse'. Consequently, there may be few opportunities to communicate in the target language in a meaningful way, particularly in the primary and secondary school contexts, where modern foreign language instruction is typically crammed into one or two hours of scheduled class time per week, is often taught by a non-specialist or generalist and has less focus on forms of 'messy experimentation' that are staples of authentic interaction.

Project-Based Learning

The machinima project explored in this book was cross-sector and cross-disciplinary and created resources for language teachers to learn how to create video-based materials and apply them in their personalised teaching contexts (Slater & Beckett, 2017). As outlined in Chapters 4 and 5, the focus of the research was teachers' technical and pedagogical skills development during two iterations of a teacher training course and how to assess their involvement in the planning, filming and editing of their machinima productions. Special emphasis was put on understanding the challenges and benefits of language learning in 3D immersive virtual environments utilising this form of creative video-based learning. Thus, special emphasis was put on the identification of opportunities for the development of skills in addition to the traditional linguistic and grammatical structures which are so often identified as most important in the second language context (Thomas & Schneider, 2018). Central to the innovative nature of the training course was the development of a supportive community of practice involving facilitators, mentors and mentees. In addition to the evaluation of the teacher training course, the field-testing phase of the project was mainly focused on the impact machinima filmmaking had on language learning with regard to learners' engagement and motivation.

Results from the field testing and teacher training course reinforced the importance and value of open educational resources (OERs) in contemporary language education. Based on our data from observation and interviews, teachers felt empowered to produce language learning materials that emphasised learner creativity, underlined the importance of collaborative forms of teaching and learning and advanced machinima as a cost-effective means of producing digital media.

The project led to collaboration with language teachers, learners and stakeholders across four main sectors of education and involved them in the process of sharing competence, expertise and feedback as part of a community of practice for language teachers. The aim was to create machinima that could be used and adapted by educators in these contexts, overcoming technical, pedagogical, educational culture and linguistic barriers and limitations to enable the use and reuse of the materials for teaching purposes.

Based on the objectives of the video project, a needs analysis of different teaching environments was initially undertaken to identify teacher development frameworks to help instructors envisage how machinima could be used in face-to-face, online and blended modes of delivery. In identifying the limitations of traditional face-to-face language teaching environments, the project grappled with the opportunities provided by Web 2.0 applications and the OER movement to place a firm emphasis on the learner as an agent and co-producer rather than a mere consumer of pedagogical content (Warschauer & Grimes, 2008). The needs analysis led to the identification of appropriate locations in-world for filming machinima which would be of value to language learners and teachers.

Much of the work in the early part of the project was aimed at creating and field-testing example machinima which could be used as resources in the teacher training course. Against the background of developments in massive open online courses in the European context, the project consortium developed a MOOT format based on similar principles of openness as well as recognisable design principles involving synchronous and asynchronous discussion, interaction and video-based learning. The course aimed to engage stakeholders in an initial pilot-testing phase before developing both facilitated and autonomous modes of study to promote engagement with machinima filmmaking techniques and the pedagogical considerations necessary to embed them productively in language lessons.

While much of the research and publication activity in the field of CALL has been in English, the video project widened its appeal by including activities in a range of less commonly taught European languages. This allowed the project to explore the meaning of dialogical modes of learning and teaching in non-English-speaking pedagogical traditions and to learn from the synergies created (Wegerif, 2013). Based on a comprehensive understanding of the history of technology-enhanced learning, one of the main aims of the project was to empower learners and teachers as producers rather than merely consumers of content. In order to succeed with this endeavour, effective teacher training that reduced barriers to entry was a key component. The project aimed to promote the attempt to rethink education by developing flexible approaches to learning based on *process* rather than *product* models in which flexibility and creativity were the engines of change.

The video production of machinima in virtual worlds did not require expensive hardware as it does in real-world filmmaking contexts. The animations in the videos were not programmed or specially created; they were filmed in a virtual world which already existed with an abundance of culturally rich authentic locations (e.g., virtual Berlin, Paris, London and Rome, among many others). These virtual worlds provided filming locations without the need for teachers and learners to travel to these places. Purchasing recording and editing software was likewise the only expense involved in the process. Since the outcomes of the project were digital in nature, the distribution was also digital and relied on free web-based services such as YouTube, Vimeo, Facebook and Google Drive, thus enabling the dissemination of project outcomes in the worldwide CALL and digital education community.

Video Project Outcomes

One of the project's main aims was to locate the use of machinima in the wider context of academic research on virtual worlds and task- and project-based language teaching in order to explore

1. structured and creative opportunities for learners and teachers to use immersive environments to create digital videos to aid language learning;
2. opportunities to investigate the pedagogical potential of immersive environments by developing resources to help teachers create videos in the target language, then experience authentic cultural artefacts;
3. the know-how of live video production to a community of language educators across a range of sectors;
4. a community of practice sustained by numerous dissemination and CPD activities that empowered teachers with the relevant pedagogical and technical know-how to integrate digital technologies effectively in a supportive environment.

Stemming from these objectives it was possible to produce an extensive list of machinima that can be used and reused by novice and experienced teachers, students and materials designers (see Appendix I).

In terms of results, it was hypothesised that machinima would be effective at engaging all target groups with the exception of those in adult education. This view was substantiated by the data collected during the project, and several factors emerged to explain this outcome. These include the lack of technology in adult education in general, the perceived time and effort required to produce high-quality video productions and the lack of incentives in this educational sector. As the case studies of the CALL teachers demonstrated in Chapter 4, the majority were enthusiastic about teaching with machinima and their students were engaged by the innovative format and user-generated content. Data suggested that the main difference between real-life video and machinima were the avatars, as the latter often lacked facial expressions and natural gestures. While this is a challenge that may be overcome as immersive and virtual reality technologies continue to evolve, it is currently perceived as an obstacle to wider acceptance by teachers.

All the teachers who participated in the survey-based research used 'ready-made' machinima that focused on a specific topic or grammar point. The majority of the teachers had only recently discovered machinima and were reluctant to create their own, either because of the lack of necessary skills and/or time constraints. According to teachers' and learners' feedback, the most effective and rewarding machinima were those that involved the learners in the production process as the group of English teacher trainees from Turkey discovered when they created a machinima for language teaching in the virtual world of SL. They worked collaboratively, involving everyone in the production process, either as part of the team, filming or acting.

For the learners, it was equally evident from the data that the process of creative production was more important than the final product. As some teachers mentioned in their feedback, making machinima could be very time-consuming, especially when they were not familiar with 3D environments or if there was a lack of technical support. Older models of computer, poor graphic cards or lack of bandwidth all contributed to preventing teachers from creating machinima. Hence, the use of ready-made machinima proved to be the optimal solution for the majority of teachers in the study. However, when technical obstacles were overcome, learning with and through machinima proved to be highly motivating and rewarding. Examples of good practice were seen in the outcome of the MOOT course which demonstrated how teachers immersed in virtual worlds and produced several effective machinima for their teaching.

Above all, the outcomes of the project underlined the importance of a dialogical approach in which intercultural communication and linguistic diversity were integral factors (Wegerif, 2013). It used innovative Web 2.0 and social media technologies, virtual online environments and OERs and promoted interactive and collaborative pedagogies in order to realise its goals (Barwell et al., 2011). It was led by a research-informed approach based on mixed-methods data collection involving questionnaires, interviews, focus groups and observation in a variety of languages. In this respect, one of the project's main achievements was to underline the significance of an evidence-based approach to inform decision-making about digital education in the European educational technology policy context.

Contribution to Language Teaching Policy

The machinima project was a direct response to key competencies identified in the Lisbon Process for Lifelong Learning as it encouraged communication in the mother tongue of several languages (English, Czech, Dutch, German, Polish and Turkish). Moreover, it identified the importance of CLIL and the role of foreign language instruction in teaching technical subjects in science and technology in a cross-curricular format (Barnes, 2015). Arising from this emphasis, the project underlined the importance of interpersonal and intercultural communication skills alongside traditional language learning skills. More than merely focusing on language acquisition, the project's findings emphasised how language learning promotes opportunities for cultural knowledge acquisition and the development of important values, such as mutual understanding, within a values-based approach to learning.

By understanding the role that language learning can play in promoting cultural understanding the project encouraged communication between students and teachers across and within European educational institutions. Learning for the new generation of learners is not merely about learning in a traditional classroom. The project demonstrated that learning is concerned with motivating trainee teachers and learners by tapping into their creativity and stimulating them to work in authentic environments to address problems and situations both in and outside the traditional language classroom. The project-based approach cast the trainee teachers and learners in a variety of interchangeable roles, as a researcher, movie director, actor and producer, and enabled them to collaborate with one another creatively.

Research Framework

The methodology chosen for the video project research followed a mixed-methods model using a case study approach (Boellstorff, 2008; Mawer, 2014; Yin, 2014) to analyse and evaluate the engagement of teachers in learning to create machinima. Furthermore, the methods explored the potential added value of machinima for language learning and teaching. Of the three types of case studies identified by Cohen et al. (2007) and Yin (2004), known as the *explanatory, descriptive* and *exploratory*, the *exploratory* case study approach was most relevant for this research, as the results provided opportunities for further studies in the field of learning with machinima.

Both Cohen et al. (2007) and Yin (2004) identify the greatest strength of case study research design in terms of how they define their boundaries. At the same time, case study research methods have often been criticised for their lack of objectivity and rigidity when compared with other social research methodologies (Rowley, 2002). Although case study research is often designed to illustrate a principle that can be generalised (Shen, 2009), the most common criticism is that the results may not be reliable, that they are not representative and, accordingly, that their findings may be subjective and difficult to substantiate. Indeed, Shen (2009) identifies how the intensive exposure to a specific case may bias the findings, and as Cohen et al. (2007) suggest, case studies often lack control as a result. Conversely, case studies can provide valuable insights into a situation, group or person which the researcher might not have gained or been aware of with a different approach (Boellstorff, 2008). Johannsson (2003) states that generalisations are based on reasoning, which are analytical rather than statistical and that generalisations from a case can be made using a combination of *deduction*, *induction* or *abduction*

The research carried out during this project focused on small groups and individuals, following a holistic approach as outlined by Cohen et al. (2007), Yin (2014) and Schneider (2014b) utilising participating observation during the training course, interviews and focus group discussions as qualitative research methods. Cohen et al. (2007) considered observation a suitable technique for case study research and distinguished between participating and non-participating observers. During the CALL teacher training evaluation process, a participating observation approach was applied, where the observer was actively involved in a number of roles, ranging from actor, film director, supervisor, technical support and participant across a range of training sessions and events. Non-participating observation was used for field-testing events, where the observer was not actively involved in the teaching units but took notes of video recordings, discussions, interviews and reports.

In order to acquire a diverse view of participants' individual background, experience, opinions and self-assessed learning progress, questionnaires were used at the beginning and the end of the training courses, as well as in the field-testing events. This approach aided the acquisition of information about the participants' age, background, interests and what they wanted to achieve. The field testing was mainly based on focus group discussion reports using guided questions, teachers' reports and questionnaires completed by teachers and students. The data were collected in the field testing raised similar issues identified by Yin (2004), who found that conflicting information could occur when comparing data. Sometimes statements students made in the questionnaires contradicted the teachers' reports, which we discovered by mapping students' responses to specific lessons. In the few conflicting cases, we based our findings on the qualitative data such as interviews rather than the anonymous quantitative data provided by the questionnaires.

The research followed the key ethical principles established by Girvan and Savage (2011) in order to secure permissions from all participants. As the research was based on different resources, each had to be carefully considered with regard to the nature and context (Eysenbach & Till, 2001; Moschini, 2010). Boellstorff (2008) used a more formal approach for some of his observational research to obtain consent in his fieldwork. During the field-testing phase of machinima in various European countries, consent was obtained by the teachers in the physical classroom. The participants in the training course did not have any physical contact with the facilitators but had been asked for permission prior to, during and after the research to publish their contributions. These included sharing their reports about experiences, live-session recordings, interviews or machinima productions. This method of triple-checking consent turned out to be valuable, because some of the participants who had already given their consent were reluctant to share their experience under their real name at a later stage. Participants' names and identities were also kept anonymous. Only interviews with experts or samples of machinima videos made publicly available on YouTube and the project website were provided with real names with the consent of the authors.

Moschini (2010) identified the specific challenge when conducting research in the context of virtual environments in that a user's privacy could be infringed when asked to reveal their real-life identity. Some researchers such as Boellstorff (2008) and Girvan and Savage (2011) try to overcome this issue by accepting avatars' names to identify participants in-world and typed names on notecards to represent agreement in a virtual context. All participants in the project were registered with their real name and email address. This meant that users could be identified and not, as suggested by Moschini (2010), hide behind their avatars or change their appearance. However, this approach becomes an issue when filming in-world, as avatars who do not belong to the film set and accidentally appear in a scene, are still required to give their permission (Bäcker, 2015). Teachers and learners need to be aware of these ethical considerations and procedures, as well as copyright issues, when creating machinima in virtual worlds and other immersive environments. Linden Labs provide guidelines for filming in SL in the form of *Terms* and *Services*, which address the community standards and policy (Moschini, 2010). These indicate that researchers must have the consent of all residents whose avatars or SL names are featured or are recognisable in a machinima. As in real life, consent for filming is not required if an avatar cannot be identified and is merely part of a crowd scene. Similar regulations apply to snapshots taken in-world. Of course, as in real life, anything with a trademark or brand requires permission to be recorded. Nevertheless, it is challenging to obtain filming permissions at times in immersive environments, as it is not always possible to find landowners' or content creators' real names or email addresses and not everyone is willing to offer this information voluntarily. In such cases, as mentioned previously, notecards are a common way of obtaining consent in-world in these situations (Boellstorff, 2008).

The Impact of the Project

According to teachers' and learners' feedback, the most effective and rewarding machinima were the ones that involved the learners in the production process as the group of English teacher trainees in Turkey discovered when they created a machinima for language teaching in SL. They worked collaboratively, involving everyone in the production process, either as part of the team, filming or acting. For the learners, on the other hand, the process of achievement was more important than the final product. As a minority of teachers mentioned in their feedback, making machinima can be very time-consuming, especially when they are not familiar with 3D environments, and challenging if there is a lack of technical support. Older or less technically advanced computers with poor graphic cards or lack of bandwidth were identified as barriers preventing teachers from using machinima. Hence, the use of ready-made machinima designed and created by other teachers or learners may be the best solution for the majority of teachers. However, when technical obstacles can be overcome, learning with and through machinima may be highly motivating and rewarding (Burns, 2015). Examples of good practice in this respect are evident in the outcome of the MOOT course which demonstrated how teachers immersed in virtual worlds were able to produce a wider range of effective machinima for their language teaching (Thomas & Schneider, 2018).

The specific research objectives arising from the project's online teacher training course and field-testing phase were to discover how immersion in the virtual environment influenced teachers' acceptance of and engagement with machinima. In what ways did the creation and use of machinima affect students' motivation, active participation and learning outcomes in terms of foreign language learning? How could machinima be utilised for self-reflection, feedback and assessment?

The quality of the finished machinima products was shown to be strongly connected with the extent to which instructors and learners either accepted or rejected machinima, whether the machinima were ready-made or self-created and to what extent the quality of machinima affected language learning. In this respect, the investment of time and effort required to produce the machinima was also a major concern of the investigation.

The review of existing research in Chapter 2 discussed how machinima developed from computer gaming to a stand-alone medium that can be utilised for pedagogical purposes in education, in general, and the specific context of foreign language learning, in particular (Morozov, 2008). Furthermore, the advantages of machinima with regard to cost and time-effectiveness, and the disadvantages concerning technical challenges, quality and lack of non-verbal cues, were identified and critically explored. The importance of experiential learning was also highlighted and its impact on interaction and learning outcomes was further explored. Moreover, the benefits and challenges of using machinima, as well as how machinima could be utilised as a tool for assessment and feedback, were evaluated. Present and recent developments of machinima and their current prominence, including the disappearance and emergence of places and events in the virtual world of SL were also discussed. The final chapters explored several case studies arising from the data collected from observation, interviews and ethnography, and their key findings are further elaborated in the following.

As the research investigated machinima created in SL as well as ready-made machinima used in the physical classroom, the study was based on the hypothesis that teachers who immerse themselves in virtual worlds understand the values and benefits of this learning environment better than those who merely use machinima without being involved in the production process. To determine the 'added value' machinima may offer for language teaching, it was necessary to study teachers' engagement with them, how they implemented machinima in their teaching and to find out to what extent immersion in the virtual environment influenced teachers' acceptance of and engagement with machinima. As the pre-course survey indicated, the main interest of teachers participating in the online teacher training course was to acquire new skills, discover new and interesting ways to approach their learners, support students' engagement and participation through 3D environments, improve the quality of their teaching materials and make the lessons generally more engaging for their learners. By the end of the six-week training course, the teachers' expectations had been met and their ability to create machinima had contributed positively to their external teaching environments. Observation confirmed that the activities in SL encouraged interaction and bonding, resulting in mutual support and motivation in the process of creating machinima from beginning to end. Several teachers expressed that they had developed their existing knowledge of digital technologies, while for others, it changed their way of thinking in the physical classroom space (Wegerif, 2013).

In order to aid the process of accepting machinima, it was necessary for instructors to understand and identify with the characters in the videos. From conversations with teachers and observations in piloting machinima, it was evident that teachers who immersed themselves in 3D environments were more likely to identify with the characters in the machinima and perceive them as 'real'. Consequently, they were more likely to be enthusiastic in terms of engaging with machinima in their teaching. The experience of immersing in virtual environments and adjusting to the skills required to create machinima and pedagogical approaches was shown to directly influence teachers' perspective when teaching with the medium.

The participants on the teacher training course reported how proud they were of their machinima creations. As a result, they experienced a self-perceived increase in motivation in their teaching context and subsequently sought to involve their students in a form of co-participation in the process of learning with machinima. In addition, it was evident that machinima focused on specific learning objectives they wanted to teach, and thus, the students reported a significant sense of enhanced motivation. For other teachers, the machinima enabled them to explain complex processes either involving the language or the content of the lesson which would otherwise have been more challenging.

Another research objective was to find out how the creation and use of machinima affected students' motivation, active participation and learning outcomes in language learning. The case studies showed that students' involvement in 3D virtual environments and, specifically, in the process of making machinima had a positive influence on their course motivation and learning outcomes, and this had a perceived positive influence on their speaking and personal skills. Furthermore, it was evident that introverted students were more outspoken in the virtual environment, and thus, machinima engaged them to be more productive (De John Derrington, 2013). All instructors who actively involved their learners in the process of creating machinima described the positive effect this had on them. It was reported that students improved their target language through interaction and collaboration as well as through rehearsing dialogues repeatedly, which helped aid vocabulary and grammar retention.

The research objective that examined how machinima could be utilised for self-reflection, feedback and assessment revealed the most interesting results from all the case studies. The visual form of feedback made available by machinima was an ideal tool for reflection, as this allowed learners the opportunity to review their interactions as well as their linguistic and extra-linguistic performance. Watching the recordings of their activities helped learners to analyse and critique their presentations and assisted them in developing an awareness of their performance; as a consequence, they were able to take responsibility for their own learning. In this respect, the most effective and rewarding machinima were those that involved the learners in the process of mutual discovery and co-creation (Barwell et al., 2011). As discussed in several case studies, this did not imply that learners created machinima by themselves and that this was the only measurable output of the process; it meant that they were involved in a collective process of design and production, in which their involvement was more important than the final material production.

The research question related to the level of machinima quality was discussed with regard to the expected outcomes of the machinima productions and the way machinima were perceived by users. To find responses to this more generic question led to an examination of the reasons for either accepting or rejecting machinima. None of the piloted machinima were highly professional from an artistic point of view, and it was concluded that non-professional machinima creators could not be expected to provide flawless end products. As the study revealed, quality in machinima was often determined by the end user and was not dependent on the overall quality of the product.

Indeed, examples demonstrated that students frequently accepted machinima with poor quality, as they were more interested in the pedagogical or linguistic content and appreciated the work their teachers had invested in them. This finding again demonstrated that the process of creating machinima was more important than the final result. The evaluation of field-testing surveys, however, showed that quite a number of machinima were considered to be poor quality because of the lack of non-verbal expressions and the unnatural appearance and movements of the avatars involved.

The next question addressed related concerns. What impact did the level of quality have on whether machinima were ready-made or self-created? The study revealed that teachers and students often critiqued ready-made machinima, because they could not identify with the avatars or even rejected them, especially when they were unfamiliar with virtual environments or 3D games. Perceptions of avatar aesthetics and the lack of seriousness also had an effect on some learners in terms of their engagement with ready-made machinima. Generally, both teachers and learners expected good-quality videos from ready-made machinima with regard to content and film and were not prepared to accept lesser quality. As mentioned in Chapter 4, teachers accepted their self-created machinima more easily as they had invested time and effort in the production and were proud of their creation, whereas poor quality did not matter as long as the machinima conveyed the learning content in a suitable form. Therefore, we further investigated to what extent the quality of machinima affected language learning. The main points raised in the discussions with teachers piloting machinima were technical challenges that determined the impact on learners' achievements. For active listening in a language class, the sound quality was essential, and for language production, it was necessary that the machinima provided an effective model of spoken language. Furthermore, the lack of body language and facial expressions was perceived as the biggest challenge when learning with machinima, as students could not lip-read to obtain a better understanding when the lip movements were not synchronised. It was evident that more advanced techniques are required in order to make avatars that are more capable of expressing human emotions.

The time and effort required to create machinima were a great concern for teachers. The study examined the impact time and effort had on machinima productions and focused in more detail on the question to what extent the creation of machinima was worth the time and effort in relation to the potential added value to teaching. As discussed in the case studies in Chapter 4, the creation of machinima was an extremely time-consuming process, especially because of the technical challenges. Teachers on the training course all managed to create machinima and were enthusiastic about the products in spite of the significant amount of time invested in the process. They were keen on integrating them in their lessons and felt motivated to create more. Overall, the more machinima they produced, the less time they needed with their productions, and thus, the time spent was worth the added value the machinima brought to their lessons.

In summary, the generally positive experiences and benefits of immersive learning in virtual environments equipped teachers with the skills to create machinima, and this, in turn, appeared to have a positive influence on their language lessons. Furthermore, the most effective and rewarding machinima were the ones that involved learners in the process as co-producers (Carroll & Cameron, 2005). Whereas technical obstacles or time constraints prevented teachers from creating their own machinima, the use of ready-made machinima tailored to their needs which focused on specific teaching points appeared to be the best solution.

Limitations and Recommendations

Arising from the study and within the wider context of research on video-based approaches, more empirical research is recommended on machinima in language learning in order to investigate the unique challenges and opportunities it presents. Further studies should involve qualitative research including ethnographic and autoethnographic approaches to better understand teacher and learner behaviour in immersive virtual environments.

Although the research has achieved its overall aim of investigating the effectiveness and added value of machinima for language learning of using machinima in virtual immersive environments, we acknowledge that this study can only be seen as a snapshot. From the overwhelming amount of data used in the piloting events, only a few cases could be represented. Apart from this, some aspects, such as learners' perspectives were missing or not fully investigated, and this would be interesting for further research, particularly in the context of netnography studies.

In terms of the CALL teacher education course, findings from the project underline the importance of an integrated approach that combines the opportunity for dialogue and support in relation to both technology and pedagogy (Hubbard, 2008; Hubbard & Levy, 2006). The process of machinima making was undertaken with an understanding of the different contexts in which teachers find themselves, as this enabled the trainee teachers to appreciate the limitations as well as the benefits of the technology. As pedagogy became more important, the training course sought to develop trainees' transferable skills rather than specific digital skills (Slaouti & Motteram, 2006), thus enabling them to build a degree of technology resilience regardless of the specific context and technologies that they may encounter in future (Motteram, Slaouti, & Onat-Stelma, 2013). CALL teacher education courses such as the video project also need to consider how they can cultivate more general digital skill sets to encourage flexible and adaptable behaviour in trainees and to underline the importance of pedagogical rather than merely technological objectives (Fuchs, 2006). Courses of this type need to aim to have a broader relevance for trainees' teaching practice and to move away from only focusing on any potentially impressive implications of the new applications or tools.

Arising from the findings of the course, Figure 6.1 shows a representation of a future iteration in its life cycle. Adapted from Picciano's (2017) 'multimodal model of online education' and Garrison, Anderson, and Archer's (2000) 'community of inquiry model', we have replaced 'CoP' (Lave & Wenger, 1991) with the notion of a 'community of critical inquiry' as collaborative criticality (via ongoing individual reflection and collaborative peer review) stands at the heart of effective teacher training in digital education contexts. This also stems from our critique of

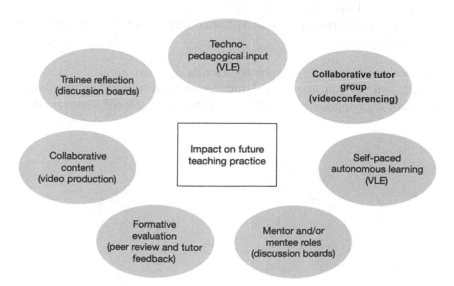

Figure 6.1 CALL Online Teacher Education: Community of Critical Inquiry Model

the influential concept of 'normalisation' in the CALL research literature (Bax, 2003); technology usage needs to be carefully considered rather than uncritically normalised in the lives of teachers and learners (Pennycook, 2018). This collaborative form of critical inquiry is underpinned by socio-constructivist learning and teaching principles that emphasise the primacy of adapting to individual teaching contexts rather than assuming that one approach to CALL teacher education fits with every context (Parks, Huot, Hamers, & Lemonnier, 2003).

Inquiry, collaboration, reflection and community are at the heart of the model, alongside a more flexible, deconstructed understanding of mentoring (trainees can be *mentors* as well as *mentees*). In addition to input that is both pedagogical and technical, the model combines *creative spaces* for collaborative group tutoring, self-paced autonomous learning, trainee reflection, collaborative content production via a technology-mediated project-based approach and an ongoing process of formative evaluation from tutors and peers. At the centre of the model is also the impact of the training on the participants' teaching context. As Egbert et al. (2002) have argued in this respect, an effective criterion of success in CALL is the extent to which a participant's subsequent teaching practice is influenced positively by it in an ongoing process of critical review and adaptation. Their questions remain influential:

> What impact does CALL course input have on teachers' post-course teaching practice?
> What factors influence CALL teachers' choice of techno-pedagogy in the classroom following CPD?
> In what ways do teachers continue their CALL training once the course is over?

These questions would be a fitting starting point for future research on CALL teacher education involving the creative technology-mediated project-based approach to teaching and learning explored in this book.

Bibliography

Abram, S. (2012). Benefits of using video in the classroom: 11 reasons every educator needs a video strategy. *Stephen's Lighthouse, Illuminating Library Industry Trends, Innovation and Information* [blog]. Retrieved from http://stephenslighthouse.com/2012/09/30/benefits-to-using-video-in-the-classroom/

Abrams, Z. I. (2006). From theory to practice: Intra-cultural CMC in the L2 classroom. In L. Ducate & N. Arnold (Eds.), *Calling on CALL: From theory to research to new directions in foreign language teaching* (pp. 181–210). San Marcos, TX: CALICO.

Adamková, E. (2015, May 19). Interview with Eva Adamcová. *YouTube* [video]. Retrieved from https://youtu.be/dfJkDMAhj9o

Aeon, C. (2015a, December 31). Machinima open studio project. *Looking Towards the Future* [blog]. Retrieved from http://machinimasl.blogspot.de/search?updated-min=2015-01-01T00:00:00-08:00&updated-max=2016-01-01T00:00:00-08:00&max-results=50

Aeon, C. (2015b, July 11). Machinima open studio project. *MOSP Takedown Update* [blog]. Retrieved from http://machinimasl.blogspot.nl/2015/07/mosp-takedown-update.html

Alan, B., & Stoller, F. L. (2005). Maximizing the benefits of project work in foreign language classrooms. *English Teaching Forum, 43*(4), 10–21.

Aldrich, C. (2009). *Learning online with games, simulations, and virtual world: Strategies for Online Instruction.* San Francisco, CA: Jossey-Bass.

Allwright, R. L. (1984). The importance of interaction in classroom language learning. *Applied Linguistics, 5*(2), 156–171.

Altberg, E. (2016, March 9). *Keynote at virtual worlds: Best practices in education (VWBPE 2016).* 06:00 PM–06:50 PM. In Burns, M. (2016, March 10). VWBPE – Ebbe Altberg. *YouTube* [video]. Retrieved from https://youtu.be/ovl-YCIO2Vc

Amaya, A., Woolf, C., Devane, N., Galliers, J., Talbot, R., Wilson, S., & Marshall, J. (2018). Receiving aphasia intervention in a virtual environment: The participants' perspective. *Aphasiology, 32*(5), 538–558.

Au, W. J. (2015, June 29). Second Life lost 100,000 monthly active users since 2014. *New World News. Wagner James Au Reports First-Hand from the Metaverse* [blog]. Retrieved from http://nwn.blogs.com/nwn/2015/06/second-life-users-900k.html

Avalon Project. (2009–2010). *Lifelong learning programme: Education and culture DG.* Retrieved from http://avalonlearning.eu

Bäcker, K. (2015). User-generated content anonymity leads to a certain feeling of 'safety'. In T. Payome (Ed.), *Checkpoint elearning special-edition* (pp. 1–8). Berlin: OnlineEduca.

Barab, S. A., & Duffy, T. M. (2000). From practice fields to communities of practice. In J. H. Jonassen & S. M. Land (Eds.), *Theoretical foundations of learning environments* (pp. 25–55). Chicago: Lawrence Erlbaum Associates Publishers.

Barnes, J. (2005). Strangely familiar: Authentic experience, teacher education and a thought-provoking environment. *Improving Schools, 8*(2), 199–206.

Barnes, J. (2015). *Cross-curricular learning 3–14.* London: Sage.

Barwell, G., Moore, C., & Walker, R. (2011). Marking machinima: A case study in assessing student use of a web 2.0 technology. *Australasian Journal of Educational Technology, 27*, 765–780.

Baş, G., & Beyhan, O. (2010). Effects of multiple intelligences supported project-based learning on students' achievement levels and attitudes towards English lessons. *International Electronic Journal of Elementary Education, 2*(3), 365–386.

Bauer-Ramazani, C. (2006). Training CALL teachers online. In M. Levy & P. Hubbard (Eds.), *Teacher education in CALL* (pp. 183–202). Philadelphia, PA: John Benjamins.

Bax, S. (2003). CALL – Past, present and future. *System, 31*, 13–28.

Bax, S. (2011a). Normalisation revisited: The effective use of technology in language education. *International Journal of Computer-Assisted Language Learning and Teaching, 1*(2), 1–15.

Bax, S. (2011b). Digital education: Beyond the 'wow' factor. In M. Thomas (Ed.), *Digital education: Opportunities for social collaboration* (pp. 239–256). London and New York: Palgrave Macmillan.

Becker, H., & Riel, M. M. (2000). *Teacher professional engagement and constructivist compatible computer use.* Center for Research on Information Technology and Organisations. Washington, DC.

Beckett, G. (2002). Teacher and student evaluations of project-based instruction. *TESL Canada Journal, 19*(2), 52–66.

Beckett, G. (2006). Project-based second and foreign language education: Theory, research and practice. In G. Beckett & P. Miller (Eds.), *Project-based second and foreign language education* (pp. 3–18). Greenwich, CT: Information Age Publishing.

Beckett, G., & Miller, P. (Eds.). (2006). *Project-based second and foreign language education.* Greenwich, CT: Information Age Publishing.

Beckett, G., & Slater, T. (2005). The project framework: A tool for language, content, and skills integration. *ELT Journal, 59*(2), 108–116.

Beckett, G., & Slater, T. (2018). Technology-integrated project-based language learning. In C. Chapelle (Ed.), *The encyclopedia of applied linguistics* (pp. 1–8). Oxford: Wiley-Blackwell.

Beckett, G., & Slater, T. (2019). *Global perspectives on project-cased language learning, teaching, and assessment: Key approaches, technology tools, and frameworks.* London and New York: Routledge.

Beetham, H., & Sharpe, R. (Eds.). (2019). *Rethinking pedagogy for a digital age: Principle and practices of design.* London: Routledge.

Black, R. W. (2008). *Adolescents and online fan fiction.* New York: Peter Lang.

Blake, R. J., & Zyzik, E. C. (2003). Who's helping whom? Learner/heritage-speakers' networked discussions in Spanish. *Applied Linguistics*, 24(4), 519–544.

Blancette, J. (2012). Participants interaction in asynchronous learning environments: Evaluating interaction analysis methods. *Linguistics and Education*, 23(1), 77–87.

Block, S. (2003). *The social turn in second language acquisition*. Washington, DC: Georgetown University Press.

Bloom, B. S., Engelhart, M. D., Furst, E. J., Hill, W. H., & Krathwohl, D. R. (1956). *Taxonomy of educational objectives: The classification of educational goals. Handbook I: Cognitive domain*. New York: David McKay Company.

Blumenfeld, P. C., Soloway, E., Marx, R. W., Krajcik, J. S., Guzdial, M., & Palinscar, A. (1991). Motivating project-based learning: sustaining the doing, supporting the learning. *Educational Psychologist*, 26(3–4), 369–398.

Blyth, C. (2017). Immersive technologies and language learning. *Foreign Language Annals*, 51(1), 225–232.

Boellstorff, T. (2008). *Coming of age in Second Life: An anthropologist explores the virtually human*. Princeton, NJ: Princeton University Press.

Bomirska, A. (2015, November 12). Interview with Alicja Bomirska. *YouTube* [video]. Retrieved from https://youtu.be/7a_QAkiDRac

Boon, A. (2007). Building bridges: Instant messenger cooperative development. *The Language Teacher*, 31(12), 9–13.

Breen, M. (1984). Process syllabus for the language classroom. In C. J. Brumfit (Ed.), *General English syllabus design ELT document* (Vol. 118 pp. 47–60). Oxford: Pergamon Press.

British Council. (2013). *TBL and PBL: Two learner-centred approaches*. Retrieved from www.teachingenglish.org.uk/article/tbl-pbl-two-learner-centred-approaches

Brooke, S. (2003). Video production in the foreign language classroom: Some practical ideas. *The Internet TESL Journal*, 9(10). Retrieved from http://iteslj.org/Techniques/Brooke-Video.html

Brown, W., & Holtmeier, M. (2013). Machinima: Cinema in a minor or multitudinous key? In J. Ng (Ed.), *Understanding machinima: Essays on filmmaking in virtual worlds* (pp. 3–21). London: Bloomsbury Publishing.

Brumfit, C., Myles, F., Mitchell, R., Johnston, B., & Ford, P. (2005). Language study in higher education and the development of criticality. *International Journal of Applied Linguistics*, 15(2), 145–168.

Bülent, A., & Stoller, F. (2005). Maximizing the benefits of project work in foreign language classrooms. *English Teaching Forum*, 43(4), 10–21.

Burns, A. (2015). Making machinima: Animation, games, and multimodal participation in the media arts. *Learning Media and Technology*, 41(2), 1–20.

Butler, D. (2012). Second Life machinima enhancing the learning of law: Lessons from successful endeavours. *Australasian Journal of Educational Technology*, 28(3), 383–399.

Bygate, M. (1996). Effects of task repetition: Appraising the development of second language learners. In J. Willis & D. Willis (Eds.), *Challenge and change in language teaching* (pp. 136–146). London: Palgrave Macmillan.

Candlin, C. N. (1978). *Teaching of English: Principles and an exercise typology*. London: Langenscheidt-Longman.

Candlin, C. N. (1987). Towards task-based learning. In C. N. Candlin & D. Murphy (Eds.), *Lancaster practical papers in English language education. Vol. 7. Language Learning Tasks* (pp. 5–22). Englewood Cliffs, NJ: Prentice Hall.

Carroll, J., & Cameron, D. (2005, June 16–20). *Machinima: Digital performance and emergent authorship.* Proceedings of Digital Games Research Association (DiGRA) 2005 Conference, Changing Views-Worlds in Play, Vancouver.

Castronova, E. (2007). *Exodus to the virtual world: How online fun is changing reality.* New York: Palgrave Macmillan.

Catak, G. (2010, March 8–10). *Using machinima as an educational model for film, animation, and architecture studies: Machinima 101.* INTED 2010 Proceedings, Valencia, Spain.

Chang, M. M. (2005). Applying self-regulated learning strategies in a web-based instruction: An investigation of motivation perception. *Computer Assisted Language Learning, 18*(3), 217–230.

Chao, C. C. (2015). Rethinking transfer: Learning from CALL teacher education as consequential transition. *Language Learning & Technology, 19*(1), 102–118.

Chapelle, C. A. (2001). *Computer applications in second language acquisition: Foundations for teaching, testing, and research.* Cambridge: Cambridge University Press.

Chapelle, C. A. (2004). Technology and language learning: Expanding methods and agendas. *System, 23*(4), 593–601.

Chapelle, C. A. (2005). Interactionist SLA theory in CALL research. In J. Egbert & G. Petrie (Eds.), *Research perspectives on CALL* (pp. 53–64). Mahwah, NJ: Laurence Erlbaum Associates.

Charara, S. (2016, January 20). Virtual worlds reborn: Can Second Life's second life democratise VR? Project Sansar is a truly virtual world, built by you. *Wareable* [Web Log]. Retrieved from www.wareable.com/vr/second-life-project-sansar-beta-2016

Chun, D. (2017). Research methods for investigating technology for language and culture learning. In C. A. Chapelle & S. Sauro (Eds.), *The handbook of technology and second language teaching and learning* (pp. 393–408). Chicago: John Wiley & Sons.

Coffman, T., & Klinger, M. (2008). Utilising virtual worlds in education: The implications for practice. *International Journal of Social Sciences, 2,* 29–33.

Cohen, L., Manion, L., & Morrison, K. (2007). *Research methods in education.* London: Routledge.

Coleman, J. (1992). Project-based learning, transferable skills, information technology and video. *The Language Learning Journal, 5*(1), 35–37.

Collins, C. M. (2008). Essayish: Traditional learning spaces in virtual worlds. *Fleep's Deep Thoughts* [blog]. Retrieved from www.fleeptuque.com/blog/2008/04/essayish-traditional-learning-spaces-in-virtual-worlds/

Collins, F., & McCormick, D. (2011). Digital selves: Lessons from Second Life. In T. Bastiaens & M. Ebner (Eds.), *Proceedings of world conference on educational multimedia, hypermedia and telecommunications* (pp. 3405–3411). Orland, FL: AACE.

Compton, L. K. L. (2007). The impact of content and context on international teaching assistants' willingness to communicate in the language classroom. *TESL EJ, 10*(4). Retrieved from http://tesl-ej.org/ej40/a2.html

Compton, L. K. L. (2009). Preparing language teachers to teach language online: A look at skills, roles, and responsibilities. *Computer Assisted Language Learning, 22*(1), 73–99.

Conkey, C. A. (2010). *Machinima and video-based soft skills training* (PhD dissertation). College of Sciences, University of Central Florida, Orlando, FL.

Constantinides, M. (2012). Making a machinima in Second Life – in 19 Steps. *TEFL Matters, Teaching, Teacher Education, New Technology* [blog]. Retrieved from http://marisaconstantinides.edublogs.org/?s=machinevo

Constantinides, M. (2014, March 23). Interview with Marisa Constantinides. *YouTube* [video]. Retrieved from https://youtu.be/yrcOPbRX-pU

Corrigan, S. (2014). Learn it town ESL/EFL students: How to improve pronunciation through performance. *YouTube* [video]. Retrieved from https://youtu.be/Ib2aQKanXKQ

Cosh, J. (1999). Peer observation: A reflective model. *ELT Journal, 53*(1), 22–27.

Council of Europe. (2001). *Common European framework of reference for languages: Learning, teaching, assessment.* Cambridge: Cambridge University Press.

Creswell, J. W. (2014). *A concise introduction to mixed methods research.* Thousand Oaks, CA: Sage Publications.

Cuban, L. (1993). Computers meet classrooms: Classroom wins. *Teachers College Record, 95*(2), 85–210.

Cuban, L. (2003). *Oversold and underused: Computers in the classroom.* Cambridge: Harvard University Press.

Dalton-Puffer, C., Nikula, T., & Smit, U. (Eds.). (2010). *Language use and language learning in CLIL classrooms.* Amsterdam, The Netherlands: John Benjamins.

Dalton-Puffer, C., & Smit, U. (Eds.). (2007). *Critical perspectives in CLIL classroom discourse.* Frankfurt: Peter Lang.

Davies, G., Otto, S., & Rüschoff, B. (2013). Historical perspectives on CALL. In M. Thomas & H. Reinders (Eds.), *Contemporary computer-assisted language learning* (pp. 19–38). London: Bloomsbury.

Debski, R. (2006). Theory and practice in teaching project-oriented CALL. In P. Hubbard & M. Levy (Eds.), *Teacher education in CALL* (pp. 99–115). Amsterdam: John Benjamins.

De Boer, P. (2015, September 2). Patrick de Boer interviewed by Christel Schneider. *YouTube* [video]. Retrieved from https://youtu.be/HAbgWoNRz1A

De Jong Derrington, M. (2013). Second language acquisition by immersive and collaborative task-based learning in a virtual world. In M. Childs & A. Peachey (Eds.), *Understanding learning in virtual worlds, human-computer interaction* (pp. 135–163). London: Springer.

Dede, C. (2004). *Design-based research strategies for studying situated learning in MUVE.* Paper presented at the 2004 International Conference on Learning Sciences, Mahwah, NJ.

Delgarno, B., & Lee, M. J. W. (2010). What are the learning affordances of 3-D virtual environments? *British Journal of Educational Technology, 41*(1), 10–32.

Desiatova, L. (2008). Project-based learning as CLIL approach to teaching language. *Humanising Language Teaching, 10*(5). Retrieved from www.hltmag.co.uk/oct08/sart02.htm

Deutschmann, M., & Panichi, L. (2009). Instructional design, teacher practice and learner autonomy. In J. Molka-Danielsen & M. Deutschmann (Eds.), *Learning and teaching in the virtual world of Second Life* (pp. 27–31). Trondheim: Tapir Academic Press.

Deutschmann, M., Panichi, L., & Molka-Danielsson, J. (2009). Designing oral participation in Second Life: A comparative study of two language proficiency courses. *ReCALL, 21*(2), 206–226.

Dewey, J. (1959). My pedagogic creed. In M. Dworkin (Ed.), *Dewey on education* (pp. 19–32). New York: Columbia University.

Dewey, J. (2011). *Democracy and education*. Milton Keynes: Simon and Brown.

Donato, R. (1994). Collective scaffolding in second language learning. In J. P. Lantolf & G. Appel (Eds.), *Vygotskian approaches to second language research* (pp. 33–56). Norwood, NJ: Ablex.

Dooly, M., & Sadler, R. (2016). Becoming little scientists: Technologically-enhanced project-based language learning. *Language Learning & Technology, 20*(1), 54–78.

Doughty, C. J., & Long, M. H. (2003). Optimal psycholinguistic environments for distance foreign language learning. *Language, Learning & Technology, 7*(3), 50–80.

Downes, S. (2006). Learning networks and connective knowledge. *Instructional Technology Forum*, Paper 92. Retrieved from http://it.coe.uga.edu/itforum/paper92/paper92.html

Drax, B. (2015, December 10). Tips for machinima makers from the expert. Bernhard Drax at MachinEVO 2014. *YouTube* [video]. Retrieved from https://youtu.be/ORfJJeWp4dg

Dreher, N., & Dreher, H. (2009, September 23–25). Using machinima documentary and virtual environments to reinvigorate student's learning in systems development. In *Conference Proceedings: Interactive Computer Aided Learning* (pp. 445–453). Villach, Austria: ICL2009.

Drigas, A. S., & Ioannidou, R. E. (2013). ICTs in special education: A review. *WSKS, 278*, 357–364.

Ducate, L., & Lomicka, L. (2008). Adventures in the blogosphere: From blog readers to blog writers. *Computer Assisted Language Learning, 21*, 9–28.

Duff, P. (1993). Tasks and interlanguage performance: An SLA research perspective. In G. Crookes & S. M. Gass (Eds.), *Tasks and language learning* (pp. 57–95). Clevedon: Multilingual Matters.

Edirisingha, P., Nie, M., Pluciennik, M., & Young, R. (2009). Socialisation for learning at a distance in a 3D multi-user virtual environment. *British Journal of Educational Technology, 40*(3), 458–479.

Egbert, J. L. (2006). The end of CALL and how to achieve it. *Teaching English with Technology: A Journal for Teachers of English, 6*(2), 1–5.

Egbert, J. L., Paulus, T. M., & Nakamichi, Y. (2002). The impact of CALL instruction on classroom computer use: A foundation for rethinking technology in teacher education. *Language, Learning & Technology, 6*(3), 108–126.

Egbert, J. L., Shahrokni, S. A., Zhang, X., Yahia, I. A., Borysenko, N., Mohamed, A. F. S., . . . Ezeh, C. (2018). Planning for future enquiry: Gaps in the CALL research. *International Journal of Computer-Assisted Language Learning and Teaching, 8*(2), 1–28.

Ellis, R. (2003). *Task-based language learning and Teaching*. Oxford: Oxford University Press.

Ellis, R. (2005a). *Instructed second language acquisition: A literature review*. Auckland, New Zealand: Ministry of Education.

Ellis, R. (2005b). Planning and task-based performance. In R. Ellis (Ed.), *Planning and task performance in a second language* (Vol. 11, pp. 3–36). Amsterdam, The Netherlands: John Benjamins.

Ellis, R. (2009). Task-based language teaching: Sorting out the misunderstandings. *International Journal of Applied Linguistics*, 19(3), 221–246.

Ellis, R. (2010). Foreword. In M. Thomas & H. Reinders (Eds.), *Task-based language learning and teaching with technology* (pp. xvi–xviii). London: Continuum.

Ellis, R. (2015). Epilogue. In M. Thomas & H. Reinders (Eds.), *Contemporary task-based language teaching in Asia* (pp. 381–384). London and New York: Bloomsbury.

Euroversity. (2014). Case studies. *pbworks* [Web]. Retrieved from http://euroversity.pbworks.com/w/page/90489107/Case%20studies

Euroversity Project. (2014). *Lifelong learning programme: Education and culture DG* [Web]. Retrieved from www.euroversity.eu

Evans-Andris, M. (1995). Barrier to computer integration: Micro-interaction among computer co-ordinators and classroom teachers in elementary schools. *Journal of Research on Computing in Education*, 28(1), 29–45.

Eysenbach, G., & Till, J. E. (2001). Ethical issues in qualitative research on internet communities. *BMJ 2001* [Web]. Retrieved from www.bmj.com/content/323/7321/1103.full

Falconer, L. (2011). *Metaxis: The transition between worlds and the consequences for education*. Presented at Innovative Research in Virtual Worlds. Retrieved from https://uwe-repository.worktribe.com/output/957720

Farley, H. (2016). The reality of authentic learning in virtual worlds. In M. J. W. Lee, B. Dalgarno, & B. Tynan (Eds.), *Learning in virtual worlds: Research and applications* (pp. 129–149). Athabasca: Athabasca University Press.

Farouck, I. (2016). A project-based language learning model for improving the willingness to communicate of EFL students. *Systemics, Cybernetics and Informatics*, 14(2), 11–18.

Fitze, M., & McGarrell, H. M. (2008). Teacher language in ESL face-to-face and written electronic discussions. *TESL-EJ*, 12(2), 1–24.

Flavin, M. (2017). *Disruptive technology enhanced learning*. London: Palgrave Macmillan.

Fosk, K. (2011). Machinima is growing up. *Journal of Visual Culture*, 10(1), 25–30.

Foster, P., & Skehan, P. (1996). The influence of planning and focus of planning on second language performance. *Studies in Second Language Acquisition, 18*, 299–323.

Fuchs, C. (2006). Exploring German preservice teachers' electronic and professional literacy skills. *ReCALL*, 18(2), 174–192.

Fujimoto, R. (2010). Educational machinima: Japanese American liberators at Dachau. In D. Gibson & B. Dodge (Eds.), *Proceedings of society for information technology, teacher education international conference* (pp. 3670–3673). Chesapeake, VA: AACE.

Galani, H. (2015, November 7). The usefulness of tutorials and language machinima in the flipped TEFL/EAP Classroom (with interdisciplinary benefits in education). In *8th international conference in open & distance learning* (pp. 111–120). Athens.

Galani, H. (2016a, April 1). Helena Galani in conversation with Christel Schneider. *YouTube* [video]. Retrieved from https://youtu.be/9pJFqLiqTgs

Galani, H. (2016b, January 8). Presentation of EVOViLLAGE 2016 at the nonprofit commons meeting in SL moderated by Joyce Bettencourt. *YouTube* [video]. Retrieved from https://youtu.be/t7bB4MQJ6vs

Galloway, J. P. (1997). How teachers use and learn to use computers. In *Technology and teacher education annual (1996): Proceedings of SITE, 96* (pp. 857–859). Norfolk, VA: Association for the Advancement of Computing.

Garrett, N. (2009). Computer-assisted language learning trends and issues revisited: Integrating innovation. *The Modern Language Journal, 93*(1), 719–740.

Garrison, D. R., Anderson, T., & Archer, W. (2000). Critical inquiry in a textbased environment: Computer conferencing in higher education model. *The Internet and Higher Education, 2*(2–3), 87–105.

Gass, S. M. (1997). *Input, interaction and the second language learner*. Mahwah, NJ: Lawrence Erlbaum Associates.

Gass, S. M. (2005). Input and interaction. In C. Doughty & M. Long (Eds.), *The handbook of second language acquisition* (pp. 224–255). Cornwall: Blackwell Publishing.

Gass, S. M., & Varonis, E. M. (1985). Non-native/non-native conversations: A model for negotiation of meaning. *Applied Linguistics, 6*(1), 71–90.

Gawliczek, P., & Poczekalewsicz, D. (2014). Distance education for the Polish armed forces' needs. *JADLET Journal of Advanced Distributed Learning Technology, 2*(6), 105–111.

Gee, J. P. (2003). *What video games have to teach us about learning and literacy*. New York: Palgrave Macmillan.

Gee, J. P. (2004). *Situated language and learning: A critique of traditional schooling*. London: Routledge.

Giroux, H. (2014). *Neoliberalism's war on higher education*. Chicago: Haymarket.

Girvan, C., & Savage, T. (2011). Ethical considerations for educational research in virtual world. *Interactive Learning Environments, 20*(3), 239–251.

Goffman, E. (1990). *The presentation of self in everyday life*. London: Penguin.

González-Lloret, M. (2017). Technology for task-based language teaching. In C. Chapelle & S. Sauro (Eds.), *The handbook of technology in second language teaching and learning* (pp. 234–247). Malden, MA: Wiley-Blackwell.

González-Lloret, M., & Ortega, L., (Eds.). (2014). *Technology-mediated TBLT: Researching technology and tasks*. Amsterdam, The Netherlands and Philadelphia, PA: John Benjamins.

Grant, S. (2017). Implementing project-based language teaching in an Asian context: A university EAP writing course case study from Macau. *Asian Journal of Second and Foreign Language Education, 2*(4). https://doi.org/10.1186/s40862-017-0027-x

Gras-Velazquez, A. (Ed.). (2019). *Project-based learning in second language acquisition: Building communities of practice in higher education*. London and New York: Routledge.

Gray, J. (2019). Critical language teacher education? In S. Walsh & S. Mann (Eds.), *The Routledge handbook of English language teacher education*. Abingdon, UK: Routledge.

Gregory, B., Gregory, S., & Gregory, M. (2013). *Machinima for immersive and authentic learning in higher education.* 30th ASCILITE Conference Proceedings, Macquarie University, Sydney.

Gregory, S., Lee, M., Dalgarno, B., & Tynan, B. (Eds.). (2016). *Learning in virtual worlds: Research and applications.* Athabasca, Canada: Athabasca University Press.

Guo, Y. (2006). Project-based English as a foreign language education in China: Perspectives and issues. In G. Beckett & P. Miller (Eds.), *Project-based second and foreign language education* (pp. 143–158). Greenwich, CT: Information Age Publishing.

Haase, E. (2015, August 6). Gespräch mit Dr. Ellinor Haase. *YouTube* [video]. Retrieved from https://youtu.be/8Y-5f-WYHFQ

Hafner, C., & Miller, L. (2011). Fostering learner autonomy in English for science: A collaborative digital video project in a technological learning environment. *Language Learning & Technology, 15*(3), 68–86.

Hall, A. N., & Velez-Colby, F. (2011). *Inclusive education: Enhancing the student experience through simple learning technologies.* Retrieved from www.ece.salford.ac.uk/programmes-2011/papers/paper_58.pdf

Hampel, R. (2006). Rethinking task design for the digital age: A framework for language teaching and learning in a synchronous online environment. *ReCALL, 18*(1), 105–121.

Hampel, R., & Stickler, U. (2005). New skills for a new classroom: Training teachers to teach languages. *Computer Assisted Language Learning, 18*(4), 311–326.

Hanaoka, O. (2007). Output, noticing, and learning: An investigation into the role of spontaneous attention to form in a four-stage writing task. *Language Teaching Research, 11*(4), 459–479.

Hanaoka, O., & Izumi, S. (2012). Noticing and uptake: Addressing pre-articulated covert problems in L2 writing. *Journal of Second Language Writing, 21*(4), 332–347.

Hancock, H. (2011). Machinima: Limited, ghettoized, and spectacularly promising. *Journal of Visual Culture* [Web]. Retrieved from http://vcu.sagepub.com/content/10/1/31

Hancock, H., & Ingram, J. (2007). *Machinima for dummies.* Indianapolis, IN: Wiley Publishing.

Hanson-Smith, E. (2006). Communities of practice for pre- and in-service teacher education. In P. Hubbard & M. Levy (Eds.), *Teacher education in CALL* (pp. 301–315). Amsterdam, The Netherlands: John Benjamins.

Harwood, T. (2011). Towards a manifesto for machinima. *Journal of Visual Culture, 10*(1), 6–12.

Harwood, T. (2013). Machinima as a learning tool. *Digital Creativity, 24*(3), 168–181.

Harwood, T. (2014). Final report. *MACHINIMA Investigating the Cultural Values* [blog]. Retrieved from www.machinima.dmu.ac.uk/project-report

Healey, M., & Jenkins, A. (2000). Kolb's experiential learning theory and its application in geography in higher education. *Journal of Geography, 99*(5), 185–195.

Hegelheimer, V. (2006). When the technology course is required. In M. Levy & P. Hubbard (Eds.), *Teacher education in CALL* (pp. 117–133). Philadelphia, PA: John Benjamins.

Henderson, M., Huang, H., & Grant, S. (2009). The impact of Chinese language lessons in a virtual world on university students' self-efficacy belief. *Australasian Journal of Educational Technology, 28*(3), 400–419.

Heo, H., Lim, K., & Kim, Y. (2010). Exploratory study on the patterns of online interaction and knowledge co-construction in project-based learning. *Computers & Education, 55*(3), 1383–1392.

Herrington, J., & Oliver, R. (1999). Using situated learning and multimedia to investigate higher-order thinking. *Journal of Educational Multimedia and Hypermedia, 8*(4), 401–422.

Hew, K. F., & Cheung, W. S. (2010). Use of three-dimensional (3-D) immersive virtual worlds in K-12 and higher education settings: A review of the research. *British Journal of Educational Technology, 41*(1), 33–55.

Hoffman, S. (2006). How to write a case study. *Marketing communications Inc. Strategic Business and Technology Writing* [Web]. Retrieved from www.hoffmanmarcom.com/docs/How-to-write-a-case-study.pdf

Holec, H. (1979). *Autonomy and foreign language learning*. Strasbourg: Council of Europe.

Hong, K. H. (2010). CALL teacher education as an impetus for L2 teachers in integrating technology. *ReCALL, 22*(1), 53–69.

Hsiao, H.-C. (2014). *Using machinima as a method for digital color practice and narrative creation*. Retrieved from www.iafor.org/offprints/acset2013-offprints/ACSET2013_offprint_0531.pdf

Hsu, H. (2015). The effect of task planning on L2 performance and L2 development in text-based synchronous computer-mediated communication. *Applied Linguistics*. doi:10.1093/applin/amv032

Huang, H.-M., & Liang, S.-S. (2018). An analysis of learners' intentions toward virtual reality learning based on constructivist and technology acceptance approaches. *International Review of Research in Open and Distributed Learning, 19*(1), 91–115.

Hubbard, P. (2004). Learner training for effective use of CALL. In S. Fotos & C. Browne (Eds.), *New perspectives on CALL for second language classrooms* (pp. 45–67). Mahwah, NJ: Lawrence Erlbaum.

Hubbard, P. (2008). CALL and the future of language teacher education. *CALICO Journal, 25*(2), 175–188.

Hubbard, P., & Levy, M. (2006). *Teacher education in CALL*. Amsterdam, The Netherlands: John Benjamins.

Hutchinson, T. (1991). *Introduction to project work*. Oxford: Oxford University Press.

Ide, N. M. (1987). Computers and the humanities courses: Philosophical bases and approach. *Computers and Humanities, 21*(4), 209–215.

Inman, C., Wright, V., & Hartman, J. A. (2010). Use of Second Life in K-12 and higher education: A review of the research. *Journal of Online Interactive Learning, 9*(1), 44–63.

Intercultural Development Research Association. (2002). *IDRA newsletter*. Retrieved from www.idra.org/IDRA_Newsletter/March_2002/Self_Renewing_Schools_Access_Equity_and_Excellence/

Iskold, L. V. (2003). Building on success, learning from mistakes: Implications for the future. *Computer Assisted Language Learning, 16*(4), 295–328.

Izumi, S. (2002). Output, input enhancement, and the noticing hypothesis. *Studies in Second Language Acquisition, 24*(4), 541–577.

Jauregi, K., & Canto, S. (2012). Impact of native-nonnative speaker interaction through video-web communication and Second Life on students' intercultural communicative competence. In *Proceedings of EUROCALL 2012 conference* (pp. 151–155). Dublin: Research-Publishing.Net.

Jauregi, K., Canto, S., De Graaff, R., Koenraad, T., & Moonen, M. (2011). Verbal interaction in Second Life: Towards a pedagogic framework for task design. *Computer Assisted Language Learning, 24*(1), 77–101.

Johannsson, R. (2003, September 22–24). *Methodologies in housing research.* A keynote speech at the International conference organised by the Royal Institute of Technology in cooperation with the International Association of People – Environment Studies, Stockholm.

Johnson, P., & Pettit, D. (2012). *Machinima: The art and practice of virtual filmmaking.* Jefferson, NC: McFarland.

Johnson, P., & Runo, R. (2011). *The fantastic and the furious: Capturing moments through machinima.* Retrieved from http://business.treet.tv/shows/bpeducation/episodes/bpe2011-051

Jones, C., & Munro, C. (2009). Using machinima to promote computer science study. In G. Weber & P. Calder (Eds.), ACS. Proc. Tenth Australasian User Interface Conference (AUIC 2009), Wellington, New Zealand. *CRPIT, 93,* 21–29.

Kadel, R. (2005). How teacher attitudes affect technology integration. *Learning and Leading with Technology, 32*(5), 34–35.

Kalyvioti, K., & Mikropoulos, T. A. (2012). Memory performance of dyslexic adults in virtual environments. *Procedia Computer Science, 14,* 410–418.

Karmali, L. (2015, November 3). *World of warcraft subscriber numbers fall to 5.5 million* [Web]. Retrieved from www.ign.com/articles/2015/11/03/world-of-warcraft-subscriber-numbers-fall-to-55-million

Kelland, M., Morris, D., & Lloyd, D. (2005). *Machinima: Making animated movies in 3D virtual environments.* Lewes, East Sussex: The ILEX Press Ltd.

Kelm, O. R. (1992). The use of synchronous computer networks in second language instruction: A preliminary report. *Foreign Language Annals, 25,* 441–445.

Kenning, J. M. (2007). *ICT and language learning: From print to mobile learning.* London: Palgrave Macmillan.

Kern, R. G. (2006). Perspectives on technology in learning and teaching languages. *TESOL Quarterly, 40*(1), 183–210.

Kern, R. G., Ware, P., & Warschauer, M. (2004). Crossing frontiers: New directions in online pedagogy and research. *Annual Review of Applied Linguistics, 24,* 243–260.

Keskitalo, T., Pyykkö, E., & Roukamo, H. (2011). Exploring the meaningful learning of students in Second Life. *Educational Technology & Society, 14*(1), 16–26.

Kessler, G. (2006). Assessing CALL teacher training: What are we doing and what could we do better? In P. Hubbard & M. Levy (Eds.), *Teacher education in CALL* (pp. 23–42). Amsterdam, The Netherlands and Philadelphia, PA: John Benjamins.

Kessler, G. (2007). Formal and informal CALL preparation and teacher attitude toward technology. *Computer Assisted Language Learning, 20*(2), 173–188.

Kessler, G., & Plakans, L. (2008). Does teachers' confidence with CALL equal innovative and integrated use? *Computer Assisted Language Learning, 21*(3), 269–282.

Kim, S. H., Lee, J., & Thomas, M. (2012). Between purpose and method: A review of educational research on 3D Virtual Worlds. *Journal of Virtual Worlds Research, 5*(1), 1–18.

Kirschner, F. (2005, November). Machinima, from subculture to a genre of its own. *Machinimag: The Online Machinima Magazine* [blog]. Retrieved from www.zeitbrand.de/machiniBlog/WhatIsMachinima.html

Kirschner, F. (2011). Machinima's promise. *Journal of Visual Culture, 10*(1), 19–24.

Kluge, S., & Riley, L. (2008). Teaching in virtual worlds: Opportunities and challenges. *Issues in Informing Science and Information Technology, 5*, 127–135.

Koenraad, A. L. M. (2005, September 21–23). *Developing network-based language learning & teaching in education and teacher training: The MICALL project*. Paper presented at the International Conference on Task Based Language Teaching, Leuven University.

Koenraad, T. (2013). Exploring teacher roles in 3D virtual worlds projects in modern language and teacher education. In R. McBride & M. Searson (Eds.), *Proceedings of society for information technology & teacher education international conference* (pp. 3514–3521). New Orleans: SITE.

Kolaitis, M., Mahoney, M. A., Pomann, H., & Hubbard, P. (2006). Training ourselves to train our students for CALL. In P. Hubbard & M. Levy (Eds.), *Teacher education in CALL* (pp. 317–332). Amsterdam, The Netherlands: John Benjamins.

Kotti, D. (2008). Experiential learning from theory to practice. *Adult Education, 13*, 35–41.

Kozinets, R. V. (1998). On netnography: Initial reflections on consumer research investigations of cyberculture. *Advances in Consumer Research, 25*(1), 366–371.

Kozinets, R. V. (2010). *Netnography: Doing ethnographic research online*. Los Angeles, CA and London: Sage Publications.

Krashen, S. D. (1981). *Second language acquisition and second language learning*. Oxford: Pergamon.

Krashen, S. D. (1987). *Principles and practice in second language acquisition*. London: Prentice-Hall International.

Kriwas, S. (1999). *Environmental education: A handbook for educators*. Athens: Ministry of Education.

Lacasa, P., Cortes, S., Martinez-Borda, R., & Mendez, L. (2012). Machinima as a way of looking for multimodal literacies. In J. Wimmer, K. Mitgutsch, & H. Rosentingl (Eds.), *Applied playfulness. Proceedings of the Vienna Games Conference 2011: Future and Reality of Gaming* (pp. 37–54). Vienna: Braumueller Verlag.

Lacasa, P., Martinez, R., & Mendez, L. (2011). *Games and machinima in adolescents' classrooms*. Retrieved from http://citeseerx.ist.psu.edu/viewdoc/download?doi=10.1.1.224.8198&rep=rep1&type=pdf

Lai, C., & Li, G. F. (2011). Technology and task-based language teaching: A critical review. *CALICO Journal, 28*(2), 498–521.

Lamy, M.-N. (2006). Interactive task design: Metachat and the whole learner. In M. del Pilar & M. Garcia (Eds.), *Investigating tasks in formal language learning* (pp. 242–264). Clevedon: Multilingual Matters.

Lansiquot, R., & Rosalia, C. (2008). Second languages, virtual worlds: Living second lives. In J. Luca & E. Weippl (Eds.), *Proceedings of ED-MEDIA 2008- World Conference on Educational Multimedia, Hypermedia & Telecommunications* (pp. 2660–2664). Vienna, Austria: Association for the Advancement of Computing in Education (AACE). Retrieved from www.learntechlib.org/primary/p/28734/

Lave, J., & Wenger, E. (1991). *Situated learning: Legitimate peripheral participation*. Cambridge, UK: Cambridge University Press.

Leahy, C. (2006). Introducing ICT to teachers of an institution-side language programme: Principal considerations. *The JALT CALL Journal*, 2(3), 3–14.

Leaver, B. L., & Willis, J. (Eds.). (2004). *Task-based instruction in foreign language education: Practices and programs*. Washington, DC: Georgetown University Press.

Leitão, D. K., & Gomes, L. G. (2012). Machinima and ethnographic research. *VIBRANT*, 9(2), 293–313.

Leominster, S. (2013). Why have virtual worlds declined? *The Metaverse Tribune* [blog]. Retrieved from http://metaversetribune.com/2013/05/15/why-have-virtual-worlds-declined/

Levy, M. (2009). Technologies in use for second language learning. *The Modern Language Journal*, 93, 769–782.

Levy, M., & Stockwell, G. (2006). *CALL dimensions: Options and issues in computer-assisted language learning*. New York: Routledge.

Lewis, T. (2006). When teaching is learning: A personal account of learning to teach online. *CALICO Journal*, 23(3), 581–600.

Lim, K. Y. T. (2009). The six learnings of Second Life: A framework for designing curricular interventions in-world. *Journal of Virtual Worlds Research. Pedagogy, Education and Innovation in 3-D Virtual Worlds*, 2(1) [Web]. Retrieved from https://journals.tdl.org/jvwr/index.php/jvwr/article/view/424/466

Linden Lab. (2011). *Snapshot and machinima policy* [Web]. Retrieved from http://wiki.secondlife.com/wiki/Linden_Lab_Official:Snapshot_and_machinima_policy

Linden Lab. (2013). *Second Life celebrates 10 year anniversary*. Retrieved from http://lindenlab.com/releases/second-life-celebrates-10-year-anniversary

Lochana, M., & Deb, G. (2006). Task based teaching: Learning English without tears. *Asian EFL Journal*, 8(3), 140–164.

Lombardi, M. (2007). *Authentic learning for the 21st century: An overview*. Retrieved from https://library.educause.edu/resources/2007/1/authentic-learning-for-the-21st-century-an-overview

Long, M. H. (1985). A role for instruction in second language acquisition: Task-based language teaching. In K. Hyltenstam & M. Pienemann (Eds.), *Modelling and assessing second language acquisition* (pp. 77–79). Clevedon: Multilingual Matters.

Long, M. H. (1990). Task, group and task-group interactions. In S. Anivan (Ed.), *Language teaching methodology for the nineties* (pp. 31–50). Singapore: Regional English Language Centre, Singapore University Press.

Lowood, H. (2011). Video capture: Machinima, documentation, and the history of virtual worlds. In H. Lowood & M. Nitsche (Eds.), *The machinima reader* (pp. 3–22). Cambridge, MA: Institute of Technology, The MIT Press.

Lowood, H., & Nitsche, M. (Eds.) (2011). *The machinima reader*. Cambridge, MA: The MIT Press, Institute of Technology.

Lu, L. (2011). Art education avatars in action: Preparing art teachers for learning and teaching in a virtual age. *Journal of Technology and Teacher Education, 19*(3), 287–301.

Luo, H., & Yang, C. (2018). Twenty years of telecollaborative practice: Implications for teaching Chinese as a foreign language. *Computer Assisted Language Learning, 31*(5), 546–571.

MachinEVO. (2013). *Filmfestival MachinEVO 2013* [pbwiki]. Retrieved from http://machinevo.pbworks.com/w/page/63642403/Film%20Festival%20MachinEVO%202013

Machinima. (n.d.). In *Wikipedia.org*. Retrieved from https://en.wikipedia.org/wiki/Machinima

Machinima Expo. (2015). *The machinima expo: The world's only virtual animation festival* [Web]. Retrieved from http://machinima-expo.com/v3/about-the-expo/who-we-are/

Makuch, E. (2014, February 26). Minecraft passes 100 million registered users. *Gamespot GDC 2016* [Web]. Retrieved from www.gamespot.com/articles/minecraft-passes-100-million-registered-users-14-3-million-sales-on-pc/1100-6417972/

Mann, S. (2005). The language teacher's development. *Language Teaching, 38*, 103–118.

Marino, P. (2004). *3D game-based filmmaking: The art of machinima*. Scottsdale, AZ: Paraglyph Press.

Marsh, D. (2002). *Content and language integrated learning: The European dimension actions, trends and foresight potential*. Retrieved from http://europa.eu.int/comm/education/languages/index/html

Matthew, A., & Butler, D. (2017). Narrative, machinima and cognitive realism: Constructing an authentic real-world learning experience for law students. *Australasian Journal of Educational Technology, 33*(1), 148–162.

Mawer, M. (2014, July 30). Observational practice in virtual worlds: Revisiting and expanding the methodological discussion. *International Journal of Social Research Methodology* [Web]. Retrieved from www.tandfonline.com/doi/abs/10.1080/13645579.2014.936738#.VKu_9yuG_To

Meissl-Egghart, G. (2014, May 23). Gerhilde Meissl-Egghart interviewed by Christel Schneider. *YouTube* [video]. Retrieved from https://youtu.be/KURArhyCJvo

Merleau-Ponty, M. (1968). *The visible and the invisible* (Claude Lefort, Ed. and Alphonso Lingis, Trans.). Evanston, IL: Northwestern University.

Meskill, C., Anthony, N., Hilliker-VanStrander, S., Tseng, C. H., & You, J. (2006). Expert-novice teacher mentoring in language learning technology. In P. Hubbard & M. Levy (Eds.), *Teacher education in CALL* (pp. 283–291). Amsterdam, The Netherlands and Philadelphia, PA: John Benjamins.

Meyers, E. M. (2014, March 4–7). Using machinima as cultural probes to study communication in children's virtual worlds: An exploratory approach. In *Breaking down the walls: Culture-context – Computing, iConference Proceedings* (pp. 669–674). Berlin.

Middleton, A. J., & Mather, R. (2008). Machinima interventions: Innovative approaches to immersive virtual world curriculum integration. *ALT-J, Research in Learning Technology, 16*(3), 207–220.

Milbrath, Y., & Kinzie, M. (2000). Computer technology training for prospective teachers: Computer attitudes and perceived self-efficacy. *Journal of Technology and Teacher Education, 8*(4), 373–396.

Miles, M. B., & Huberman, A. M. (1994). *Qualitative data analysis: An expanded sourcebook* (2nd ed.). Thousand Oaks, CA, London, and New Delhi: Sage Publications.

Miller, C., & Conrad, K. (2009, November 28). Social presence: An introduction. *YouTube* [video]. Retrieved from http://youtu.be/lJVLHAA90jc

Mitchell, P., Parson, S., & Leonard, A. (2006). Virtual environments for social skills training: Comments from two adolescents with autistic spectrum disorder. *Computers & Education, 47*, 186–206.

Mitchell, R. (2010). Policy and practice in foreign language education: Case studies in three European settings. *European Journal of Language Policy, 2*(2), 151–180.

Mitchell, R., & Myles, F. (2019). Learning French in the UK setting: Policy, classroom engagement and attainable learning outcomes. *Journal of Applied Language Studies, 13*(1), 69–93.

Molka-Danielsen, J. (2009). The new learning and teaching environment. In M. Deutschmann & L. Panichi (Eds.), *Instructional design, teacher practice and learner autonomy* (pp. 13–25). Trondheim: Tapir Academic Press.

Molka-Danielsen, J., & Deutschmann, M. (2009). *Learning and teaching in the virtual world of second life*. Trondheim: Tapir Academic Press.

Monsour, F. (2003). Mentoring to develop and retain new teachers. *Kappa Delta Pi Record, 39*(3), 134–135.

Montague, N. S. (1997). Critical components for dual language programs. *Bilingual Research Journal, 21*(4), 334–342.

Morozov, A. (2008). Machinima learning: Prospects for teaching and learning digital literacy skills through virtual filmmaking. *World Conference on Educational Multimedia, Hypermedia and Telecommunications, 2008*(1), 5898–5907.

Moschini, E. (2010). The Second Life researcher toolkit: An exploration of inworld tools, methods and approaches for researching educational projects in Second Life. In N. Peachey, J. Gillen, D. Livingstone, & S. Smith-Robbins (Eds.), *Researching learning in virtual worlds* (pp. 37–49). London: Springer.

Mosier, G. G., Bradley-Levine, J., & Perkins, T. (2016). Students' perceptions of project-based learning within the New Tech School model. *International Journal of Education Reform, 25*(1), 2–15.

Motteram, G., Slaouti, D., & Onat-Stelma, Z. (2013). Second language teacher education for CALL: An alignment of practice and theory. In M. Thomas, H. Reinders, & M. Warschauer (Eds.), *Contemporary computer-assisted language learning* (pp. 55–71). London: Bloomsbury.

Moviestorm (2011). *Using animation in schools: A practical handbook for teachers* [Web]. Retrieved from http://cloud.moviestorm.co.uk/edu/Using%20Animation%20in%20Schools%20-%20A%20practical%20handbook%20for%20teachers.pdf

Muldoon, N., & Kofoed, J. (2009). Second Life machinima: Creating new opportunities for curriculum and instruction. In G. Siemens & C. Fulford

(Eds.), *Proceedings of world conference on educational multimedia, hyperme-dia and telecommunications* (pp. 2243–2252). Chesapeake, VA.

Muldoon, N., & Kofoed, J. (2011). Exploring the affordances of Second Life machinima as an anchor for classroom-based apprenticeship. *International Journal on E-Learning*, *10*(4), 419–439.

Mumtaz, S. (2000). Factors affecting teachers' use of information and communi-cations technology: A review of the literature. *Journal of Information Technol-ogy for Teacher Education*, *9*(3), 319–342.

Murray, L. (1998). CALL and Web training with teacher self-empowerment: A departmental and long-term approach. *Computers & Education*, *31*, 17–23.

Myers, H. (2014, September 1). Conversation with Helen Myers at EuroCALL 2014. *YouTube* [video]. Retrieved from https://youtu.be/iDhdcU-Zi1A

Navés, T. (2002). Successful CLIL programmes. In G. Langé & P. Bertaux (Eds.), *The CLIL professional development course* (pp. 93–102). Milan: Min-istero della' Istruzione della' Università e della Ricerca. Direzione Region-ale per la Lombardia. New Jersey State Dept. of Education.

Navés, T., & Muñoz, C. (1999). Implementation of CLIL in Spain. In D. Marsh & G. Langé (Eds.), *Implementing content and language integrated learning: A research-driven TIE CLIL foundation course reader* (pp. 145–158). Jyväskylä, Finland: Continuing Education Centre, University of Jyväskylä on behalf of TIE- CLIL (European Lingua Project).

Newton, J. (1991). *Negotiation: Negotiating what?* Paper given at SEAMEO Conference on Second Language Acquisition and the Second/Foreign Lan-guage Classroom, RELC, Singapore.

Ng, J. (Ed.). (2013). *Understanding machinima: Essays on filmmaking in virtual worlds*. London: Bloomsbury.

Ng, J., & Barrett, J. (2013). A pedagogy of craft: Teaching culture analysis with machinima. In J. Ng (Ed.), *Understanding machinima: Essays on filmmaking in virtual worlds* (pp. 227–244). New York: Bloomsbury Academic.

Novelli, B., & McQueen, B. (2014, May 23). Barbara Novelli interview with Carol Rainbow. *YouTube* [video]. Retrieved from https://youtu.be/ADbK-zWYvqo

Nowak, A. (2015, August 17). Ann Nowak interviewed by Christel Schneider. *YouTube* [video]. Retrieved from https://youtu.be/DBdP_G0AJXs.

NTTI. (n.d.). Why use video in the classroom? National teacher training institute transforming the way teachers teach and students learn. *Thirteen-Ed Online* [online]. Retrieved from www.thirteen.org/edonline/ntti/resources/video1.html

Numrich, C. (1989). *Cognitive strategies for integrating ESL and content area instruction*. ERIC Education Resources Information Center (ED314959) (ERIC Document Reproduction Service No. ED 314 959).

O'Connor, E. (2008). Becoming a virtual instructor: How can higher education faculty prepare for Second Life? In C. Bonk et al. (Eds.), *Proceedings of world conference on e-Learning in corporate, government, healthcare, and higher education* (pp. 1144–1149). Montreal, Canada.

O'Dowd, R. (2018). From telecollaboration to virtual exchange: State-of-the-art and the role of UNI collaboration in moving forward. *Journal of Virtual Exchange*, (1), 1–23.

Ortega, L. (1997). Processes and outcomes in networked classroom interaction: Defining the research agenda for L2 computer-assisted classroom discussion. *Language Learning & Technology*, *1*(1), 82–93.

Ortega, L. (1999). Planning and focus on form in L2 oral performance. *Studies in Second Language Acquisition, 21*, 109–148.

Palfrey, J., & Gasser, U. (2010). *Born digital: Understanding the first generation of digital natives*. New York: Basic Books.

Panichi, L. (2015). A critical analysis of learner participation in virtual worlds: How can virtual worlds inform our pedagogy? In F. Helm, L. Bradley, M. Guarda, & S. Thouësny (Eds.), *Critical CALL – Proceedings of the 2015 EUROCALL Conference*, Padova, Italy (pp. 464–469). Dublin: Research-Publishing.Net.

Panichi, L., & Deutschmann, M. (2012). Language learning in virtual worlds: Research issues and methods. In M. Dooly & R. O'Dowd (Eds.), *Researching online foreign language interaction and exchange: Theories, methods and challenges* (pp. 205–232). Bern: Peter Lang Publishing Group.

Panichi, L., & Schneider, C. (2012, November 15–16). Getting started in virtual worlds with the Euroversity network. *International Conference: ICT for language learning* (5th Conference ed., pp. 199–202). Florence: libreriauniversitaria.it.

Papandreou, A. P. (1994). An application of the projects approach to EFL. *English Teaching Forum, 32*(3), 41–42.

Parks, S., Huot, D., Hamers, J., & Lemonnier, F. H. (2003). Crossing boundaries: Multimedia technology and pedagogical innovation in a high school class. *Language Learning & Technology, 7*(1), 28–45.

Parsons, S., Beardon, L., Neale, H. R., Reynard, G., Eastgate, R., Wilson, J. R., . . . Hopkins, E. (2000). *Development of social skills amongst adults with Asperger's Syndrome using virtual environments: The 'AS Interactive' project.* Proceedings from 3rd International Conference on Disability, Virtual Reality & Associated Technologies, Alghero, Italy.

Parson, S., & Mitchell, P. (2002). The potential of virtual reality in social skills training for people with autistic spectrum disorders. *Journal of Intellectual Disability Research, 5*, 430–443.

Peachey, A., Gillen, J., Livingstone, D., & Smith-Robbins, S. (Eds.). (2011). *Researching learning in virtual worlds*. London: Springer.

Pennycook, A. (1994). *The cultural politics of English as an international language*. London: Longman.

Pennycook, A. (2018). *Posthumanist applied linguistics*. Oxford and New York: Routledge.

Peters, M. (2006). Developing computer competencies for pre-service language teachers: Is one course enough? In P. Hubbard & M. Levy (Eds.), *Teacher education in CALL* (pp. 153–165). Amsterdam, The Netherlands and Philadelphia, PA: John Benjamins.

Peterson, C., & Nassaji, H. (2016). Project-based learning through the eyes of teachers and students in the adult ESL classroom. *The Canadian Modern Language Review, 72*(1), 13–39.

Peterson, M. (2010). Learner participation patterns and strategy use in Second Life: An exploratory case study. *ReCALL, 22*, 273–292.

Peterson, M. (2011). Toward a research agenda for the use of three-dimensional virtual worlds in language learning. *CALICO Journal, 29*(1), 67–80.

Pica, T., & Doughty, C. (1985). Input and interaction in the communicative language classroom: A comparison of teacher-fronted and group activities. In

S. Gass & C. Madden (Eds.), *Input and second language acquisition* (pp. 115–132). Rowley, MA: Newbury House.

Pica, T., Kanagy, R., & Falodun, J. (1993). Choosing and using communication tasks for second language instruction. In G. Crooks & S. Gass (Eds.), *Tasks and language learning: Integrating theory and practice* (pp. 9–34). Clevedon: Multilingual Matters.

Pica, T., Young, R., & Doughty, C. (1987). The impact of interaction on comprehension. *TESOL Quarterly*, *21*(4), 737–758.

Picard, M. (2006). *Machinima: Video as an art game*. Proceedings of CGSA 2006 Symposium, Canadian Games Study Association, Montreal.

Picciano, A. G. (2017). Theories and frameworks for online education: Seeking an integrated model. *Online Learning*, *21*(3), 166–190.

Pilus, Z. (1995). Teachers' interest in CALL and their level of computer literacy: Some implications. *On-CALL*, *9*(3), 8–11.

Pinchbeck, D., & Gras, R. (2011). Machinima: From art object to cultural practice. In H. Lowood & M. Nitsche (Eds.), *The machinima reader* (pp. 143–158). Cambridge, MA and London: MIT Press.

Player-Koro, C., Rensfeldt, A. B., & Selwyn, N. (2017). Selling tech to teachers: Education trade shows as policy events. *Journal of Education Policy*, *33*, 682–703.

Plonsky, L., & Ziegler, N. (2016). The CALL-SLA interface: Insights from a second-order synthesis. *Language Learning & Technology*, *20*, 17–37.

Plough, I., & Gass, S. (1993). Interlocutor and task familiarity: Effects on interactional structure. In G. Crookes & S. Gass (Eds.), *Tasks and language learning: Integrating theory and practice* (pp. 35–56). Philadelphia, PA: Multilingual Matters.

Prabhu, N. S. (1987). *Second language pedagogy*. Oxford: Oxford University Press.

Prendergast, G. (2000). *Creating effective online collaborative educators*. Conference Proceedings. Abacus Learning Systems, Networked Learning 2000, Lancaster University and University of Sheffield.

Prensky, M. (2001). Digital natives, digital immigrants part 1. *On the Horizon*, *9*(5), 1–6.

Rainbow, C. (2015, May 11). Interview with Carol Rainbow. *YouTube* [video]. Retrieved April 19, 2016, from https://youtu.be/FOqlEPGG2fE

Rainbow, C., & Schneider, C. (2014). *Making and using machinima in the language classroom*. London: The Round.

Richardson, W. (2010). *Weblogs, wikis, and podcasts and other powerful web tools that are transforming classrooms* (3rd ed.). London: Corwin Press.

Robb, T. (2006). Helping teachers to help themselves. In P. Hubbard & M. Levy (Eds.), *Teacher education in CALL* (pp. 335–347). Amsterdam, The Netherlands: John Benjamins.

Rooij, S. (2009). Scaffolding project-based learning with the project management body of knowledge (PMBOK®). *Computers & Education*, *52*(1), 210–219.

Rosen, L. D., & Weil, M. M. (1995). Computer availability, computer experience, and technophobia among public school teachers. *Computer in Human Behavior*, *11*(1), 9–31.

Rowley, J. (2002). Using case studies in research. *Management Research News*, *25*(1), 16–27.

Ryan, J., & Scott, A. (2008). Integrating technology into teacher education: How online discussion can be used to develop informed and critical literacy teachers. *Teacher and Teacher Education, 24,* 1635–1644.

Sadler, R. (2012). Virtual worlds: An overview and pedagogical examination. *Bellaterra Journal of Teaching & Learning Language & Literature, 5*(1), 1–22.

Sadler, R., & Dooly, M. (2013). Language learning in virtual worlds: Research and practice. In M. Thomas, M. Warschauer, & H. Reinders (Eds.), *Contemporary computer-assisted language learning* (pp. 183–200). London: Bloomsbury.

Salmon, G. (2009). The future for (Second) Life and learning. *British Journal of Educational Technology, 40*(3), 526–538.

Samuda, V., & Bygate, M. (2008). *Tasks in second language learning.* Houndmills and New York: Palgrave Macmillan.

Sant, T. (2009). Performance in Second Life: Some possibilities for learning and teaching. In J. Molka-Danielsen & M. Deutschmann (Eds.), *Learning and teaching in the virtual world of Second Life* (pp. 160–161). Trondheim: Tapir Academic Press.

Sauro, C., & Smith, B. (2010). Investigating L2 performance in text chat. *Applied Linguistics, 31,* 1–24.

Sauro, S. (2017). Online fan practices and CALL. *CALICO Journal, 34*(2), 131–146.

Sauro, S., & Sundmark, B. (2016,) Report from Middle Earth: Fanfiction tasks in the EFL classroom. *ELT Journal, 70*(4), 414–423.

Savery, J. (2015). Overview of problem-based learning: Definitions and distinctions. In A. Walker, H. Leary, C. Hmelo-Silver, & P. Ertmer (Eds.), *Essential readings in problem-based learning* (pp. 5–16). West Lafayette: Purdue University Press.

Savignon, S. (1993). Communicative language teaching: State of the art. *TESOL Quarterly, 25*(2), 261–277.

Savin-Baden, M. (2010). *A practical guide to using Second Life in higher education.* Maidenhead: McGraw-Hill Education (UK), Open University Press.

Schneider, C. (2003). Zur Didaktik von Online Seminaren. Erfahrungen und Beispiele. In H. Apel & S. Kraft (Eds.), *Online lehren.* Bielefeld: Bertelsmann wbv.

Schneider, C. (2004, May 6–8). *Encouragement and motivation in online training.* Conference Proceedings of the First Central European International Multimedia and Virtual Reality Conference, Veszprém University Press, Vesprém.

Schneider, C. (2013, February 13). Why Second Life? *YouTube* [video]. Retrieved from https://youtu.be/km_afd0_dEI

Schneider, C. (2014a, November 13–14). CAMELOT-Using and creating machinima for language teaching. In *International Conference Proceedings: ICT for language learning* (pp. 134–138). Florence: libreriauniversitaria.it [Web]. Retrieved from http://conference.pixel-online.net/ICT4LL/files/ict4ll/ed0007/FP/0586-ICL772-FP-ICT4LL7.pdf

Schneider, C. (2014b, November 17). Euroversity interview with Christel Schneider. *YouTube* [video]. Retrieved from https://youtu.be/hiKGL-Dwpzk?list=UU40YZ-21PhI2-K5Nhqgr8dA

Schrage, M. (2001). *The relationship revolution.* Retrieved seedwiki.com/wiki/Yi-Tan/TheRelationshipRevolution.htm?wikipageversionid=417577&edit=yes&i=87

Schroeder, R. (2008). Defining virtual worlds and virtual Environments. *Journal of Virtual Worlds Research, 1*(1), 2–3.

Seedhouse, P. (1999). Task-based interaction. *English Language Teaching Journal, 53*(3), 149–156.

Seedhouse, P., & Almutairi, S. (2009). A holistic approach to task-based interaction. *International Journal of Applied Linguistics, 19*(3), 311–338.

Sefton-Green, J. (2014). From 'othering' to incorporation: The dilemmas of crossing informal and formal learning boundaries. In K. Sandford, T. Rogers & M. Kendrick (Eds.), *Everyday youth literacies: Critical perspectives for new times* (pp. 175–189). Singapore: Springer.

Shen, Q. (2009). Case study in contemporary educational research: Conceptualization and critique [Etudes de cas dans la recherche pedagogique contemporaine: conceptualisation et critique]. *Cross-Cultural Communication, 5*(4), 21–31.

Shintani, N. (2012). Input-based tasks and the acquisition of vocabulary and grammar: A process-product study. *Language Teaching Research, 16*(2), 253–279.

Shintani, N. (2016). The effects of computer-mediated synchronous and asynchronous direct corrective feedback on writing: A case study. *Computer Assisted Language Learning, 29*(3), 517–538.

Shintani, N., & Aubrey, S. (2016). The effectiveness of synchronous and asynchronous written corrective feedback on grammatical accuracy in a computer-mediated environment. *The Modern Language Journal, 100*(1), 296–319.

Shrestha, S., & Harrison, T. (2019). Using machinima as teaching and learning materials: A Nepalese case study. *International Journal of Computer Assisted Language Learning and Teaching, 4*(1), 37–52.

Shrosbree, M. (2008). Digital video in the language classroom. *JALTCALL Journal, 4*(1), 75–84.

Skehan, P. (1998). *A cognitive approach to language learning.* Oxford: Oxford University Press.

Skehan, P. (2002). A non-marginal role for tasks. *ELT Journal, 56*(3), 289–295.

Slaouti, D., & Motteram, G. (2006). Reconstructing practice: Language teacher education and ICT. In P. Hubbard & M. Levy (Eds.), *Teacher education in CALL* (pp. 81–98). Amsterdam, The Netherlands: John Benjamins.

Slater, T., & Beckett, G. H. (2017). Integrating language, content, technology, and skills development through project-based language learning: Blending frameworks for successful unit planning. *MexTESOL, 43*(1).

Smith, K. (2010, February 7). *The use of virtual worlds among people with disabilities.* Presented at Interaction 10 (IxDA10) Conference. Retrieved from https://tcf.pages.tcnj.edu/files/2013/12/kelSmith_virtual_worlds_disabilities_032409.pdf

Snelson, C. (2010, April 20–22). *Virtual movie sets and branching video: Developing interactive educational machinima with Second Life and YouTube.* Conference Proceedings, 15th Annual TCC Online Conference.

Son, J.-B. (2002). Online discussion in a CALL course for distance language teachers. *CALICO Journal, 20*(1), 127–144.

Son, J.-B. (2004). Teacher development in e-learning environments. In J.-B. Son (Ed.), *Computer-assisted language learning: Concepts, contexts and practices* (pp. 107–122). Lincoln, NE: APACALL.

Sotillo, S. M. (2000). Discourse functions and syntactic complexity in synchronous and asynchronous communication. *Language Learning & Technology*, 4(1), 82–119.

Spiller, J. M. (2004). *The design and construction of a machinima-based language instruction tool.* A Master's paper submitted to the faculty of the School of Information and Library Science of the University of North Carolina at Chapel Hill.

Stanford. (2005). Steve Jobs' 2005 commencement address. *YouTube* [video]. March 7, 2008. Retrieved from https://youtu.be/UF8uR6Z6KLc

Statista. (2019). Statistics and facts about YouTube. *The Statistics Portal*. Statistics and studies from more than 18,000 sources [Web]. Retrieved from www.statista.com/topics/2019/youtube/

Stockwell, G. (2007). A review of technology choice for teaching language skills in the CALL literature. *ReCALL*, 19(2),105–120.

Stockwell, G. (2013). Mobile-assisted language learning. In M. Thomas, H. Reinders, & M. Warschauer (Eds.), *Contemporary computer-assisted language learning* (pp. 201–216). London: Bloomsbury.

Stoller, F. (2006). Establishing a theoretical foundation for project-based learning in second and foreign language contexts. In G. H. Beckett & P. C. Miller (Eds.), *Project-based second and foreign language education: Past, present, and future* (pp. 19–40). Greenwich, CT: Information Age Publishing.

Stommel, J. (2014). Critical digital pedagogy: A definition. *Hybrid Pedagogy: A Digital Journal of Learning, Teaching and Technology*. Retrieved from www.hybridpedagogy.com/journal/critical-digital-pedagogy-definition/

Suler, J. (2005). The online disinhibition effect. *International Journal of Applied Psychoanalytic Studies*, 2(2), 184–188.

Swain, M., & Lapkin, S. (1982). *Evaluating bilingual education: A Canadian case study*. Clevedon: Multilingual Matters.

Swan, M. (2005). Legislation by hypothesis: The case of task-based instruction. *Applied Linguistics*, 26(3), 376–401.

Sykes, J. M. (2005). Synchronous CNC and pragmatic development: Effects of oral and written chat. *CALICO Journal*, 22(3), 399–431.

Takeda, N. (2015). Bridging communicative language teaching and task-based language teaching in Cambodia: Learners' reactions to an integrated programme in the non-formal education sector. In M. Thomas & H. Reinders (Eds.), *Contemporary task-based language teaching in Asia* (pp. 46–64). London: Bloomsbury Academic.

Tang, X. (2012). *Language, discipline or task? A comparison study of the effectiveness of different methods for delivering content-based instructions to EFL students of business studies* (Unpublished doctoral dissertation). Durham University, Durham, UK.

Tapscott, D. (2009). *Grown up digital: How the net generation is changing your world*. New York: McGraw-Hill.

Tellis, W. (1997, September). Application of a case study methodology. *The Qualitative Report*, 3(3) [Web]. Retrieved from www.nova.edu/ssss/QR/QR3-3/tellis2.html

Thomas, H. (2010). Learning spaces, learning environments and the displacement of learning. *British Journal of Educational Technology*, 41(3), 502–511.

Thomas, M. (2010, November 11–12). *Task-based language teaching and collaborative problem-solving with Second Life: A case study of Japanese EFL learners.* 3rd International Conference ICT for Language Learning, Florence.

Thomas, M. (Ed.). (2011). *Deconstructing digital natives: Young people, technologies and the new literacies.* New York: Routledge.

Thomas, M. (2014, March 10–12). *Machinima and learner-generated content in 3D immersive environments: A case study of the EU CAMELOT project.* INTED2014 Proceedings, 8th International Technology, Education and Development Conference, Valencia [online]. Retrieved from http://library.iated.org/view/THOMAS2014MAC

Thomas, M. (2015). Researching machinima in project-based language learning: Learner generated content in the CAMELOT project. In E. Dixon & M. Thomas (Eds.), *Researching language learner interactions online: From social media to MOOCs* (Vol. 13, pp. 129–148). Austin, TX: CALICO.

Thomas, M. (2017). *Project-based language learning with technology: Learner collaboration in an EFL classroom in Japan.* London: Routledge.

Thomas, M., & Reinders, H. (Eds.). (2010). *Task-based language learning and teaching with technology.* London and New York: Continuum.

Thomas, M., & Reinders, H. (Eds.). (2015). *Contemporary task-based language teaching in Asia.* London and New York: Bloomsbury.

Thomas, M., Reinders, H., & Warschauer, M., (Eds.) (2013). *Contemporary computer-assisted language learning.* London: Bloomsbury Academic.

Thomas, M., & Schneider, C. (2018). Language learning with machinima: Video production in 3D immersive environments. In P. Hubbard & S. Ioannou-Georgiou (Eds.), *Teaching English reflectively with technology.* Canterbury: IATEFL.

Thomassen, A., & Rive, P. (2010). How to enable knowledge exchange in Second Life in design education? *Learning, Media & Technology, 35*(2), 155–169.

TILA Project. (2015). *Telecollaboration for intercultural language acquisition.* Lifelong Learning Programme [Web]. Retrieved from http://tilaproject.eu/

Tomlinson, B. (2015). TBLT materials and curricula: From theory to practice. In M. Thomas & H. Reinders (Eds.), *Contemporary task-based language teaching in Asia* (pp. 328–340). London: Bloomsbury.

Torsani, S. (2016). *CALL teacher education: Language teachers and technology integration.* London: Springer.

Trowbridge, S., & The British Council. (2013). *Teaching English: TBL and PBL: Two learner-centred approaches.* Retrieved from www.teachingenglish.org.uk/article/tbl-pbl-two-learner-centred-approaches

Tsou, W. (2011). The application of readers theatre to FLES (Foreign Language in the Elementary Schools) reading and writing. *Foreign Language Annals, 44*(4), 727–747.

University of Leicester. (n.d.). *David Kolb. Taken from: How to be an e-tutor by Dr Richard Mobbs* [Web]. Retrieved from http://www2.le.ac.uk/departments/gradschool/training/eresources/teaching/theories/kolb.

Ushioda, E. (2011). Language learning motivation, self and identity: Current theoretical perspectives. *Computer Assisted Language Learning, 24*(3), 199–210.

Van de Craen, P., & Pérez-Vidal, C. (Eds.). (2003). *The multilingual challenge* [Le défi multilingue]. Barcelona: Printulibro.

Van den Branden, K. (Ed.). (2006). *Task-based language education: From theory to practice*. Cambridge: Cambridge University Press.

Van den Branden, K., Bygate, M., & Norris, J. M. (Eds.). (2009). *Task-based language teaching: A reader*. Amsterdam, The Netherlands and Philadelphia, PA: John Benjamins.

Van Lier, L. (1996). *Interaction in the language curriculum: Awareness, autonomy, and authenticity*. London: Longman.

Vandagriff, J., & Nitsche, M. (2009). Women creating machinima. *Digital Creativity. Special Issue: Women in Games, 20*(4), 277–290.

VirtualPREX. (2012). *Virtual professional experience. Innovative assessment using a 3D virtual world with pre-service teachers*. VirtualPREX Framework for Assessment Activities Using Machinima [Web]. Retrieved from www.virtualprex.com/assessment.html

Vodanovich, S. J., & Piotrowski, C. (2004–2005). Faculty attitudes toward web-based instruction may not be enough: Limited use and obstacles to implementation. *Journal of Educational Technology Systems, 33*, 309–318.

VWBP. (2015, March 18–21). *Crossroads*. 8th Annual Virtual Worlds Best Practices in Education Conference [blog]. Retrieved from http://vwbpe.org/blog/vwbpe-2015-crossroads

Vygotsky, L. S. (1978). Interaction between learning and development (M. Lopez-Morillas, Trans.). In M. Cole, V. John-Steiner, S. Scribner, & E. Souberman (Eds.), *Mind in society: The development of higher psychological processes* (pp. 79–91). Cambridge, MA: Harvard University Press.

Wajnryb, R. (1992). *Classroom observation tasks: A resource book for language teachers and trainers*. Cambridge, UK: Cambridge University Press.

Wang, S., & Vasquez, C. (2012). Web 2.0 and second language learning: What does the research tell us? *CALICO Journal, 29*(3), 412–430.

Warburton, S. (2009). Second Life in higher education: Assessing potential for and the barriers to deploying virtual worlds in learning and teaching. *British Journal of Educational Technology, 40*(3), 414–426.

Warburton, S., & Pérez Garcia, M. (2009). 3D design and collaboration in massively multi-user virtual environments. In D. Russell (Ed.), *Cases on collaboration in virtual learning environments: Processes and interactions* (pp. 27–41). Hershey, PA: IGI Global.

Ward-Penny, R. (2010). *Cross-curricular teaching and learning in the secondary school . . . mathematics*. London: Routledge.

Warner, C. N. (2004). It's just a game, right? Types of play in foreign language CMC. *Language Learning & Technology, 8*(2), 69–87.

Warschauer, M. (2006). *Laptops and literacy: Learning in the wireless classroom*. Columbia: Teachers College Press.

Warschauer, M., & Grimes, D. (2008). Audience, authorship, and artifact: The emergent semiotics of Web 2.0. *Annual Review of Applied Linguistics, 27*, 1–23.

Wegerif, R. (2007). *Dialogic, education and technology: Expanding the space of learning*. New York and Berlin: Springer.

Wegerif, R. (2013). *Dialogic: Education for the internet age*. London and New York: Routledge.

Wegerif, R. (2017). *Defining 'dialogic education'*. Retrieved from www.rupert-wegerif.name/blog/defining-dialogic-education

Wells, G. (1999). *Dialogic inquiry: Towards a sociocultural practice and theory of education*. Cambridge: Cambridge University Press.

Wendt, U. (2013, March 4–5). *The praxis of online computer games and consoles in education at the Faculty SAGP (social work, health and care)*. INTED2013 Proceedings 7th International Technology, Education and Development Conference, Valencia, Spain.

Wheeler, S. (2005, November 11). *Creating social presence in digital learning environments: A presence of mind?* Featured Paper for the TAFE Conference, Queensland, Australia.

Whitton, N. (2014). *Digital games and learning: Research and theory*. New York, NY: Routledge.

Willis, J. (1996). *A framework for task-based learning*. Harlow: Longman.

Yamazaki, K. (2018). Computer-assisted learning of communication (CALC): A case study of Japanese learning in a 3D virtual world. *ReCALL, 30*(2), 214–231.

Yin, R. K. (2004, January 20). *Case study methods, revised draft*. COSMOS Corporation [online]. Retrieved from https://de.scribd.com/doc/37102046/Robert-Yin-Case-Study-Research

Yin, R. K. (2014). *Case study research: Design and methods*. London: Sage.

Yogeswar, D. (2015, September 5). Using avatars effectively in e-learning courses. *Ideas to transform your training*. Commlab, India for effective learning [blog]. Retrieved from: http://blog.commlabindia.com/elearning-design/avatars-in-elearning-courses-infographic

Zheng, D., Newgarden, K., & Young, M. F. (2012). Multimodal analysis of language learning in World of Warcraft Play: Languaging as values-realizing. *ReCALL, 24*(3), 339–360.

Appendices

Appendices

Appendix I
Machinima Resources and Examples

Machinima Resources

- *First! Many2Many, Programming Service for Fandom and Gamer Culture:*
  www.machinima.com/
- *The online YouTube network for gamers, creators, and fans:*
  www.youtube.com/machinima
- *Machinima – The YouTube Wiki:*
  http://youtube.wikia.com/wiki/Machinima
- *The Machinima Archive.org:*
  https://archive.org/details/machinima?&sort=-downloads&page=2
- *Second Life YouTube channel:*
  www.youtube.com/user/Secondlife
- *Second Life Machinima Wiki:*
  http://wiki.secondlife.com/wiki/Machinima
- *Making Machinima in Second Life:*
  http://marisaconstantinides.edublogs.org/2012/01/14/making-a-machinima-in-second-life-in-19-steps/#.VtlaF_nhDcs
- *Second Life Portal (Linden Scripting Language):*
  http://wiki.secondlife.com/wiki/LSL_Portal

The Drax Files: World Makers

The Drax Files: World Makers' profiles the creative people behind the avatars who move the virtual world of Second Life forward with their passion and persistence:
www.youtube.com/playlist?list=PLI0b2jAH3oFvr6J0AhWroB9lmOXRN2xLV

Educational Machinima on YouTube

- *A list of machinima produced for the video project grouped by genre:*
  http://camelotproject.eu/machinima-list/
- *Carol Rainbow YouTube channel:*
  www.youtube.com/user/carolrb/videos

- *Christel Schneider YouTube channel:* www.youtube.com/user/ChristelSchneider/featured
- *The CAMELOT YouTube Channel:* www.youtube.com/user/camelotprojecteu

Machinima Training Sessions – Wiki

- *MachinEVO, one of the EVO (Electronic Village Online) sessions that were offered by TESOL:* http://machinevo.pbworks.com/w/page/47494320/MachinEVO2014%20-%20Startpage
- *Film Festival MachinEVO 2013:* http://machinevo.pbworks.com/w/page/63642403/Film%20Festival%20MachinEVO%202013
- *Why Second Life? An award-winning machinima for the categories, best informative machinima and best digital storytelling:* https://youtu.be/km_afd0_dEI

Machinima Investigating the Cultural Values

- *This is part of an Arts & Humanities Research Council funded (UK funding council) investigation into the cultural impacts of machinima:* http://machinima.dmu.ac.uk/

Research Artefacts: Machinima Panel Videos

- *Machinima and me:* http://machinima.dmu.ac.uk/project-report/machinima-focus-groups
- *Barriers to machinima:* https://vimeo.com/101793863
- *The future of machinima:* https://vimeo.com/101793784
- *Machinima community creators:* https://vimeo.com/101793864

Branching Video Examples on YouTube
(Snelson, 2010, p. 30)

- *Playlist of Interactive Adventures:*
- www.youtube.com/view_play_list?p=FF71721629BAE928
- *Playlist of Interactive Games:*
  www.youtube.com/view_play_list?p=7215176DBCFB548F
- *Playlist of Interactive Tours and Maps:*
  www.youtube.com/view_play_list?p=4427BD3E28B63522

Real-Time 3D Animation Technologies

- *Snagit from Techsmith: allows free evaluation trials:*
  www.techsmith.com/tutorial-snagit-current.html
- *Screencast O Matic:*
  The free version does not allow audio from the computer sound card.
  http://screencast-o-matic.com/home
- *CamStudio from Sourceforge:*
  http://camstudio.org
- *Camtasia Studio: allows free evaluation trials:*
  www.techsmith.com/camtasia.html
- *Windows live movie maker:*
  http://windows.microsoft.com/en-GB/windows/get-movie-maker-download
- *Audacity sound recorder/editor software:*
  http://audacity.sourceforge.net/
- *Free Sound Effect Archive:*
  www.grsites.com/archive/sounds/

Screencasting Software

- Fraps is a screen-casting software that records anything that is happening on a screen.
  The free version allows to record 30 seconds of video and has a watermark.
  www.fraps.com

3D Animation Software

- *Moviestorm:*
  www.moviestorm.co.uk/
- *iClone:*
  www.reallusion.com/iClone/
- *Second Life:*
  http://secondlife.com/

Video-Publishing tools

- *Robin Good: Directory of 350+ of the best tools and services to capture, edit, publish and distribute video online.*
  https://video-publishing.zeef.com/robin.good
- *Mashable, Video Toolbox:* 150+ Online Video tools and Resources
  http://mashable.com/2007/06/27/video-toolbox/#aKCRzryajgqb

Appendix II
Self-Assessment Questionnaire

For Participants in the Machinima Open Online Training Course

The self-evaluation questionnaire was to the trainees to be completed prior to the beginning of the facilitated MOOT course and at the end of the course to evaluate their achievements.

Questionnaire

Part I

Essential things that I understand:
1. I understand the term *viewer* in the context of SL
2. I understand the term *avatar* in the context of SL
3. I understand the term *landmark* in the context of SL
4. I understand the term *SLURL* in the context of SL
5. I understand the term *rez* in the context of SL
6. I understand the term *inventory* in the context of SL
7. I understand the term *sandbox* in the context of SL
8. I understand the term *lag* in the context of SL
9. I understand the term *holodeck* in the context of SL
10. I understand the term *screen casting* in the context of SL

Part II

I can:
1. Walk, run and fly
2. Use text chat to talk to people near me
3. Use voice chat to talk to people near me
4. Send an instant message (IM) to someone
5. Make someone my friend
6. Accept a friendship invitation from someone
7. Teleport to a location
8. Accept an invitation from someone to teleport to their location
9. Switch audio streaming on and off in a location
10. View a slideshow on a projection screen
11. View a video stream on a projection screen
12. Add a new landmark to my inventory

13. Navigate to an existing landmark which is in your inventory
14. Add an object that I have bought or obtained free of charge to my inventory
15. Rez an object from my inventory and take it back
16. Read a notecard and add it to my inventory
17. Use the mini-map to assist me to navigate
18. Use the world map to assist me to navigate
19. Change my avatar's appearance and clothing
20. Use the search facility to find people, places and objects
21. Rez and clear a holodeck
22. Take a snapshot from Second Life and save it onto my computer's hard drive
23. Use my camera controls
24. Set the window size for machinima (720 × 1280)
25. Set appropriate light for taking footage
26. Hide my User Interface (UI)
27. Take video footage with a screencasting software (Fraps, Camtasia, Screencast, QuickTime)

Part III

Editing Machinima

1. I know how to import media to Camtasia or other video editor
2. I know how to add media to the timeline
3. I know how to split media
4. I know how to control audio
5. I know how to add transitions
6. I know how to add callouts
7. I know how to use Audacity to create audio files
8. I know how to add music, audio and sound effects
9. I know how to add a title and credits
10. I know how to publish a video
11. I know how to upload a video to my choice of video host (YouTube, Vimeo, Camtasia etc.)
12. I know how to share my video

Appendix III
Call Teacher Training Course Overview

This course is designed as a facilitated self-study course. It has been designed in six modules over six weeks. Progress in the course will be monitored, and general feedback will be provided through the forums. It is important to respond to other participants' posts as everyone has knowledge to share.

After three weeks where participants will mostly be learning about *Second Life* the course moves on to the making of machinima. If you know *Second Life* very well you can start working on machinima much earlier, though it would be worth looking at the interviews in the *Reflection* section of each module. There is much to be learned from the interviewees.

The software mentioned in the course is *Fraps*, *Windows Movie Maker* and *Camtasia*, they each have free or evaluation trial periods. If you have a *Mac* then you have the built-in *iMovie* which you can use. If you have other software that you already use then there is no need to change, continue to use whatever you know the software is not important.

We hope that you enjoy the course, good luck and we look forward to seeing your first machinima!

Week 1

- Starting to get familiar with *Second Life*.
- Considering why people use machinima in their teaching and/or learning.

Week2

- Learning to dress your avatar
- Changing avatars
- Mixing and matching avatar clothing
- Working with gestures and animations
- Using a holodeck
- Controlling light
- Starting to screencast

Week 3

- Moving around *Second Life*
- Controlling your camera
- Using the mini-map to get around
- Using the World Map
- Giving inventory items to others
- Making a lesson plan outline and storyboard

Week 4

- Finding places to film
- Requesting permissions
- Making landmarks
- Starting to film and edit your machinima

Week 5

- Working on your machinima
- Sharing and improving your machinima
- Evaluating machinima

Week 6

- Finishing all work
- A reflective task

Structure of Weekly Tasks and Discussion, Example Week 1 on Moodle

Week 1 Learning Activities

Task 1.1 Introduce Yourself

Task 1.2 Communication, Chat, IM, Call, and making Friends in Second Life Assignment

Task 1.3 Turn the volume up of individuals in a group

Task 1.4 Change the Sound Settings Assignment

Task 1.5 Change name above head and make a profile

Task 1.6 How are you getting on in Second Life?

Week 1 Reflection

Task 1.7 Reflect on the use of machinima in a language lesson

Week 1 Discussions

Week 1 Discussions

This forum is where you will respond to all of the week 1 tasks. Please look for my message with the topic heading and reply to that.

Week 1 Pedagogical Reading

Read the sample from "Making and Using Machinima in the Language Classroom" which looks at the pedagogies from Kolb, Lave and Wenger and Lim regarding using a virtual world as a teaching medium. Even if you do not teach in a virtual world reflect on these pedagogies in the light of the course you are taking in Second Life. Follow the link listed below and then download the book extract.

 Task 1.8 Making and Using Machinima in the Language Classroom

Appendix IV
Video Teacher Training Course
Self – Evaluation

1. How to do you feel about your own skills of using *Second Life*?
2. Do you feel confident to create a simple machinima?
3. Did you make a machinima for use in class?
4. Would you include your students in making future machinima?
5. Did the course meet your expectations? If yes, in what way?
6. What could be improved in the training course?
7. Did you face any challenges (i.e. time/ language/ technological)? If yes, what were they?
8. How might you use machinima in the future?
9. Any additional comments you would like to make?
10. Would you recommend this course to others?

Appendix V
Machinima Piloted in the Field Testing

Machinima Piloted in Germany

Three self-contained Machinima, Level A1 according to the CEFR:

1. "Reisen mit Musik" (www.youtube.com/watch?v=b_oviCmXrCw& feature=youtu.be)
2. "An Sport interessiert sein" (www.youtube.com/watch?v=IeF6kzoZ NSk&feature=youtu.be)
3. "Paula feiert Geburtstag" (www.youtube.com/watch?v=xJWuG3uK gko&feature=youtu.be)

Five Interrelated Machinima Level A2 According to the CEFR

1. "Conversation With the Waiter" (www.youtube.com/watch?v=IBF M920w2R4&feature=youtu.be)
2. "Buying a Painting" (www.youtube.com/watch?v=UiPariAw3oU&fe ature=youtu.be)
3. "In the Gallery Part 1" (www.youtube.com/watch?v=6YXlCAGtVp 4&feature=youtu.be)
4. "In the Gallery Part 2" (www.youtube.com/watch?v=IyHqeD3UIho &feature=youtu.be)
5. "Conversation With Police" (www.youtube.com/watch?v=AlxPUO4 YFDg&feature=youtu.be)

Machinima Piloted in the Czech Republic

1. Do You Really Need a Hard Hat?" (www.youtube.com/watch?v=7d gyx2qdYNA&feature=youtu.be)

2. "When No Smoking Really Means 'No Smoking'" (www.youtube.com/watch?v=xA-jPtJq2dQ&feature=youtu.be)
3. "How High Is Too High?" (www.youtube.com/watch?v=GCSE3-58RQA&feature=youtu.be)

Machinima Piloted in the Netherlands

1. "The Pythagoras Theorem Made Easy" (https://youtu.be/BF_-Dt5K7jY)

Appendix VI
Interviews

A list of expert interviews conducted the video project which are available on YouTube.

Project Partners	URL
Dr Ellinor Haase, ICC, Chairperson, DE	https://youtu.be/8Y-5f-WYHFQ
Ton Koenraad, TellConsult, Manager, NL	https://youtu.be/pDvbmXpGKzw
Sandra Gasber, LinguaTV, Manager, DE	https://youtu.be/X6dBZUTjzUw
Carol Rainbow, UCLan, Teacher, UK	https://youtu.be/FOqlEPGG2fE
Heike Philp, Lets, Organiser, BE	https://youtu.be/QQZ4Di9sToE
Jana Cepickova, UWB, Teacher, CZ	https://youtu.be/FWUIKmN9-fU
Dr Tuncer Can, UIST, Teacher, TR	https://youtu.be/rgXu4lqlNVw
Interviews with teachers and machinima experts	
Alicja Bomirska, Secondary School Teacher, PL	https://youtu.be/7a_QAkiDRac
Patrick de Boer, Secondary School Teacher/CLIL – Utrecht, NL	https://youtu.be/HAbgWoNRz1A
Helena Galani, EFL Teacher, GR	https://youtu.be/9pJFqLiqTgs
Ann Nowak, FH Düsseldorf, Teacher, DE	https://youtu.be/DBdP_G0AJXs
Stephanie Wössner, Teacher/ MachinEVO Project, DE	https://youtu.be/YRL9x6vsxtc
Eva Adamcova, UWB, Field Testing Machinima, CZ	https://youtu.be/dfJkDMAhj9o
Dr. Hanna Outakoski, University Umea, Teacher, SE	https://youtu.be/bTJTuQ6OYKA
Christel Schneider, UCLan, Researcher, DE/ UK	https://youtu.be/hiKGL-Dwpzk?list=UU40YZ-21PhI2-K5Nhqgr8dA
Yağmur Damla Aslan, Tugay Elmas, Nelida Nita, UIST, Teacher Trainees. TR	https://youtu.be/l1uTS90zlTo
Serap Yildiz, UIST, Teacher Trainee. TR	https://youtu.be/NKNwKMm-u3c

Project Partners	URL
Anabel Nowak, FH Düsseldorf, Teacher, DE	https://youtu.be/R2TwrTiMsm8
Dr. Luisa Panichi, Euroversity Project, Teacher, IT	https://youtu.be/NDK9bWT6ak8
Edith Paillat, Organiser, NZ	https://youtu.be/nuwj-IUr4JA
Helen Myers, Secondary School London, Teacher, UK	https://youtu.be/iDhdcU-Zi1A
Chantal Harvey, Author and Machinimatographer, NL	https://youtu.be/4p-cUkRVLew
Alina Dobos, EUROCALL Workshop2014, Researcher, IE	https://youtu.be/iXPlPI9Gf88
Prof. Liz Falconer, UWE, Researcher, Lecturer, UK	https://youtu.be/yqc2j4-0QyM
Dennis Newson, Retired Teacher, DE	https://youtu.be/b4SCq_PiRWI
Gerhilde Meissl-Egghart, Talkademie, Teacher, AT	https://youtu.be/KURArhyCJvo
Prof. Rod Ellis, University of Auckland, Research Professor, AU	https://youtu.be/sv2Tiw-Rtgk
Dr. Mari Carmen Gil Otega, UWE, Lecturer,Teacher, UK	https://youtu.be/zsYebLl8hKc
Barbara McQueen, Private School, Teacher, USA	https://youtu.be/ADbK-zWYvqo
Shelwyn Corrigan, University San Francisco and Learn it Town, Teacher, USA	https://youtu.be/bgtF2bwt18c
Marisa Constantinides, DELTA Teacher Trainer, GR	https://youtu.be/yrcOPbRX-pU
Bernhard Drax, Machinimatographer, USA	https://youtu.be/Ov4_PLXR1Uk
Kamera Muggins, Retired Animator, UK	https://youtu.be/vOVsdeoIHjM

Appendix VII
Final Course Feedback MOOT2

Statements	Strongly Agree	Agree	Disagree	Strongly Disagree
Support was provided to help prior to the start of the training.	83.33%	0%	0%	16.67%
The goals of the training were clearly defined and well displayed.	83.33%	16.67%	0%	0%
Each learning unit stated the objectives clearly.	83.33%	16.67%	0%	0%
There were sufficient opportunities for interactive communication.	100%	0%	0%	0%
The format of the course allowed me to get to know other participants on the course.	50%	50%	0%	0%
The materials for the training given on the course were very helpful.	83.33%	16.67%	0%	0%
The training was too technical and difficult to understand.	16.67%	16.67%	16.67%	50%
The training experience will be useful for my language teaching.	100%	0%	0%	0%
The materials provided were the appropriate level for me.	83.33%	16.67%	0%	0%
The schedule for the training provided was sufficient to cover all the proposed activities.	83.33%	16.67%	0%	0%
The sessions were well balanced as regards to input and activities.	83.33%	16.67%	0%	0%

Statements	Strongly Agree	Agree	Disagree	Strongly Disagree
The schedule was very tight and it was difficult to manage all the tasks and materials.	16.67%	0%	83.33%	0%
The materials provided for the course were good quality.	83.33%	16.67%	0%	0%
The training was appropriate for my level of learning.	66.67%	33.33%	0%	0%
The units taught lasted for about the right amount of time.	50%	33.33 %	0%	16.67%
I learned a lot about producing machinima and feel confident in producing my own machinima.	50%	50%	0%	0%
I am still struggling with producing machinima.	0%	0%	83.33%	16.67%
The course facilitator was knowledgeable about training in 3D worlds and making machinima.	100%	0%	0%	0%
The course facilitator encouraged active participation.	100%	0%	0%	0%
The facilitator responded to all questions in a comprehensive way'	100%	0%	0%	0%
The facilitator used a variety of training methods.	60%	40%	0%	0%
The facilitator gave sufficient instructions for homework.	83.33%	16.67%	0%	0%

Index

3D MUVE 23
3D virtual world 17, 25, 38

abstract conceptualization 33
academic skills 55
achievement 21, 34, 110, 120, 170, 179, 182, 185
ActiveWorlds 16, 23
Adobe Connect 11, 114, 117, 118, 122, 136, 138, 140, 145, 158, 159, 166
analysis: of collaboration 52, 119; critical 42, 53, 119, 159; of feedback 120; lessons 11; meta-analysis 60; needs 10, 14, 19, 176
animation 13, 25, 26, 29, 30, 34, 73, 75, 169, 177
applying: Bloom's Cognitive Domain 54
apprentice-style learning 5, 28
architecture of participation 54, 57, 58
Asperger's syndrome 32, 54
assessment 11, 13, 15, 30, 33–34, 38, 43, 47, 49, 50, 63–64, 87, 106, 111–113, 135–136, 141, 142, 166, 181–184
asynchronous 11, 52, 58, 60, 114, 121–123, 130, 176
Audacity 144, 145
audiolingualism 47
authentic: communication 42; content 62, 152, 161; cultural artefacts 177; dialogues 162; environments 32, 58, 71, 99, 163, 173, 177, 179; facial expression 128; health and safety 154; immersive environment 10, 28, 152; interaction 175; language learning 7, 24, 49, 50, 172; learning 31, 39, 46, 48, 54–55, 59; machinima 12;

pronunciation 96; situations 4, 44, 155; tasks 5, 13, 22, 56, 117
authorship-based education 57
autistic spectrum 32, 81; Autism Society of America Island 32
autonomy 38, 43, 48, 53, 113
avatar 23–24, 25, 27, 29, 30, 34, 37, 58, 70, 73, 75, 79, 82, 85, 87, 97–111, 115, 120, 125, 141, 149–165, 178–185
awareness: intercultural 62; metacognitive 13, 44; of performance 184; pragmatic 24; training courses 14

barriers to entry: to creating machinima 110, 176; institutional 21; introverted students 81; novice teachers 7, 177, 182; use of digital environments 37
bandwidth 7, 37, 110, 120, 171, 178, 181
Bax, Stephen 19, 27, 42, 103, 142, 188
behavioural challenges 58
behaviouristic: learning principles 17; theoretical approaches 6, 12, 15, 21, 47–48, 52, 55, 57, 58, 110, 124, 153, 164, 175, 186–187
blended learning 114
blogs 8, 34, 57, 114
Bloom's taxonomy 53, 58, 149
Blyth, Carl 16
browser-based technologies 58

CALL: CALL-IS 35; computer-assisted language learning 1, 56; online training course 3, 129, 136, 139, 218; teacher education 113–171, 186, 188; techno-pedagogical model 4, 129

Printed in the United States
by Baker & Taylor Publisher Services

Printed in the United States
by Baker & Taylor Publisher Services